1 MONTH OF
FREE
READING

at

www.ForgottenBooks.com

By purchasing this book you are eligible for one month membership to ForgottenBooks.com, giving you unlimited access to our entire collection of over 1,000,000 titles via our web site and mobile apps.

To claim your free month visit:
www.forgottenbooks.com/free517999

ISBN 978-0-483-01748-1
PIBN 10517999

This book is a reproduction of an important historical work. Forgotten Books uses
state-of-the-art technology to digitally reconstruct the work, preserving the original format
whilst repairing imperfections present in the aged copy. In rare cases, an imperfection in
the original, such as a blemish or missing page, may be replicated in our edition. We do,
however, repair the vast majority of imperfections successfully; any imperfections that
remain are intentionally left to preserve the state of such historical works.

LETTERS

OF

JUNIUS, *pseud.*

STAT NOMINIS UMBRA.

SECOND AMERICAN EDITION.

PHILADELPHIA:

PUBLISHED BY M. CAREY,

NO. 122, MARKET STREET.

X, GRAVES, PRINTER, NO. 40, NORTH FOURTH STREET.

1807.

DEDICATION

TO THE

ENGLISH NATION.

——◆:❋:◆——

I . DEDICATE to you a collection of letters, written by one of yourselves for the common benefit of us all.
They would never have grown to this size, without your
continued encouragement and applause. To me they
originally owe nothing but a healthy, sanguine constitution. Under your care they have thriven. To you
they are indebted for whatever strength or beauty they
possess. When Kings and Ministers are forgotten, when
the force and direction of personal satire is no longer understood, and when measures are only felt in their re-
motest consequences, this book will, I believe, be found
to contain principles worthy to be transmitted to posterity.
When you leave the unimpaired hereditary freehold to
your children, you do but half your duty. Both liberty
and property are precarious, unless the possessors have
sense and spirit enough to defend them. This is not the
language of vanity. If I am a vain man, my gratification lies within a narrow circle. I am the sole deposi-
tary of my own secret, and it shall perish with me.

If an honest, and I may truly affirm, a laborious zeal
for the public service, has given me any weight in your
esteem, let me exhort and conjure you never to suffer an
invasion of your political constitution, however minute
the instance may appear, to pass by, without a determined, persevering resistance. One precedent creates
another.—They soon accumulate and constitute law.
What yesterday was fact, to-day is doctrine. Examples
are supposed to justify the most dangerous measures;
and where they do not suit exactly, the defect is supplied
by analogy. Be assured, that the laws which protect us
in our civil rights, grow out of the constitution, and that

they must fall or flourish with it. 'This is not the cause of faction or of party, or of any individual, but the common interest of every man in Britain. Although the King should continue to support his present system of government, the period is not very distant at which you will have the means of redress in your own power. It may be nearer perhaps than any of us expect, and I would warn you to be prepared for it. The King may possibly be advised to dissolve the present parliament a year or two before it expires of course, and precipitate a new election, in hopes of taking the nation by surprise. If such a measure be in agitation, this very caution may defeat or prevent it.

I cannot doubt that you will unanimously assert the freedom of election, and vindicate your exclusive right to choose your representatives. But other questions have been started, on which your determination should be equally clear and unanimous. Let it be impressed upon your minds, let it be instilled into your children, that the liberty of the press is the palladium of all the civil, political, and religious rights of an Englishman; and that the right of juries to return a general verdict, in all cases whatsoever, is an essential part of our constitution, not to be controuled or limited by the judges, nor in any shape questionable by the legislature. The power of King, Lords, and Commons, is not an arbitrary power.[a] They are the trustees, not the owners of the estate. The fee-simple is in us. They cannot alienate, they cannot waste. When we say that the legislature is supreme, we mean, that it is the highest power known to the constitution;—that it is the highest in comparison with the other subordinate powers established by the laws. In this sense the word supreme is relative, not absolute. The power of the legislature is limited, not only by the general rules of natural justice, and the welfare of the community, but by the forms and principles of our particular constitution. If this doctrine be not true, we must admit that King, Lords, and Commons have no rule to direct their resolutions, but merely their own will and pleasure. They might unite the legislative and executive power in the same hands, and dissolve the constitution by an act of parliament. But I am persuaded you will not leave it to the choice of seven hundred persons, notoriously corrupted by the Crown, whether seven millions of their equals shall be freemen or slaves.' The certainty of forfeiting their own rights, when they sacrifice those of the nation, is no check to a brutal, degenerate mind. Without insisting upon the extravagant concession made to Harry the Eighth, there are instances in the history of other countries, of a formal, deliberate surrender of the public liberty into the hands of the Sovereign. If England does not share the same fate, it is because we have better resources than in the virtue of either house of parliament.

I said that the liberty of the press is the palladium of all your rights, and that the right of the juries to return a general verdict, is part of your constitution. To preserve the whole system, you must correct your legislature. With regard to any influence of the constituent over the conduct of the representative, there is little difference between a seat in parliament for seven years, and a seat for life. The prospect of your resentment is too remote; and although the last session of a septennial parliament be usually employed in courting the favour of the people, consider, that at this rate your representatives have six years for offence, and but one for atonement. A deathbed repentance seldom reaches to restitution. If you reflect, that in the changes of administration which have marked and disgraced the present reign, although your warmest patriots have in their turn been invested with the lawful and unlawful authority of the crown, and though other reliefs or improvements have been held forth to the people, yet, that no one man in office has ever promoted or encouraged a bill for shortening the duration of parliaments, but that (whoever was minister) the opposition to this measure, ever since the septennial act passed, has been constant and uniform on the part of government.—You cannot but conclude, without the possibility of a doubt, that long parliaments are the foundation of the undue influence of the crown. This influence answers every purpose of arbitrary power to the crown, with an expence and oppression to the people, which would be unnecessary in an arbitrary government. The best of our ministers find it the easiest and most compendious mode of conducting the King's affairs ; and all ministers have a general interest in adhering to a system, which of itself is sufficient to support them in office, without any assistance from personal virtue, popularity, labour, abilities, or experience. It promises every gratification to avarice and ambition, and secures impunity. These are truths unquestionable. If they make no impression, it is because they are too vulgar and notorious. But the inattention or indifference of the nation has continued too long. You are roused at last to a sense of your danger. The remedy will soon be in your power. If Junius lives, you shall often be reminded of it. If, when the opportunity presents itself, you neglect to do your duty to yourselves and to posterity,—to God and to your country, I shall have one consolation left, in common with the meanest and basest of mankind. Civil liberty may still last the life of - -

Junius.

PREFACE.

THE encouragement given to a multitude of spurious, mangled publications of the letters of Junius, persuades me, that a complete edition, corrected and improved by the author, will be favourably received. The printer will readily acquit me of any view to my own profit. I undertake this troublesome task, merely to serve a man who has deserved well of me, and of the public; and who, on my account, has been exposed to an expensive, tyrannical prosecution. For these reasons, I give to Mr. Henry Sampson Woodfall, and to him alone, my right, interest, and property in these letters, as fully and completely, to all intents and purposes, as an author can possibly convey his property in his own works to another.

This edition contains all the letters of Junius, Philo Junius, and of Sir William Draper and Mr. Horne to Junius, with their respective dates, and according to the order in which they appeared in the Public Advertiser. The auxiliary part of Philo Junius was indispensably necessary to defend or explain particular passages in Junius, in answer to plausible objections; but the subordinate character is never guilty of the indecorum of praising his principal. The fraud was innocent, and I always intended to explain it. The notes will be found not only useful, but necessary. References to facts not generally known, or allusions to the current report or opinion of the day, are in a little time unintelligible. Yet the reader will not find himself overloaded with explanations. I was not born to be a commentator, even upon my own works.

It remains to say a few words upon the liberty of the press. The daring spirit, by which these letters are supposed to be distinguished, seems to require that something serious should be said in their defence. I am no lawyer by profession, nor do I pretend to be more deeply read than every English gentleman should be in the laws of his country. If, therefore, the principles I maintain are truly constitutional, I shall not think myself answered, though I should be convicted of a mistake in terms, or of misap-

A 2

plying the language of the law. I speak to the plain understanding of the people, and appeal to their honest, liberal construction of me.

Good men, to whom alone I address myself, appear to me to consult their piety as little as their judgment and experience, when they admit the great and essential advantages accruing to society from the freedom of the press, yet indulge themselves in peevish or passionate exclamations against the abuses of it. Betraying an unreasonable expectation of benefits pure and entire from any human institution, they in effect arraign the goodness of Providence, and confess that they are dissatisfied with the common lot of humanity. In the present instance, they really create to their own minds, or greatly exaggerate, the evil they complain of. The laws of England provide as effectually as any human laws can do, for the protection of the subject, in his reputation, as well as in his person and property. If the characters of private men are insulted or injured, a double remedy is open to them, by action and indictment. If, through indolence, false shame, or indifference, they will not appeal to the laws of their country, they fail in their duty to society, and are unjust to themselves. If, from an unwarrantable distrust of the integrity of juries, they would wish to obtain justice by any mode of proceeding more summary than a trial by their peers, I do not scruple to affirm, that they are in effect greater enemies to themselves than to the libeller they prosecute.

With regard to strictures upon the characters of men in office, and the measures of government, the case is a little different. A considerable latitude must be allowed in the discussion of public affairs, or the liberty of the press will be of no benefit to society. As the indulgence of private malice and personal slander should be checked and resisted by every legal means, so a constant examination into the characters and conduct of ministers and magistrates should be equally promoted and encouraged. They who conceive that our newspapers are no restraint upon bad men, or impediment to the execution of bad measures, know nothing of this country. In that state of abandoned servility and prostitution, to which the undue influence of the crown has reduced the other branches of the legislature, our ministers and magistrates, have in reality little punishment to fear, and few difficulties to contend with, beyond the censure of the press, and the spirit of resistance which it excites among the people. While this censorial power is maintained, to speak in the words of a most ingenious foreigner, both minister and magistrate is compelled, in almost every instance, to choose between his duty and his reputation. A dilemma of this kind perpetually before him, will not indeed work a miracle in his heart, but it will assuredly operate in some degree upon his conduct. At all events, these are not times to admit of any relaxation in the little discipline we have left.

But it is alleged that the licentiousness of the press is carried beyond all bounds of decency and truth;—that our excellent ministers are continually exposed to the public hatred or derision;—that, in prosecutions for libels on government, juries are partial to the popular side;—and that, in the most flagrant cases, a verdict cannot be obtained for the King. If the premises were admitted, I should deny the conclusion. It is not true that the temper of the times has in general an undue influence over the conduct of juries. On the contrary, many signal instances may be produced of verdicts returned for the King, when the inclinations of the people led strongly to an undistinguishing opposition to government. Witness the cases of Mr. Wilkes and Mr. Almon. In the late persecutions of the printers of my address to a great personage, the juries were never fairly dealt with. Lord Chief Justice Mansfield, conscious that the paper in question contained no treasonable or libellous matter, and that the severest parts of it, however painful to the King, or offensive to his servants, were strictly true, would fain have restricted the jury to the finding of special facts, which, as to guilty or not guilty, were merely indifferent. This particular motive, combined with his general purpose to contract the power of juries, will account for the charge he delivered in Woodfall's trial. He told the jury, in so many words, that they had nothing to determine except the fact of printing and publishing, and whether or no the blanks or inuendos were properly filled up in the information:—but that, whether the defendant had

committed a crime or not, was no matter of consideration
to twelve men, who yet, upon their oaths, were to pronounce their peer guilty or not guilty. When we hear
such nonsense delivered from the bench, and find it supported by a laboured train of sophistry, which a plain understanding is unable to follow, and which an unlearned
jury, however it may shock their reason, cannot be supposed qualified to refute, can it be wondered that they
should return a verdict perplexed, absurd, or imperfect?
Lord Mansfield has not yet explained to the world why
he accepted of a verdict which the court afterwards set
aside as illegal; and which, as it took no notice of the
inuendos, did not even correspond with his own charge.
If he had known his duty, he should have sent the jury
back. I speak advisedly, and am well assured that no
lawyer of character in Westminster-hall will contradict
me. To show the falsehood of Lord Mansfield's doctrine, it is not necessary to enter into the merits of the
paper which produced the trial. If every line of it were
treason, his charge to the jury would still be false, absurd,
illegal, and unconstitutional. If I stated the merits of my
letter to the King, I should imitate Lord Mansfield, and
^btravel out of the record. When law and reason speak
plainly, we do not want authority to direct our understandings. Yet, for the honour of the profession, I am
content to oppose one lawyer to another, especially when
it happens that the King's Attorney General has virtually
disclaimed the doctrine by which the Chief Justice meant
to ensure success to the prosecution. The opinion of the
plaintiff's counsel (however it may be otherwise insignificant,) is weighty in the scale of the defendant. My Lord
Chief Justice De Grey, who filed the information *ex officio*, is directly with me. If he had concurred in Lord
Mansfield's doctrine, the trial must have been a very short
one. The facts were either admitted by Woodfall's counsel, or easily proved to the satisfaction of the jury. But
Mr. De Grey, far from thinking he should acquit himself
of his duty by barely proving the facts, entered largely,
and, I confess, not without ability, into the demerits of
the paper, which he called a seditious libel. He dwelt
but lightly upon those points which (according to Lord
Mansfield) were the only matter of consideration to the

jury. The criminal intent, the libellous matter, the pernicious tendency of the paper itself, were the topics on which he principally insisted, and of which for more than an hour he tortured his faculties to convince the jury.—. If he agreed in opinion with Lord Mansfield, his discourse was impertinent, ridiculous, and unreasonable. But, understanding the law as I do, what he said was at least consistent and to the purpose.

If any honest man should still be inclined to leave the construction of libels to the court, I would entreat him to consider what a dreadful complication of hardships he imposes upon his fellow-subjects. In the first place, the prosecution commences by information of an officer of the crown, not by the regular constitutional mode of indictment before a grand jury. As the fact is usually admitted, or in general can easily be proved, the office of the petty jury is nugatory. The court then judges of the nature and extent of the offence, and determines *ad arbitrium* the *quantum* of the punishment, from a small fine to a heavy one, to repeated whipping, to pillory, and unlimited imprisonment. Cutting off ears and noses might still be inflicted by a resolute judge; but I will be candid enough to suppose that penalties, so apparently shocking to humanity, would not be hazarded in these times. In all other criminal prosecutions, the jury decides upon the fact and the crime in one word; and the court pronounces a certain sentence, which is the sentence of the law, not of the judge. If Lord Mansfield's doctrine be received, the jury must either find a verdict of acquittal, contrary to evidence (which, I can conceive, might be done by very conscientious men, rather than trust a fellow-creature to Lord Mansfield's mercy,) or they must leave to the court two offices, never but in this instance united, of finding guilty, and awarding punishment.

But, says this honest Lord Chief Justice, " If the pa-. " per be not criminal, the defendant (though found guil- " ty by his peers) is in no danger, for he may move the " court in arrest of judgment."—True, my good Lord; but who is to determine upon the motion?—Is not the court still to decide, whether judgment shall be entered up or not? and is not the defendant this way as effectually deprived of judgment by his peers, as if he were tried in a court of civil law, or in the chambers of the inquisition? It is you, my Lord, who then try the crime, not the jury. As to the probable effect of the motion in arrest of judgment, I shall only observe, that no reasonable man would be so eager to possess himself of the invidious power of inflicting punishment, if he were not predetermined to make use of it.

Again:—We are told, that judge and jury have a distinct office ;—that the jury is to find the fact, and the judge, to deliver the law. *De jure respondent judices, de facto jurati.* The *dictum* is true, though not in the sense given to it by Lord Mansfield. The jury are undoubtedly to determine the fact, that is, whether the defendant did or did not commit the crime charged against him. The judge pronounces the sentence annexed by law to that fact so found ; and if, in the course of the trial, any question of law arises, both the counsel and the jury must, of necessity, appeal to the judge, and leave it to his decision. An exception, or plea in bar, may be allowed by the court ; but when issue is joined, and the jury have received their charge, it is not possible, in the nature of things, for them to separate the law from the fact, unless they think proper to return a special verdict.

It has also been alleged, that, although a common jury are sufficient to determine a plain matter of fact, they are not qualified to comprehend the meaning, or to judge of the tendency of a seditious libel. In answer to this objection (which, if well founded, would prove nothing as to the strict right of returning a general verdict,) I might safely deny the truth of the assertion. Englishmen of that rank, from which juries are usually taken, are not so illiterate as (to serve a particular purpose) they are now represented. Or, admitting the fact, let a special jury be summoned in all cases of difficulty and importance, and the objection is removed. But the truth is, that if a paper, supposed to be a libel upon government, be so obscurely worded, that twelve common men cannot possibly see the seditious meaning and tendency of it, it is in effect no libel. It cannot inflame the minds of the people, nor alienate their affections from government ; for they no more understand what it means, than if it were published in a language unknown to them.

Upon the whole matter, it appears to my understanding, clear beyond a doubt, that if, in any future prosecution for a seditious libel, the jury should bring in a verdict of acquittal not warranted by the evidence, it will be owing to the false and absurd doctrines laid down by Lord Mansfield. Disgusted by the odious artifices made use of by the judge to mislead and perplex them, guarded against his sophistry, and convinced of the falsehood of his assertions, they may perhaps determine to thwart his detestable purpose, and defeat him at any rate. To him at least they will do substantial justice.——Whereas, if the whole charge, laid in the information, be fairly and honestly submitted to the jury, there is no reason whatsoever to presume that twelve men, upon their oaths, will not decide impartially between the King and the defendant. The numerous instances in our state-trials, of verdicts recovered for the king, sufficiently refute the false and scandalous imputations thrown by the abettors of Lord Mansfield upon the integrity of juries.——But even admitting the supposition, that in times of universal discontent, arising from the notorious maladministration of public affairs, a seditious writer should escape punishment, it makes nothing against my general argument. If juries are fallible, to what other tribunal shall we appeal?——If juries cannot safely be trusted, shall we unite the offices of judge and jury, so wisely divided by the constitution, and trust implicitly to Lord Mansfield?——Are the judges of the court of King's Bench more likely to be unbiassed and impartial, than twelve yeomen, burgesses, or gentlemen, taken indifferently from the county at large?——Or, in short, shall there be no decision, until we have instituted a tribunal, from which no possible abuse or inconvenience whatever can arise?——If I am not grossly mistaken, these questions carry a decisive answer along with them.

Having cleared the freedom of the press from a restraint equally unnecessary and illegal, I return to the use which has been made of it in the present publication.

National reflections, I confess, are not justified in theory, nor upon any general principles. To know how well they are deserved, and how justly they have been applied, we must have the evidence of facts before us. We must be conversant with the Scots in private life, and ob-

serve their principles of acting to us, and to each other;
—the characteristic prudence, the selfish nationality, the
indefatigable smile, the persevering assiduity, the everlast-
ing profession of a discreet and moderate resentment. If
the instance were not too important for an experiment, it
might not be amiss to confide a little in their integrity.—
Without any abstract reasoning upon causes and effects,
we shall soon be convinced by experience, that the Scots,
transplanted from their own country, are always a distinct and separate body from the people who receive
them. In other settlements, they only love themselves;
—In England, they cordially love themselves, and as cordially hate their neighbors. For the remainder of their
good qualities, I must appeal to the reader's observation,
unless he will accept of my Lord Barrington's authority.
In a letter to the late Lord Melcombe, published by Mr.
Lee, he expresses himself with a truth and accuracy not
very common in his Lordship's lucubrations:—And Cock-
burn, like most of his countrymen, "is as abject to those
" above him, as he is insolent to those below him."—I
am far from meaning to impeach the articles of the Union.
If the true spirit of those articles were religiously adhered
to, we should not see such a multitude of Scotch common-
ers in the lower-house, as representatives of English boroughs, while not a single Scotch borough is ever represented by an Englishman. We should not see English
peerages given to Scotch ladies, or to the elder sons of
Scotch peers, and the number of sixteen doubled and
trebled by a scandalous evasion of the act of Union.—If
it should ever be thought advisable to dissolve an act,
the violation or observance of which is invariably directed by
the advantage and interest of the Scots, I shall say, very
sincerely, with Sir Edward Coke, c " When poor England
" stood alone, and had not the access of another king-
" dom, and yet had more and as potent enemies as it
" now hath, yet the King of England prevailed."

Some opinion may now be expected from me, upon a
point of equal delicacy to the writer, and hazard to the
printer. When the character of the chief magistrate is
in question, more must be understood than may safely be
expressed. If it be really a part of our constitution, and
not a mere *dictum* of the law, that the King can do no

wrong, it is not the only instance in the wisest of human institutions, where theory is at variance with practice.— That the Sovereign of this country is not amenable to any form of trial known to the laws, is unquestionable. But exemption from punishment is a singular privilege annexed to the royal character, and no way excludes the possibility of deserving it. How long, and to what extent, a King of England may be protected by the forms, when he violates the spirit of the constitution, deserves to be considered. A mistake in this matter proved fatal to Charles and his son.—For my own part, far from thinking that the King can do no wrong, far from suffering myself to be deterred or imposed upon by the language of forms in opposition to the substantial evidence of truth, if it were my misfortune to live under the inauspicious reign of a prince, whose whole life was employed in one base contemptible struggle with the free spirit of his people, or in the detestable endeavour to corrupt their moral principles, I would not scruple to declare to him,—
" Sir, You alone are the author of the greatest wrong to
" your subjects and to yourself. Instead of reigning in
" the hearts of your people, instead of commanding their
" lives and fortunes through the medium of their affec-
" tions, has not the strength of the crown, whether in-
" fluence or prerogative, been uniformly exerted, for
" eleven years together, to support a narrow, pitiful sys-
" tem of government, which defeats itself, and answers
" no one purpose of real power, profit, or personal satis-
" faction to you ?—With the greatest unappropriated re-
" venue of any prince in Europe, have we not seen you
" reduced to such vile and sordid distresses, as would
" have conducted any other man to a prison ?—With a
" great military, and the greatest naval power in the
" known world, have not foreign nations repeatedly in-
" sulted you with impunity ?—Is it not notorious, that
" the vast revenues, extorted from the labor and industry
" of your subjects, and given you to do honor to your-
" self and to the nation, are dissipated in corrupting their
" representatives ?——Are you a prince of the house of
" Hanover, and do you exclude all the leading Whig fa-
" milies from your councils ?—Do you profess to govern
" according to law ; and is it consistent with that pro-

B

" fession, to impart your confidence and affection to those
" men only, who, though now perhaps detached from
" the desperate cause of the Pretender, are marked in
" this country by an hereditary attachment to high and
" arbitrary principles of government?—Are you so infa-
" tuated as to take the sense of your people from the re-
" presentation of ministers, or from the shouts of a mob,
" notoriously hired to surround your coach, or stationed
" at a theatre?—And if you are, in realty, that public
" man, that King, that Magistrate, which these questions
" suppose you to be, is it any answer to your people, to
" say, That among your domestics you are good-humour-
" ed;—that to one lady you are faithful;—that to your
" children you are indulgent?——Sir, the man who ad-
" dresses you in these terms is your best friend. He
" would willingly hazard his life in defence of your title
" to the crown; and, if power be your object, would
" still show you how possible it is for a King of England,
" by the noblest means, to be the most absolute prince in
" Europe. You have no enemies, Sir, but those who
" persuade you to aim at power without right, and who
" think it flattery to tell you, that the character of King
" dissolves the natural relation between guilt and punish-
" ment."

I cannot conceive that there is a heart so callous, or an
understanding so depraved, as to attend to a discourse of
this nature, and not to feel the force of it. But where
is the man, among those who have access to the closet,
resolute and honest enough to deliver it? The liberty of
the press is our only resource. It will command an audience, when every honest man in the kingdom is excluded. This glorious privilege may be a security to the
King, as well as a resource to his people. Had there
been no star-chamber, there would have been no rebellion against Charles the First. The constant censure and
admonition of the press would have corrected his conduct,
prevented a civil war, and saved him from an ignominious death. I am no friend to the doctrine of precedents
exclusive of right: though lawyers often tell us, that
whatever has been once done may lawfully be done
again.

I shall conclude this preface with a quotation applica-

ble to the subject, from a foreign writer [d]; whose essay
on the English constitution I beg leave to recommend to
the public, as a performance deep, solid, and ingenious.

" In short, whoever considers what it is that consti-
" tutes the moving principle of what we call great af-
" fairs, and the invincible sensibility of man to the opi-
" nion of his fellow-creatures, will not hesitate to affirm,
" that if it were possible for the liberty of the press to
" exist in a despotic government, and (what is not less
" difficult) for it to exist without changing the con-
" stitution, this liberty of the press would alone form a
" counterpoise to the power of the prince. If, for ex-
" ample, in an empire of the East, a sanctuary could be
" found, which, rendered respectable by the ancient re-
" ligion of the people, might ensure safety to those who
" should bring thither their observations of any kind ;
" and that, from thence, printed papers should issue,
" which, under a certain seal, might be equally respect-
" ed ; and which, in their daily appearance, should ex-
" amine and freely discuss the conduct of the Cadis, the
" Bashaws, the Vizir, the Divan, and the Sultan him-
" self ; that would introduce immediately some degree of
" liberty."

LETTERS OF JUNIUS.

——:✸:——

LETTER I.

TO THE PRINTER OF THE PUBLIC ADVERTISER.

SIR,   *January* 21, 1769.

THE submission of a free people to the executive authority of government is no more than a compliance with laws, which they themselves have enacted. While the national honour is firmly maintained abroad, and while justice is impartially administered at home, the obedience of the subject will be voluntary, cheerful, and I might almost say unlimited. A generous nation is grateful even for the preservation of its rights, and willingly extends the respect due to the office of a good prince into an affection for his person. Loyalty, in the heart and understanding of an Englishman, is a rational attachment to the guardian of the laws. Prejudices and passion have sometimes carried it to a criminal length ; and, whatever foreigners may imagine, we know that Eglishmen have erred as much in a mistaken zeal for particular persons and families, as they ever did in defence of what they thought most dear and interesting to themselves.

It naturally fills us with resentment, to see such a temper insulted and abused. In reading the history of a free people, whose rights have been invaded, we are interested in their cause. Our own feelings tell us how they ought to have submitted, and at what moment it would have been treachery to themselves not to have resisted. How much warmer will be our resentment, if experience should bring the fatal example home to ourselves !

The situation of this country is alarming enough to rouse the attention of every man who pretends to a concern for the public welfare. Appearances justify suspicion ; and when the safety of a nation is at stake, suspicion is a just ground of inquiry. Let us enter into it with candour and decency. Respect is due to the station of ministers ; and, if a resolution must at last be taken,

B 2

there is none so likely to be supported with firmness as that which has been adopted with moderation.

The ruin or prosperity of a state depends so much upon the administration of its government, that, to be acquainted with the merit of a ministry, we need only observe the condition of the people. If we see them obedient to the laws, prosperous in their industry, united at home, and respected abroad, we may reasonably presume that their affairs are conducted by men of experience, abilities, and virtue. If, on the contrary, we see an universal spirit of distrust and dissatisfaction, a rapid decay of trade, dissentions in all parts of the empire, and a total loss of respect in the eyes of foreign powers, we may pronounce without hesitation, that the government of that country is weak, distracted, and corrupt. The multitude, in all countries, are patient to a certain point. Ill-usage may rouse their indignation, and hurry them into excesses; but the original fault is in government. Perhaps there never was an instance of a change, in the circumstances and temper of a whole nation, so sudden and extraordinary as that which the misconduct of ministers has, within these few years, produced in Great Britain. When our gracious Sovereign ascended the throne, we were a flourishing and a contented people. If the personal virtues of a king could have ensured the happiness of his subjects, the scene could not have altered so entirely as it has done. The idea of uniting all parties, of trying all characters, and distributing the offices of state by rotation, was gracious and benevolent to an extreme, though it has not yet produced the many salutary effects which were intended by it. To say nothing of the wisdom of such a plan, it undoubtedly arose from an unbounded goodness of heart in which folly had no share. It was not a capricious partiality to new faces :—it was not a natural turn for low intrigue ;—nor was it the treacherous amusement of double and triple negotiations. No, Sir ; it arose from a continued anxiety, in the purest of all possible hearts, for the general welfare. Unfortunately for us, the event has not been answerable to the design. After a rapid succession of changes, we are reduced to that state, which hardly any change can mend. Yet there is no extremity of distress, which of itself ought to reduce a great nation to despair. It is not the disorder, but the physician;—it is not a casual concurrence of calamitous circumstances;—it is the pernicious hand of government, which alone can make a whole people desperate.

Without much political sagacity, or any extraordinary depth of observation, we need only mark how the principal departments of the state are bestowed, and look no farther for the true cause of every mischief that befals us.

a The finances of a nation, sinking under its debts and expences, are committed to a young nobleman already ruined by play. Introduced to act under the auspices of Lord Chatham, and left at the head of affairs by that nobleman's retreat, he became minister by accident; but deserting the principles and professions which gave him a moment's popularity, we see him, from every honorable engagement to the public, an apostate by design. As for business, the world yet knows nothing of his talents or resolution; unless a wayward, wavering inconsistency be a mark of genius, and caprice a demonstration of spirit. It may be said, perhaps, that it is his Grace's province, as surely it is his passion, rather to distribute than to save the public money; and that while Lord North is Chancellor of the Exchequer, the First Lord of the Treasury may be as thoughtless and extravagant as he pleases. I hope, however, he will not rely too much on the fertility of Lord North's genius for finance. His Lordship is yet to give us the first proof of his abilities: It may be candid to suppose that he has hitherto voluntarily concealed his talents; intending perhaps to astonish the world, when we least expect it, with a knowledge of trade, a choice of expedients, and a depth of resources, equal to the necessities, and far beyond the hopes, of his country. He must now exert the whole power of his capacity, if he would wish us to forget, that since he has been in office, no plan has been formed, no system adhered to, nor any one important measure adopted for the relief of public credit. If his plan for the service of the current year be not irrevocably fixed on, let me warn him to think seriously of the consequence before he ventures to increase the public debt. Outraged and oppressed as we are, this nation will not bear, after a six years peace, to see new millions borrowed, without an eventual diminution of debt, or reduction of interest. The attempt might rouse a spirit of resentment which might reach beyond the sacrifice of a minister. As to the debt upon the civil list, the people of England expect that it will not be paid without a strict inquiry how it was incurred. If it must be paid by parliament, let me advise the Chancellor of the Exchequer to think of some better expedient than a lottery. To support an expensive war, or in circumstances of absolute necessity, a lottery may perhaps be allowable ; but, besides that it is at all times the very worst way of raising money upon the people, I think it ill becomes the Royal dignity, to have the debts of a King provided for, like the repairs of a country bridge, or a decayed hospital. The management of the King's affairs in the House of Commons cannot be more disgraced than it has been. [b] A leading minister repeatedly called down for absolute ignorance ;—ridiculous motions ridiculously withdrawn ;—deliberate plans disconcerted, and a week's preparation of graceful oratory lost in a moment, give us some, though not adequate idea, of Lord North's parliamentary abilities and influence. Yet before he had the misfortune of being Chancellor of the Exchequer, he was neither an object of derision to his enemies, nor of melancholy pity to his friends.

A series of inconsistent measures has alienated the colonies from their duty as subjects, and from their natural affection to their common country. When Mr. Grenville was placed at the head of the Treasury, he felt the impossibility of Great Britain's supporting such an establishment as her former successes had made indispensable, and at the same time of giving any sensible relief to foreign trade, and to the weight of the public debt. He thought it equitable that those parts of the empire which had been benefited most by the expences of the war, should contribute something to the expences of the peace, and he had no doubt of the constitutional right vested in parliament to raise the contribution. But, unfortunately for this country, Mr. Grenville was at any rate to be distressed because he was minister, and Mr. Pitt [c] and Lord Cambden were to be the patrons of America because they were in opposition. Their declaration gave spirit and argument to the colonies; and while perhaps they meant no more than the ruin of a minister, they in effect divided one half of the empire from the other.

Under one administration the stamp-act is made; under the second, it is repealed; under the third, in spite of all experience, a new mode of taxing the colonies is invented, and a question revived which ought to have been buried in oblivion. In these circumstances a new office is established for the business of the plantations, and the Earl of Hilsborough called forth, at a most critical season, to govern America. The choice at least announced to us a man of superior capacity and knowledge. Whether he be so or not, let his dispatches as far as they have appeared, let his measures as far as they have operated, determine for him. In the former, we have seen strong assertions without proof, declamation without argument, and violent censures without dignity or moderation; but neither correctness in the composition, nor judgment in the design. As for his measures, let it be remembered, that he was called upon to conciliate and unite; and that when he entered into office, the most refractory of the colonies were still disposed to proceed by the constitutional methods of petition and remonstrance. Since that period they have been driven into excesses little short of rebellion. Petitions have been hindered from reaching the throne; and the continuance of one of the principal assemblies rested upon an arbitrary condition[d]; which, considering the temper they were in, it was impossible they should comply with, and which would have availed nothing as to the general question if it had been complied with. So violent, and I believe I may call it so unconstitutional, an exertion of the prerogative, to say nothing of the weak injudicious terms in which it was conveyed, gives us as humble an opinion of his lordship's capacity as it does of his temper and moderation. While we are at peace with other nations, our military force may perhaps be spared to support the Earl of Hilsborough's measures in America. Whenever that force shall be necessarily withdrawn or diminished, the dismission of such a minister will neither console us for his imprudence, nor remove the settled resentment of a people,

who, complaining of an act of the legislature, are outraged by an unwarrantable stretch of prerogative, and,
supporting their claims by argument, are insulted with declamation.

Drawing lots would be a prudent and reasonable method of appointing the officers of state, compared to a
late disposition of the secretary's office. Lord Rochford
was acquainted with the affairs and temper of the south-
ern courts : Lord Weymouth was equally qualified for
either department [e]. By what unaccountable caprice has
it happened, that the latter, who pretends to no experience whatsoever, is removed to the most important of
the two departments, and the former by preference placed
in an office where his experience can be of no use to
him ? Lord Weymouth had distinguished himself in his
first employment by a spirited, if not judicious conduct.
He had animated the civil magistrate beyond the tone of
civil authority, and had directed the operations of the
army to more than military execution. Recovered from
the errors of his youth, from the distraction of play, and
the bewitching smiles of Burgundy, behold him exerting
the whole strength of his clear, unclouded faculties in the
service of the crown. It was not the heat of midnight
excesses, nor ignorance of the laws, nor the furious spirit
of the house of Bedford : No, Sir, when this respectable
minister interposed his authority between the magistrate
and the people, and signed the mandate, on which, for
aught he knew, the lives of thousands depended, he did
it from the deliberate motion of his heart, supported by
the best of his judgment.

It has lately been a fashion to pay a compliment to the
bravery and generosity of the commander in chief [f] at
the expence of his understanding. They who love him
least make no question of his courage, while his friends
dwell chiefly on the facility of his disposition. Admitting him to be as brave as a total absence of all feeling
and reflection can make him, let us see what sort of merit
he derives from the remainder of his character. If it be
generosity to accumulate in his own person and family a
number of lucrative employments ; to provide, at the
public expence, for every creature that bears the name
of Manners ; and, neglecting the merit and services of

the rest of the army, to heap promotions upon his favourites and dependants ; the present commander in chief is the most generous man alive. Nature has been sparing of her gifts to this noble lord ; but where birth and fortune are united, we expect the noble pride and independence of a man of spirit, not the servile humiliating complaisance of a courtier. As to the goodness of his heart, if a proof of it be taken from the facility of never refusing, what conclusion shall we draw from the indecency of never performing? And if the discipline of the army be in any degree preserved, what thanks are due to a man, whose cares, notoriously confined to filling up vacancies, have degraded the office of commander in chief into a broker of commissions?

With respect to the navy, I shall only say, that this country is so highly indebted to Sir Edward Hawke, that no expence should be spared to secure to him an honourable and affluent retreat.

The pure and impartial administration of justice is perhaps the firmest bond to secure a cheerful submission of the people, and to engage their affections to government. It is not sufficient that questions of private right or wrong are justly decided, nor that judges are superior to the vileness of pecuniary corruption. Jefferies himself, when the court had no interest, was an upright judge. A court of justice may be subject to another sort of bias more important and pernicious, as it reaches beyond the interest of individuals, and affects the whole community. A judge, under the influence of government, may be honest enough in the decision of private causes, yet a traitor to the public. When a victim is marked out by the ministry, this judge will offer himself to perform the sacrifice. He will not scruple to prostitute his dignity, and betray the sanctity of his office, whenever an arbitrary point is to be carried for government, or the resentment of a court to be gratified.

These principles and proceedings, odious and contemptible as they are, in effect are no less injudicious. A wise and generous people are roused by every appearance of oppressive, unconstitutional measures, whether those measures are supported only by the power of government, or masked under the forms of a court of justice. Prudence and self-preservation will oblige the most moderate dispositions to make common cause, even with a man whose conduct they censure, if they see him persecuted in a way which the real spirit of the laws will not justify. The facts, on which these remarks are founded, are too notorious to require an application.

This, Sir, is the detail. In one view, behold a nation overwhelmed with debt; her revenues wasted; her trade declining; the affections of her colonies alienated: the duty of the magistrate transferred to the soldiery: a gallant army, which never fought unwillingly but against their fellow-subjects, mouldering away for want of the direction of a man of common abilities and spirit; and in their last instance, the administration of justice become odious and suspected to the whole body of the people. This deplorable scene admits of but one addition—that we are governed by counsels, from which a reasonable man can expect no remedy but poison, no relief but death.

If, by the immediate interposition of Providence, it were possible for us to escape a crisis so full of terror and despair, posterity will not believe the history of the present times. They will either conclude that our distresses were imaginary, or that we had the good fortune to be governed by men of acknowledged integrity and wisdom: they will not believe it possible that their ancestors could have survived or recovered from so desperate a condition, while a Duke of Grafton was Prime Minister, a Lord North Chancellor of the Exchequer, a Weymouth and a Hilsborough Secretaries of State, a Granby Commander in Chief, and Mansfield chief criminal Judge of the kingdom.

JUNIUS.

LETTER II.

TO THE PRINTER OF THE PUBLIC ADVERTISER.

SIR, *Jan.* 26, 1769.

THE kingdom swarms with such numbers of felonious robbers of private character and virtue, that no honest or good man is safe; especially as these cowardly base assassins stab in the dark, without having the courage to sign their real names to their malevolent and wicked productions. A writer, who signs himself Junius, in the Public Advertiser of the 21st instant, opens the deplorable situation of his country in a very affecting manner; with a pompous parade of his candour and decency, he tells us, that we see dissentions in all parts of the empire, an universal spirit of distrust and dissatisfaction, and a total loss of respect towards us in the eyes of foreign powers. But this writer, with all his boasted candour, has not told us the real cause of the evils he so pathetically enumerates. I shall take the liberty to explain the cause for him. Junius and such writers as himself occasion all the mischief complained of, by falsely and maliciously traducing the best characters in the kingdom. For when our deluded people at home, and foreigners abroad, read the poisonous and inflammatory libels that are daily published with impunity, to vilify those who are any way distinguished by their good qualities and eminent virtues; when they find no notice taken of, or reply given to, these slanderous tongues and pens; their conclusion is, that both the ministers and the nation have been fairly described; and they act accordingly. I think it therefore the duty of every good citizen to stand forth, and endeavor to undeceive the public, when the vilest arts are made use of to defame and blacken the brightest characters among us. An eminent author affirms it to be almost as criminal to hear a worthy man traduced, without attempting his justification, as to be the author of the calumny against him. For my own part, I think it a sort of misprision of treason against society. No man, therefore, who knows Lord Granby, can possibly hear so good and great a character most vilely abused, without a warm and just indignation against this Junius, this high-priest of envy, malice, and all uncharitableness, who has endeavored to sacrifice our beloved commander in chief at the altars of his horrid deities. Nor is the injury done to his lordship alone, but to the whole nation, which may too soon feel the contempt, and consequently the attacks, of our late enemies, if they can be induced to believe that the person, on whom the safety of these kingdoms so much depends, is unequal to his high station, and destitute of those qualities which form a good general. One would have thought that his lord-ship's services in the cause of his country, from the battle of Culloden to his most glorious conclusion of the late war, might have entitled him to common respect and decency at least; but this uncandid, indecent writer, has gone so far as to turn one of the most amiable men of the age into a stupid, unfeeling, and senseless being; possessed indeed of personal courage, but void of those essential qualities which distinguish the commander from the common soldier.

A very long, uninterrupted, impartial, I will add a most disinterested, friendship with Lord Granby, gives me the right to affirm, that all Junius's assertions are false and scandalous. Lord Granby's courage, though of the brightest and most ardent kind, is among the lowest of his numerous good qualities; he was formed to excel in war by nature's liberality to his mind as well as person. Educated and instructed by his most noble father, and a most spirited as well as excellent scholar, the present Bishop of Bangor, he was trained to the nicest sense of honour, and to the truest and noblest sort of pride, that of never doing or suffering a mean action. A sincere love and attachment to his king and country, and to their glory, first impelled him to the field, where he never gained aught but honour. He impaired, through his bounty, his own fortune: for his bounty, which this writer would in vain depreciate, is founded upon the noblest of the human affections; it flows from a heart melting to goodness from the most refined humanity. Can a man, who is described as unfeeling and void of reflection, be constantly employed in seeking proper objects on whom to exercise those glorious virtues of compassion and generosity? The distressed officer, the soldier, the widow, the orphan, and a long list besides, know that vanity has no share in his frequent donations; he gives, because he feels their distresses. Nor has he ever been rapacious with one hand, to be bountiful with the other: yet this uncandid Junius would insinuate, that the dignity of the commander in chief is depraved into the base office of commission-broker: that is, Lord Granby bargains for the sale of commissions; for it must have this meaning, if it has any at all. But where is the man living who can justly charge

his lordship with such mean practices? Why does not
Junius produce him? Junius knows that he has no other
means of wounding this hero, than from some missile weapon, shot from an obscure corner: He seeks, as all defa-
matory writers do,

————————*spargere voces*
In vulgum ambiguas————

to raise a suspicion in the minds of the people. But I
hope that my countrymen will be no longer imposed upon by artful, and designing men, or by wretches, who,
bankrupts in business, in fame, and in fortune, mean nothing more than to involve this country in the same common ruin with themselves. Hence it is, that they are
constantly aiming their dark and too often fatal weapons
against those who stand forth as the bulwark of our national safety. Lord Granby was too conspicuous a mark
not to be their object. He is next attacked for being un-
faithful to his promises and engagements: Where are Junius's proofs? Although I could give some instances,
where a breach of promise would be a virtue, especially
in the case of those who would pervert the open, unsuspecting moments of convivial mirth, into sly, insidious applications for preferment or party-systems, and would endeavor to surprise a good man, who cannot bear to see
any one leave him dissatisfied, into unguarded promises.
Lord Granby's attention to his own family and relations is
called selfish. Had he not attended to them, when fair
and just opportunities presented themselves, I should have
thought him unfeeling, and void of reflection indeed.——
How are any man's friends or relations to be provided for
but from the influence and protection of the patron? It
is unfair to suppose that Lord Granby's friends have not as
much merit as the friends of any other great man: If he
is generous at the public expence, as Junius invidiously
calls it, the public is at no more expence for his lordship's
friends than it would be if any other set of men possessed
those offices. The charge is ridiculous!

The last charge against Lord Granby, is of a most alarming nature indeed. Junius asserts, that the army is mouldering away for want of the direction of a man of common abilities and spirit. The present condition of the
army gives the directest lie to his assertions. It was never

upon a more respectable footing with regard to discipline, and all the essentials that can form good soldiers. Lord Ligonier delivered a firm and noble palladium of our safeties into Lord Granby's hands, who has kept it in the same good order in which he received it. The strictest care has been taken to fill up the vacant commissions, with such gentlemen as have the glory of their ancestors to support, as well as their own, and they are doubly bound to the cause of their king and country, from motives of private property as well as public spirit. The adjutant-general, who has the immediate care of the troops after Lord Granby, is an officer that would do great honour to any service in Europe, for his correct arrangements, good sense and discernment upon all occasions, and for a punctuality and precision which give the most entire satisfaction to all who are obliged to consult him. The reviewing generals, who inspect the army twice a-year, have been selected with the greatest care, and have answered the important trust reposed in them in the most laudable manner. Their reports of the condition of the army are much more to be credited than those of Junius, whom I do advise to atone, for his shameful aspersions, by asking pardon of Lord Granby and the whole kingdom, whom he has offended by his abominable scandals. In short, to turn Junius's own battery against him, I must assert, in his own words, " that he has given strong assertions without proof, decla- ".mation without argument, and violent censures without " dignity or moderation."

WILLIAM DRAPER.

LETTER III.

TO SIR WILLIAM DRAPER, KNIGHT OF THE BATH.

SIR,   *Feb.* 7, 1769.

Your defence of Lord Granby does honour to the goodness of your heart. You feel, as you ought to do, for the reputation of your friend, and you express yourself in the warmest language of your passions. In any other cause, I doubt not, you would have cautiously weighed the consequences of committing your name to the licentious discourses and malignant opinions of the

world. : But here I presume, you thought it would be a
breach of friendship to lose one moment in consulting
your understanding: as if an appeal to the public were
no more than a military *coup de main*, where a brave man
has no rules to follow but the dictates of his courage.—
Touched with your generosity, I freely forgive the excesses
into which it has led you : and, far from resenting those
terms of reproach, which, considering that you are an advocate for decorum, you have heaped upon me rather too
liberally, I place them to the account of an honest unre-
flecting indignation, in which your cooler judgment and
natural politeness had no concern. I approve of the spirit with which you have given your name to the public ;
and, if it were a proof of any thing but spirit, I should
have thought myself bound to follow your example. I
should have hoped that even my name might have carried
some authority with it, if I had not seen how very little
weight or consideration a printed paper receives even from
the respectable signature of Sir William Draper.

You begin with a general assertion, that writers, such
as I am, are the real cause of all the public evils we complain of. And do you really think, Sir William, that the
licentious pen of a political writer is able to produce such
important effects ? A little calm reflection might have
shown you, that national calamities do not arise from the
description, but from the real character and conduct of
ministers. To have supported your assertion, you should
have proved that the present ministry are unquestionably
the best and brightest characters of the kingdom ; and
that, if the affections of the colonies have been alienated,
if Corsica has been shamefully abandoned, if commerce
languishes, if public credit is threatened with a new debt,
and your own Manilla ransom most dishonorably given
up, it has all been owing to the malice of political writers, who will not suffer the best and brightest characters
(meaning still the present ministry) to take a single right
step for the honour or interest of the nation. But it seems
you were a little tender of coming to particulars. Your
conscience insinuated to you, that it would be prudent
to leave the characters of Grafton, North, Hilsborough,
Weymouth, and Mansfield, to shift for themselves ; and

truly, Sir William, the part you have undertaken is at least as much as you are equal to.

Without disputing Lord Granby's courage, we are yet to learn in what articles of military knowledge nature has been so very liberal to his mind. If you have served with him, you ought to have pointed out some instances of able disposition and well concerted enterprise, which might fairly be attributed to his capacity as a general. It is you, Sir William, who make your friend appear awkward and ridiculous, by giving him a laced suit of tawdry qualifications, which nature never intended him to wear.

You say he has acquired nothing but honour in the field. Is the Ordnance nothing? Are the Blues nothing? Is the command of the army, with all the patronage annexed to it, nothing? Where he got these nothings, I know not; but you at least ought to have told us where he deserved them.

As to his bounty, compassion, &c. it would have been but little to the purpose, though you had proved all that you have asserted. I meddle with nothing but his character as commander in chief; and, though I acquit him of the baseness of selling commissions, I still assert that his military cares have never extended beyond the disposal of vacancies; and I am justified by the complaints of the whole army, when I say, that in this distribution he consults nothing but parliamentary interest, or the gratification of his immediate dependants. As to his servile submission to the reigning ministry, let me ask whether he did not desert the cause of the whole army when he suffered Sir Jefferey Amherst to be sacrificed, and what share he had in recalling that officer to the service? Did he not betray the just interest of the army, in permitting Lord Percy to have a regiment? And does he not at this moment give up all character and dignity as a gentleman, in receding from his own repeated declarations in favour of Mr. Wilkes?

In the two next articles I think we are agreed. You candidly admit that he often makes such promises as it is a virtue in him to violate, and that no man is more assiduous to provide for his relations at the public expence. I did not urge the last as an absolute vice in his disposition, but to prove that a careless disinterested spirit is no part of his character ; and as to the other, I desire it may be remembered that I never descended to the indecency of inquiring into his convivial hours. It is you, Sir William Draper, who have taken care to represent your friend in the character of a drunken landlord, who deals out his promises as liberally as his liquor, and will suffer no man to leave his table either sorrowful or sober. None but an intimate friend, who must frequently have seen him in these unhappy, disgraceful moments, could have described him so well.

The last charge, of the neglect of the army, is indeed the most material of all. I am sorry to tell you, Sir William, that, in this article, your first fact is false ; and as there is nothing more painful to me than to give a direct contradiction to a gentleman of your appearance, I could wish that, in your future publications, you would pay a greater attention to the truth of your premises, before you suffer your genius to hurry you to a conclusion. Lord Ligonier did not deliver the army (which you, in classical language, are pleased to call a palladium) into Lord Granby's hands. It was taken from him much against his inclination, some two or three years before Lord Granby was commander in chief. As to the state of the army, I should be glad to know where you have received your intelligence. Was it in the rooms at Bath, or at your retreat at Clifton ? The reports of reviewing generals comprehend only a few regiments in England, which, as they are immediately under the royal inspection, are perhaps in some tolerable order. But do you know any thing of the troops in the West Indies, the Mediterranean, and North America, to say nothing of a whole army absolutely ruined in Ireland ? Inquire a little into facts, Sir William, before you publish your next panegyric upon Lord Granby ; and believe me, you will find there is a fault at head-quarters, which even the acknowledged care and abilities of the adjutant-general cannot correct.

Permit me now, Sir William, to address myself personally to you, by way of thanks for the honor of your correspondence. You are by no means undeserving of notice ; and it may be of consequence even to Lord Granby to have it determined, whether or no the man, who has praised him so lavishly, be himself deserving of praise. When you returned to Europe, you zealously undertook the cause of that gallant army, by whose bravery at Manilla your own fortune had been established. You complained, you threatened, you even appealed to the public in print. By what accident did it happen, that, in the midst of all this bustle, and all these clamours for justice to your injured troops, the name of the Manilla ransom was suddenly buried in a profound, and, since that time, an uninterrupted silence? Did the ministry suggest any motives to you, strong enough to tempt a man of honour to desert and betray the cause of his fellow-soldiers? Was it that blushing ribband, which is now the perpetual ornament of your person? Or was it that regiment, which you afterwards (a thing unprecedented among soldiers) sold to Colonel Gisborne? Or was it that government, the full pay of which you are contented to hold, with the half-pay of an Irish colonel? And do you now, after a retreat not very like that of Scipio, presume to intrude yourself, unthought of, uncalled for, upon the patience of the public? Are your flatteries of the commander in chief directed to another regiment, which you may again dispose of on the same honourable terms? We know your prudence, Sir William, and I should be sorry to stop your preferment.

JUNIUS.

LETTER IV.

TO JUNIUS.

SIR, *Feb.* 17, 1769.

I RECEIVED Junius's favour last night: he is determined to keep his advantage by the help of his mask; it is an excellent protection, it has saved many a man from an untimely end. But whenever he will be honest enough to lay it aside, avow himself, and produce the face which has so long lurked behind it, the world will be able to judge of his motives for writing such infamous invectives. His real name will discover his freedom and independency, or his servility to a faction. Disappointed am bition, resentment for defeated hopes, and desire of revenge, assume but too often the appearance of public spirit; but be his designs wicked or charitable, Junius should learn that it is possible to condemn measures, without a barbarous and criminal outrage against men. Junius delights to mangle carcases with a hatchet; his language and instrument have a great connexion with Clare-Market; and, to do him justice, he handles his weapon most admirably. One would imagine he had been taught to throw it by the savages of America. It is therefore high time for me to step in once more to shield my friend from this merciless weapon, although I may be wounded in the attempt. But I must first ask Junius, by what forced analogy and construction the moments of convivial mirth are made to signify indecency, a violation of engagements, a drunken landlord, and a desire that every one in company should be drunk likewise? He must have culled all the flowers of St. Giles's and Billingsgate to have produced such a piece of oratory. Here the hatchet descends with tenfold vengeance; but, alas! it hurts no one but its master! For Junius must not think to put words into my mouth, that seem too foul even for his own.

My friend's political engagements I know not; so cannot pretend to explain them, or assert their consistency. I know not whether Junius be considerable enough to belong to any party; if he should be so, can he affirm that he has always adhered to one set of men and measures? Is he sure that he has never sided with those whom he was first hired to abuse? Has he never abused those he was hired to praise? To say the truth, most men's politics sit much too loosely about them. But as my friend's military character was the chief object that engaged me in this controversy, to that I shall return.

Junius asks what instances my friend has given of his military skill and capacity as a general? When and where he gained his honour? When he deserved his emoluments? The united voice of the army which served under him, the glorious testimony of Prince Ferdinand, and of vanquished enemies, all Germany will tell him. Junius repeats the complaints of the army against parliamentary influence. I love the army too well not to wish that such influence were less. Let Junius point out the time when it has not prevailed. It was of the least force in the time of that great man, the late Duke of Cumberland, who, as a prince of the blood, was able as well as willing to stem a torrent which would have overborne any private subject. In time of war, this influence is small. In peace, when discontent and faction have the surest means to operate, especially in this country, and when, from a scarcity of public spirit, the wheels of government are rarely moved but by the power and force of obligations, its weight is always too great. Yet, if this influence at present has done no greater harm than the placing Earl Percy at the head of a regiment, I do not think that either the rights or best interests of the army are sacrificed and betrayed, or the nation undone. Let me ask Junius if he knows any one nobleman in the army who has had a regiment by seniority? I feel myself happy in seeing young noblemen of illustrious name and great property come among us. They are an additional security to the kingdom from foreign or domestic slavery. Junius needs not be told, that, should the time ever come when this nation is to be defended only by those who have nothing more to lose than their arms and their pay, its danger will be great indeed. A happy mixture of men of quality with soldiers of fortune is always to be wished for. But the main point is still to be contended for, I mean the discipline and condition of the army; and I must still maintain, though contradicted by Junius, that it was never upon a more respectable footing, as to all the essentials that can form good soldiers, than it is at present. Junius is forced to allow that our army at home may be in some tolerable order; yet how kindly does he invite our late enemies to the invasion of Ireland, by assuring them that the army in that kingdom is totally ruined! (The colonels of that army are much obliged to him.) I have too great an opinion of the military talents of the lord lieutenant, and of all their diligence and capacity, to believe it. If from some strange, unaccountable fatality, the people of that kingdom cannot be induced to consult their own security by such an effectual augmentation as may enable the troops there to act with power and energy, is the commander in chief here to blame? Or is he to blame, because the troops in the Mediterranean, in the

West Indies, in America, labour under great difficulties from the scarcity of men, which is but too visible all over these kingdoms? Many of our forces are in climates unfavorable to British constitutions; their loss is in proportion. Britain must recruit all these regiments from her own emaciated bosom, or more precariously, by Catholics from Ireland. We are likewise subject to the fatal drains to the East Indies, to Senegal, and the alarming emigrations of our people to other countries: Such depopulation can only be repaired by a long peace, or by some sensible bill of naturalization.

I must now take the liberty to talk to Junius on my own account. He is pleased to tell me that he addresses himself to me personally; I shall be glad to see him. It is his impersonality that I complain of, and his invisible attacks: for his dagger in the air is only to be regarded because one cannot see the hand which holds it; but had it not wounded other people more deeply than myself, I should not have obtruded myself at all on the patience of the public.

Mark how a plain tale shall put him down, and transfuse the blush of my ribband into his own cheeks. Junius tells me, that, at my return, I zealously undertook the cause of the gallant army by whose bravery at Manilla my own fortunes were established: that I complained, that I even appealed to the public. I did so; I glory in having done so, as I had an undoubted right to vindicate my own character, attacked by a Spanish memorial, and to assert the rights of my brave companions. I glory likewise that I have never taken up my pen but to vindicate the injured. Junius asks by what accident did it happen, that in the midst of all this bustle, and all the clamours for justice to the injured troops, the Manilla ransom was suddenly buried in a profound, and, since that time, an uninterrupted silence? I will explain the cause to the public. The several ministers who have been employed since that time have been very desirous to do justice, from two most laudable motives, a strong inclination to assist injured bravery, and to acquire a well-deserved popularity to themselves. Their efforts have been in vain. Some were ingenuous enough to own that they could not think of involving this distressed nation into another war for our private-concerns. In short, our rights for the present are sacrificed to national convenience ; and I must confess, that although I may lose five and twenty thousand pounds by their acquiescence to this breach of faith in the Spaniards, I think they are in the right to temporize, considering the critical situation of this country, convulsed in every part by poison infused by anonymous, wicked and incendiary writers. Lord Shelburne will do me the justice to own, that, in September last, I waited upon him with a joint memorial from the admiral Sir S. Cornish and myself, in behalf of our injured companions. His Lordship was as frank upon the occasion as other secretaries had been before him. He did not deceive us by giving any immediate hopes of relief.

Junius would basely insinuate that my silence may have been purchased by my government, by my blushing ribband, by my regiment, by the sale of that regiment, and by half-pay as an Irish colonel.

His majesty was pleased to give me my government for my service at Madras. I had my first regiment in 1757. Upon my return from Manilla, his Majesty, by Lord Egremont, informed me that I should have the first vacant red ribband, as a reward for many services in an enterprise, which I had planned as well as executed. The Duke of Bedford and Mr. Grenville confirmed those assurances many months before the Spaniards had protested the ransom bills. To accommodate Lord Clive, then going upon a most important service to Bengal, I waved my claim to the vacancy which then happened. As there was no other vacancy until the Duke of Grafton and Lord Rockingham were joint ministers, I was then honored with the order: and it is surely no small honour to me, that, in such a succession of ministers, they were all pleased to think that I had deserved it ; in my favor they were all united. Upon the reduction of the 79th regiment, which had served so gloriously in the East Indies, his Majesty, unsolicited by me, gave me the 16th of foot as an equivalent. My motives for retiring afterwards are foreign to the purpose : let it suffice, that his Majesty was pleased to approve of them ; they are such as no man can think indecent, who knows the shocks that repeated vicissitudes of heat and cold, of dangerous and sickly climates, will give to the best constitutions in a pretty long course of service. I resigned my regiment to Colonel Gisborne, a very good officer, for his half pay, 200l. Irish annuity; so that, according to Junius, I have been bribed to say nothing more of the Manilla ransom, and sacrifice those brave men, by the strange avarice of accepting three hundred and eighty pounds per annum, and giving up eight hundred! If this be bribery, it is not the bribery of these times. As to my flattery, those who know me will judge of it. By the asperity of Junius's style, I cannot indeed call him a flatterer, unless he be as a cynic, or a mastiff; if he wags his tail, he will still growl, and long to bite. The public will now judge of the credit that ought to be given to Junius's writings, from the falsities that he has insinuated with respect to myself.

WILLIAM DRAPER.

LETTER V.

TO SIR WILLIAM DRAPER, KNIGHT OF THE BATH.

SIR, *Feb.* 21, 1769.

I SHOULD justly be suspected of acting upon motives of more than common enmity to Lord Granby, if I continued to give you fresh materials or occasion for writing in his defence. Individuals who hate, and the public who despise, have read your letters, Sir William, with infinitely more satisfaction than mine. Unfortunately for him, his reputation, like that unhappy country to which you refer me for his last military achievements, has suffered more by his friends than his enemies. In mercy, to him, let us drop the subject. For my own part, I willingly leave it to the public to determine whether your vindication of your friend has been as able and judicious, as it was certainly well intended; and you, I think, may be satisfied with the warm acknowledgments he already owes you for making him the principal figure in a piece, in which, but for your amicable assistance, he might have passed without particular notice or distinction.

In justice to your friends, let your future labours be

D

confined to the care of your own reputation. Your declaration, that you are happy in seeing young noblemen
come among us, is liable to two objections. With respect
to Lord Percy, it means nothing, for he was already in
the army. He was aid-de-camp to the King, and had
the rank of Colonel. A regiment therefore could not
make him a more military man, though it made him
richer, and probably at the expence of some brave, deserving, friendless officer.—The other concerns yourself.
—After selling the companions of your victory in one instance, and after selling your profession in the other, by
what authority do you presume to call yourself a soldier?
The plain evidence of facts is superior to all declarations.
Before you were appointed to the 16th regiment, your
complaints were a distress to government;—from that
moment you were silent. The conclusion is inevitable.
You insinuate to us that your ill state of health obliged
you to quit the service. The retirement necessary to repair a broken constitution, would have been as good a
reason for not accepting, as for resigning the command
of a regiment. There is certainly an error of the press,
or an affected obscurity in that paragraph, where you
speak of your bargain with Colonel Gisborne. Instead of
attempting to answer what I do not really understand,
permit me to explain to the public what I really know.
In exchange for your regiment, you accepted of a colonel's half-pay (at least 220l. a-year,) and an annuity of
200l. for your own and Lady Draper's life jointly.—And
is this the losing bargain, which you would represent to
us, as if you had given up an income of 800l. a-year for
380l.? Was it decent, was it honourable, in a man
who pretends to love the army, and calls himself a soldier, to make a traffic of the royal favour, and turn the
highest honour of an active profession into a sordid provision for himself and his family? It were unworthy of
me to press you farther. The contempt with which the
whole army heard of the manner of your retreat assures
me, that as your conduct was not justified by precedent,
it will never be thought an example for imitation.

The last and most important question remains. When
you receive your half-pay, do you, or do you not take a
solemn oath, or sign a declaration upon your honour, to

the following effect? " That you do not actually hold any
" place of profit, civil or military, under his Majesty." The
charge which the question plainly conveys against you, is
of so shocking a complexion, that I sincerely wish you
may be able to answer it well, not merely for the colour
of your reputation, but for your own peace of mind.

JUNIUS.

LETTER VI.

TO JUNIUS.

SIR, *Feb.* 27, 1769.

I HAVE a very short answer for Junius's important question; I do not either take an oath, or declare upon honour, that I have no place of profit, civil or military, when I receive the half-pay as an Irish colonel.——
My most gracious Sovereign gives it me as a pension;
he was pleased to think I deserved it. The annuity of
200l. Irish, and the equivalent for the half-pay, together,
produce no more than 380l. per annum, clear of fees and
perquisites of office. I receive 167l. from my government of Yarmouth. Total 547l. per annum. My conscience is much at ease in these particulars; my friends
need not blush for me.

Junius makes much and frequent use of interrogations:
they are arms that may be easily turned against himself.
I could, by malicious interrogation, disturb the peace of
the most virtuous man in the kingdom. I could take the
decalogue, and say to one man, Did you never steal?
To the next, Did you never commit murder? And to
Junius himself, who is putting my life and conduct to
the rack, Did you never bear false witness against thy
neighbour? Junius must easily see, that unless he affirms
to the contrary in his real name, some people who may
be as ignorant of him as I am, will be apt to suspect him
of having deviated a little from the truth: therefore let
Junius ask no more questions. You bite against a file:
cease, viper.

W. D.

LETTER VII.

TO SIR WILLIAM DRAPER, KNIGHT OF THE BATH.

SIR,   *March* 3, 1769.

An academical education has given you an unlimited command over the most beautiful figures of speech.
Masks, hatchets, racks and vipers, dance through your
letters in all the mazes of metaphorical confusion. These
are the gloomy companions of a disturbed imagination ;
the melancholy madness of poetry, without the inspiration. I will not contend with you in point of composition. You are a scholar, Sir William ; and, if I am
truly informed, you write Latin with almost as much purity as English. Suffer me, then, for I am a plain unlettered man, to continue that style of interrogation, which
suits my capacity ; and to which, considering the readi-
ness of your answers, you ought to have no objection.
Even &c Mr. Bingly promises to answer, if put to the
torture.

Do you then really think, that, if I were to ask a most
virtuous man whether he ever committed theft, or murder, it would disturb his peace of mind? Such a question might perhaps discompose the gravity of his muscles,
but I believe it would little affect the tranquility of his
conscience. Examine your own breast, Sir William, and
you will discover, that reproaches and inquiries have no
power to afflict either the man of unblemished integrity,
or the abandoned profligate. It is the middle compound
character which alone is vulnerable ; the man who, without firmness enough to avoid a dishonourable action, has
feeling enough to be ashamed of it.

I thank you for the hint of the decalogue, and shall
take an opportunity of applying it to some of your most
virtuous friends in both houses of parliament.

You seem to have dropped the affair of your regiment ;
so let it rest. When you are appointed to another, I
dare say you will not sell it either for a gross sum, or for
an annuity upon lives.

I am truly glad (for really, Sir William, I am not your
enemy, nor did I begin this contest with you) that you
have been able to clear yourself of a crime, though at the

expence of the highest indiscretion. You say that your half-pay was given you by way of pension. I will not dwell upon the singularity of uniting in your own person two sorts of provision, which in their own nature, and in all military and parliamentary views, are incompatible ; but I call upon you to justify that declaration, wherein you charge your Sovereign with having done an act in your favor notoriously against law. The half-pay, both in Ireland and England, is appropriated by Parliament; and if it be given to persons who, like you, are legally incapable of holding it, it is a breach of law. It would have been more decent in you to have called this dishonourable transaction by its true name ; a job to accommodate two persons, by particular interest and management at the Castle. What sense must government have had of your services, when the rewards they have given you are only a disgrace to you ?

And, now, Sir William h, I shall take my leave of you for ever. Motives very different from any apprehension of your resentment, make it impossible you should ever know me. In truth, you have some reason to hold yourself indebted to me. From the lessons I have given you, you may collect a profitable instruction for your future life. They will either teach you so to regulate your conduct, as to be able to set the most malicious inquiries at defiance ; or, if that be a lost hope, they will teach you prudence enough not to attract the public attention to a character which will only pass without censure, when it passes without observation.

JUNIUS.

LETTER VIII.

TO THE DUKE OF GRAFTON.

MY LORD,   *March* 18, 1769.

BEFORE you were placed at the head of affairs, it had been a maxim of the English government, not unwillingly admitted by the people, that every ungracious or severe exertion of the prerogative should be placed to the account of the Minister; but that, whenever an act of grace or benevolence was to be performed, the whole

D 2

merit of it should be attributed to the Sovereign himself[i].
It was a wise doctrine, my Lord, and equally advantageous to the King and his subjects ; for while it preserved
that suspicious attention, with which the people ought
always to examine the conduct of ministers, it tended at
the same time rather to increase than diminish their attachment to the person of the Sovereign. If there be not
a fatality attending every measure you are concerned in,
by what treachery, or by what excess of folly, has it happened, that those ungracious acts which have distinguished
your administration, and which I doubt not were entirely
your own, should carry with them a strong appearance of
personal interest, and even of personal enmity, in a quarter where no such interest or enmity can be supposed to
exist without the highest injustice, and the highest dishonour ? On the other hand, by what injudicious management have you contrived it, that the only act of mercy to
which you have ever advised your Sovereign, far from
adding to the lustre of a character truly gracious and benevolent, should be received with universal disapprobation
and disgust? I shall consider it as a ministerial measure,
because it is an odious one ; and as your measure, my
Lord Duke, because you are the minister.

As long as the trial of this chairman was depending,
it was natural enough that government should give him
every possible encouragement and support. The honourable service for which he was hired, and the spirit with
which he performed it, made a common cause between
your Grace and him. The minister, who by secret corruption invades the freedom of elections, and the ruffian,
who, by open violence, destroys that freedom, are em-
barked in the same bottom. They have the same interests,
and mutually feel for each other. To do justice to your
Grace's humanity, you felt for M'Quirk as you ought to
do ; and if you had been contented to assist him indirectly, without a notorious denial of justice, or openly
insulting the sense of the nation, you might have satisfied every duty of political friendship, without commuting
the honour of your Sovereign, or hazarding the reputation of his government. But when this unhappy man
had been solemnly tried, convicted, and condemned ;—
when it appeared that he had been frequently employed

in the same services, and that no excuse for him could be
drawn either from the innocence of his former life, or the
simplicity of his character; was it not hazarding too
much to interpose the strength of the prerogative between
this felon and the justice of his country k? You ought
to have known, that an example of this sort was never so
necessary as at present; and certainly you must have
known that the lot could not have fallen upon a more
guilty-object. What system of government is this? You
are perpetually complaining of the riotous disposition of
the lower class of people; yet when the laws have given
you the means of making an example in every sense unexceptionable, and by far the most likely to awe the multitude, you pardon the offence, and are not ashamed to
give the sanction of government to the riots you complain
of, and even to future murders. You are partial perhaps
to the military mode of execution; and had rather see a
score of these wretches butchered by the guards, than
one of them suffer death by regular course of law. How
does it happen, my Lord, that, in your hands, even the
mercy of the prerogative is cruelty and oppression of the
subject?

The measure, it seems, was so extraordinary, that you
thought it necessary to give some reasons for it to the
public. Let them be fairly examined.

1: You say that Messrs. Bromfield and Starling were
not examined at M'Quirk's trial. I will tell your Grace
why they were not. They must have been examined upon oath; and it was foreseen, that their evidence would
either not benefit, or might be prejudicial to the prisoner.
Otherwise, is it conceivable that his counsel should neglect to call in such material evidence?

You say that Mr. Foot did not see the deceased
until after his death. A surgeon, my Lord, must know
very little of his profession, if, upon examining a wound
or a contusion, he cannot determine whether it was mor-
tal or not.—While the party is alive, a surgeon will be
cautious of pronouncing; whereas, by the death of the
patient, he is enabled to consider both cause and effect in
one view, and to speak with a certainty, confirmed by experience.

Yet we are to thank your Grace for the establishment

of a new tribunal. Your *inquisitio post mortem* is unknown to the laws of England, and does honor to your invention. The only material objection to it is, that if Mr. Foot's evidence was insufficient, because it did not examine the wound till after the death of the party, much less can a negative opinion, given by gentlemen who never saw the body of Mr. Clarke, either before or after his decease, authorise you to supersede the verdict of a jury, and the sentence of the law.

Now, my Lord, let me ask you, Has it never occurred to your Grace, while you were withdrawing this desperate wretch from that justice which the laws had awarded, and which the whole people of England demanded against him, that there is another man, who is the favourite of his country, whose pardon would have been accepted with gratitude, whose pardon would have healed all our divisions? Have you quite forgotten that this man was once your Grace's friend? Or is it to murderers only that you will extend the mercy of the crown?

These are questions you will not answer, nor is it necessary. The character of your private life, and the tenour of your public conduct, is an answer to them all.

JUNIUS.

LETTER IX.

TO HIS GRACE THE DUKE OF GRAFTON.

MY LORD, *April* 10, 1769.

I HAVE so good an opinion of your Grace's discernment, that when the author of the vindication of your conduct assures us, that he writes from his own mere motion, without the least authority from your Grace, I should be ready enough to believe him, but for one fatal mark, which seems to be fixed upon every measure in which either your personal or your political character is concerned.—Your first attempt to support Sir William Proctor, ended in the election of Mr. Wilkes; the second ensured success to Mr. Glynn. The extraordinary step you took to make Sir James Lowther lord paramount of Cumberland, has ruined his interest in that country for ever. The House List of Directors was cursed with the con-

currence of government; and even the miserable [1] Dingley could not escape the misfortune of your Grace's protection. With this uniform experience before us, we
are authorised to suspect, that when a pretended vindication of your principles and conduct, in reality contains
the bitterest reflections upon both; it could not have been
written without your immediate direction and assistance.
The author indeed calls God to witness for him, with all
the sincerity, and in the very terms of an Irish evidence,
to the best of his knowledge and belief. My Lord, you
should not encourage these appeals to Heaven. The pious Prince from whom you are supposed to descend, made
such frequent use of them in his public declarations, that
at last the people also found it necessary to appeal to
Heaven in their turn. Your administration has driven us
into circumstances of equal distress; beware at least how
you remind us of the remedy.

You have already much to answer for. You have provoked this unhappy gentleman to play the fool once more
in public life, in spite of his years and infirmities; and to
show us, that, as you yourself are a singular instance of
youth without spirit, the man who defends you is a no less
remarkable example of age without the benefits of experience. To follow such a writer minutely would, like his
own periods, be a labour without end. The subject too has
been already discussed, and is sufficiently understood. I
cannot help observing, however, that, when the pardon of
M'Quirk was the principal charge against you, it would
have been but a decent compliment to your Grace's understanding, to have defended you upon your own principles. What credit does a man deserve, who tells us
plainly, that the facts set forth in the King's proclamation
were not the true motives on which the pardon was
granted: and that he wishes that those chirurgical reports, which first gave occasion to certain doubts in the
royal breast, had not been laid before his Majesty? You
see, my Lord, that even your friends cannot defend your
actions, without changing your principles; nor justify a
deliberate measure of government, without contradicting
the main assertion on which it was founded.

The conviction of M'Quirk had reduced you to a dilemma, in which it was hardly possible for you to recon-

cile your political interest with your duty. You were obliged either to abandon an active useful partisan, or to protect a felon from public justice. With your usual spirit, you preferred your interest to every other consideration; and with your usual judgment, you founded your determination upon the only motives which should not have been given to the public.

I have frequently censured Mr. Wilkes's conduct, yet your advocate reproaches me with having devoted myself to the service of sedition. Your Grace can best inform us, for which of Mr. Wilkes's good qualities you first honoured him with your friendship; or how long it was before you discovered those bad ones in him, at which, it seems, your delicacy was offended. Remember, my Lord, that you continued your connexion with Mr. Wilkes long after he had been convicted of those crimes which you have since taken pains to represent in the blackest colours of blasphemy and treason. How unlucky is it that the first instance you have given us of a scrupulous regard to decorum is united with the breach of a moral obligation! For my own part, my Lord, I am proud to affirm, that if I had been weak enough to form such a friendship, I would never have been base enough to betray it. But let Mr. Wilkes's character be what it may, this at least is certain, that, circumstanced as he is with regard to the public, even his vices plead for him. The people of England have too much discernment to suffer your Grace to take advantage of the failings of a private character, to establish a precedent by which the public liberty is affected, and which you may hereafter, with equal ease and satisfaction, employ to the ruin of the best men in the kingdom.——Content yourself, my Lord, with the many advantages which the unsullied purity of your own character has given you over your unhappy deserted friend. Avail yourself of all the unforgiving piety of the court you live in, and bless God that you " are not as other men " are, extortioners, unjust, adulterers, or even as this " publican." In a heart void of feeling, the laws of honour and good faith may be violated with impunity, and there you may safely indulge your genius : But the laws of England shall not be violated, even by your holy zeal to oppress a sinner ; and though you have succeeded in

making him a tool, you shall not make him the victim of
your ambition.

JUNIUS.

LETTER X.

TO MR. EDWARD WESTON.

SIR, *April* 21, 1769.

    I SAID you were an old man without the benefit
of experience. It seems you are also a volunteer with the
stipend of twenty commissions ; and at a period when all
prospects are at an end, you are still looking forward to
rewards which you cannot enjoy. No man is better acquainted with the bounty of government than you are.
———————————*ton impudence,*
    Temeraire vicillard, aura sa recompense.

    But I will not descend to an altercation either with the
impotence of your age, or the peevishness of your diseases.
Your pamphlet, ingenious as it is, has been so little read,
that the public cannot know how far you have a right
to give me the lie, without the following citation of your
own words.

    Page 6.—' 1. That he is persuaded that the motives
' which he (Mr. Weston) has alleged, must appear ful-
' ly sufficient, with or without the opinions of the sur-
' geons.

    ' 2. That those very motives MUST HAVE BEEN the
' foundation on which the Earl of Rochfort thought pro-
' per, &c.

    ' 3. That he CANNOT BUT REGRET that the Earl of
' Rochfort seems to have thought proper to lay the chi-
' rurgical reports before the King, in preference to all the
' other sufficient motives,' &c.

    Let the public determine whether this be defending go-
vernment on their principles or your own.

    The style and language you have adopted are, I con-
fess, not ill suited to the elegance of your own manners,
or the dignity of the cause you have undertaken. Every
common dauber writes rascal and villain under his pictures, because the pictures themselves have neither character nor resemblance. But the works of a master re-

quire no index. His features and colouring are taken from nature. The impression they make is immediate and uniform; nor is it possible to mistake his characters, whether they represent the treachery of a minister, or the abused simplicity of a king.

JUNIUS.

LETTER XI.

TO HIS GRACE THE DUKE OF GRAFTON.

MY LORD,   *April* 24, 1769.

THE system you seemed to have adopted, when Lord Chatham unexpectedly left you at the head of affairs, gave us no promise of that uncommon exertion of vigour which has since illustrated your character and distinguished your administration. Far from discovering a spirit bold enough to invade the first rights of the people, and the first principles of the constitution, you were scrupulous of exercising even those powers with which the executive branch of the legislature is legally invested. We have not yet forgotten how long Mr. Wilkes was suffered to appear at large, nor how long he was at liberty to canvas for the city and county, with all the terrors of an outlawry hanging over him. Our gracious Sovereign has not yet forgotten the extraordinary care you took of his dignity, and of the safety of his person, when, at a crisis which courtiers affected to call alarming, you left the metropolis exposed for two nights together to every species of riot and disorder. The security of the Royal residence from insult was then sufficiently provided for in Mr. Conway's firmness, and Lord Weymouth's discretion; while the prime minister of Great Britain, in a rural retirement, and in the arms of faded beauty, had lost all memory of his Sovereign, his country, and himself. In these instances you might have acted with vigour, for you would have had the sanction of the laws to support you. The friends of government might have defended you without shame; and moderate men, who wish well to the peace and good order of society, might have had a pretence for applauding your conduct. But these, it seems, were not occasions worthy of your Grace's interposition. You re-

served the proofs of your intrepid spirit for trials of great‑
er hazard 'and .importance: and now, as if the most disgraceful relaxation of the executive authority had given
you a claim of credit to indulge in excesses still more dangerous, you seem determined to compensate amply for
your former negligence, and to balance the non-execution
of the laws with a breach of the constitution. From one
extreme you suddenly start to the other, without leaving,
between the weakness and the fury of the passions, one
moment's interval for the firmness of the understanding.

These observations, general as they are, might easily be
extended into a faithful history of your Grace's administration, and perhaps may be the employment of a future
hour. But the business of the present moment will not
suffer me to look back to a series of events, which cease
to be interesting or important, because they are succeeded
by a measure so singularly daring, that it excites all our attention, and engrosses all our resentment:

Your patronage of Mr. Luttrell has been crowned with
success. With this precedent before you, with the
principles on which it was established, and with a future House of Commons, perhaps less virtuous than the
present, every county in England under the auspices of
the treasury, may be represented as completely as the
county of Middlesex. Posterity will be indebted to your
Grace for not contenting yourself with a temporary expedient, but entailing upon them the immediate blessings of your administration. Boroughs were already too
much at the mercy of government. Counties could
neither be purchased not intimidated. But their solemn
determined election may be rejected, and the man they
detest may be appointed, by another choice, to represent
them in parliament. Yet it is admitted, that the sheriffs
obeyed the laws and performed their duty[m]. The return they made must have been legal and valid, or undoubtedly they would have been censured for making it.
With every good natured allowance for your Grace's
youth and inexperience, there are some things which you
cannot but know. You cannot but know that the right
of the freeholders to adhere to their choice (even supposing it improperly exerted) was as clear and indisputable as that of the House of Commons to exclude one

of their own members.—Nor is it possible for you not to see the wide distance there is between the negative power of rejecting one man, and the positive power of appointing another. The right of expulsion, in the most favourable sense, is no more than the custom of parliament. The right of election is the very essence of the constitution. To violate that right, and much more to transfer it to any other set of men, is a step leading immediately to the dissolution of all government. So far forth as it operates, it constitutes a House of Commons which does not represent the people. A House of Commons so formed would involve a contradiction and the grossest confusion of ideas ; but there are some ministers, my Lord, whose views can only be answered by reconciling absurdities, and making the same proposition, which is false and absurd in argument, true in fact.

This measure, my Lord, is however attended with one consequence favourable to the people, which I am persuaded you did not foresee[n]. While the contest lay between the ministry and Mr. Wilkes, his situation and private character gave you advantages over him, which common candour, if not the memory of your former friendship, should have forbidden you to make use of. To religious men, you had an opportunity of exaggerating the irregularities of his past life ;—to moderate men, you held forth the pernicious consequences of faction. Men, who with this character looked no farther than to the object before them, were not dissatisfied at seeing Mr. Wilkes excluded from parliament. You have now taken care to shift the question ; or rather, you have created a new one, in which Mr. Wilkes is no more concerned than any other English gentleman. You have united this country against you on one grand constitutional point, on the decision of which our existence, as a free people, absolutely depends. You have asserted, not in words but in fact, that the representation in parliament does not depend upon the choice of the freeholders. If such a case can possibly happen once, it may happen frequently ; it may happen always : —and if three hundred votes, by any mode of reasoning whatsoever, can prevail against twelve hundred, the same reasoning would equally have given Mr. Luttrell his seat with ten votes, or even with one. The consequences of this attack upon the constitution are too plain and palpable not to alarm the dullest apprehension. I trust you will find, that the people of England are neither deficient in spirit nor understanding, though you have treated them as if they had neither sense to feel, nor spirit to resent. We have reason to thank God and our ancestors, that there never yet was a minister in this country who could stand the issue of such a conflict; and with every prejudice in favour of your intentions, I see no such abilities in your Grace as should entitle you to succeed in an enterprise, in which the ablest and basest of your predecessors have found their destruction. You may continue to deceive your gracious master with false representations of the temper and condition of his subjects. You may command a venal vote, because it is the common established appendage of your office. But never hope that the freeholders will make a tame surrender of their rights, or that an English army will join with you in overturning the liberties of their country. They know that their first duty as citizens is paramount to all subsequent engagements; nor will they prefer the discipline, or even the honours of their profession, to those sacred original rights, which belonged to them before they were soldiers, and which they claim and possess as the birth-right of Englishmen.

Return, my Lord, before it be too late, to that easy, insipid system which you first set out with. Take back your mistress;°—the name of friend may be fatal to her, for it leads to treachery and persecution. Indulge the people. Attend Newmarket. Mr. Luttrell may again vacate his seat; and Mr. Wilkes, if not persecuted, will soon be forgotten. To be weak and inactive, is, safer than to be daring and criminal; and, wide is the distance between a riot of the populace and a convulsion of the whole kingdom. You may live to make the experiment, but no honest man can wish you should survive it.

JUNIUS,

TO HIS GRACE THE DUKE OF GRAFTON.

MY LORD,   May 30. 1769.

IF the measures in which you have been most successful had been supported by any tolerable appearance of argument, I should have thought my time not ill employed in continuing to examine your conduct as a minister, and stating it fairly to the public. But when I see, questions of the highest national importance carried as they have been, and the first principles of the constitution openly violated, without argument or decency, I confess I give up the cause in despair. The meanest of your predecessors had abilities sufficient to give a colour to their measures. If they invaded the rights of the people, they did not dare to offer a direct insult to their understanding ; and in former times, the most venal parliaments made it a condition in their bargain with the minister, that he should furnish them with some plausible pretences for selling their country and themselves. You have had the merit of introducing a more compendious system of government and logic. You neither address yourself to the passions, nor to the understanding, but simply to the touch. You apply yourself immediately to the feelings of your friends ; who, contrary to the forms of parliament, never enter heartily into a debate until they have divided.

Relinquishing, therefore, all idle views of amendment to your Grace, or of benefit to the public, let me be permitted to consider your character and conduct merely as a subject of curious speculation.—There is something in both, which distinguishes you not only from all other ministers, but all other men ; it is not that you do wrong by design, but that you should never do right by mistake. It is not that your indolence and your activity have been equally misapplied ; but that the first uniform principle, or, if I may call it, the genius of your life, should have carried you through every possible change and contradiction of conduct, without the momentary imputation or colour of a virtue ; and that the wildest spirit of inconsistency should never once have betrayed you into a wise

or honourable action. This I own gives an air of singularity to your fortune as well as to your disposition. Let
us look back together to a scene in which a mind like
yours will find nothing to repent of. Let us try, my
Lord, how well you have supported the various relations
in which you stood, to your sovereign, your country, your
friends, and yourself. Give us, if it be possible, some
excuse to posterity; and to ourselves, for submitting to
your administration. If not the abilities of a great minister, if not the integrity of a patriot, or the fidelity of
a friend, show us at least the firmness of a man.—For
the sake of your mistress, the lover shall be spared. I
will not lead her into public, as you have done, nor will
I insult the memory of departed beauty. Her sex, which
alone made her amiable in your eyes, makes her respectable in mine.

The character of the reputed ancestors of some men,
has made it possible for their descendants to be vicious in
the extreme, without being degenerate. Those of your
Grace, for instance, left no distressing examples of virtue even to their legitimate posterity; and you may look
back with pleasure to an illustrious pedigree, in which
heraldry has not left a single good quality upon record to
insult or upbraid you. You have better proofs of your
descent, my Lord, than the register of a marriage, or any
troublesome inheritance of reputation. There are some
hereditary strokes of character, by which a family may
be as clearly distinguished, as by the blackest features of
the human face. Charles the First lived and died a hypocrite. Charles the Second was a hypocrite of another
sort, and should have died upon the same scaffold. At
the distance of a century, we see their different characters happily revived and blended in your Grace. Sullen
and severe without religion, profligate without gaiety, you
live like Charles the Second, without being an amiable
companion; and, for aught I know, may die as his father
did, without the reputation of a martyr.

You had already taken your degrees with credit in
those schools in which the English nobility are formed to
virtue, when you were introduced to Lord Chatham's
protection[p]. From Newmarket, White's, and the opposition, he gave you to the world with an air of popularity,

which young men usually, set out with, and seldom preserve :--grave and plausible enough to be thought fit for business ; too young for treachery ; and, in short, a patriot of no unpromising expectations. Lord Chatham was the earliest object of your political wonder and attachment ; yet you deserted him, upon the first hopes that offered of an equal share of power with Lord Rockingham. When the Duke of Cumberland's first negotiation failed, and when the favourite was pushed to the last extremity, you saved him by joining with an administration in which Lord Chatham had refused to engage. Still, however, he was your friend : and you are yet to explain to the world, why you consented to act without him ; or why, after uniting with Lord Rockingham, you deserted and betrayed him. You complained that no measures were taken to satisfy your patron ; and that your friend Mr. Wilkes, who had suffered so much for the party, had been abandoned to his fate. They have since contributed, not a little, to your present plenitude of power : yet, I think, Lord Chatham has less reason than ever to be satisfied ; and as for Mr. Wilkes , it is, perhaps, the greatest misfortune of his life that you should have so many compensations to make in the closet for your former friendship with him. Your gracious master understands your character ; and makes you a persecutor, because you have been a friend.

Lord Chatham formed his last administration upon principles, which you certainly concurred in, or you could never have been placed at the head of the Treasury. By deserting those principles, and by acting in a direct contradiction to them, in which he found you were secretly supported in the closet, you soon forced him to leave you to yourself, and to withdraw his name from an administration which had been formed on the credit of it. You had then a prospect of friendships better suited to your genius, and more likely to fix your disposition. Marriage is the point on which every rake is stationary at las : and truly, my Lord, you may well be weary of the circuit you have taken ; for you have now fairly travelled through every sign in the political zodiac, from the Scorpion, in which you stung Lord Chatham, to the hopes of a Virgin ? in the house of Bloomsbury. One would think that you had had sufficient experience of the frailty of nuptial engagements, or, at least, that such a friendship as the Duke of Bedford's might have been secured to you by the auspicious marriage of your late Duchess with his nephew. But ties of this tender nature cannot be drawn too close; and it may possibly be a part of the Duke of Bedford's ambition, after making her an honest woman, to work a miracle of the same sort upon your Grace. This worthy nobleman has long dealt in virtue. There has been a large consumption of it in his own family; and, in the way of traffic, I dare say, he has bought and sold more than half the representative integrity of the nation.

In a political view, this union is not imprudent. The favour of princes is a perishable commodity. You have now a strength sufficient to command the closet; and if it be necessary to betray one friendship more, you may set even Lord Bute at defiance. Mr. Stuart Mackenzie may possibly remember what use the Duke of Bedford usually makes of his power; and our gracious Sovereign, I doubt not, rejoices at this first appearance of union among his servants. His late Majesty, under the happy influence of a family connection between his ministers was relieved from the cares of the government. A more active prince may perhaps observe, with suspicion, by what degrees an artful servant grows-upon his master, from the first unlimited professions of duty and attachment, to the painful representation of the necessity of the royal service, and soon, in regular progression, to the humble insolence of dictating in all the obsequious forms of peremptory submission. The interval is carefully employed in forming connections, creating interests, collecting a party, and laying the foundation of double marriages; until the deluded prince, who thought he had found a creature prostituted to his service, and insignificant enough to be always dependent upon his pleasure, finds him at last too strong to be commanded, and too formidable to be removed.

Your Grace's public conduct, as a minister, is but the counter part of your private history;—the same inconsistency, the same contradictions. In America we trace you from the first opposition to the Stamp Act, on principles of convenience, to Mr. Pitt's surrender of the right: then forward to Lord Rockingham's surrender of the fact; then back again to Lord Rockingham's declaration of the right; then forward to taxation with Mr. Townshend; and in the last instance, from the gentle Conway's undetermined discretion, to blood and compulsion with the Duke of Bedford: Yet, if we may believe the simplicity of Lord North's eloquence, at the opening of next sessions, you are once more to be the patron of America. Is this the wisdom of a great minister? or is it the ominous vibration of a pendulum? Had you no opinion of your own, my Lord? or was it the gratification of betraying every party with which you have been united, and of deserting every political principle in which you had concurred?

Your enemies may turn their eyes without regret from this admirable system of provincial government. They will find gratification enough in the survey of your domestic and foreign policy.

If instead of disowning Lord Shelburne, the British court had interposed with dignity and firmness, you know, my Lord, that Corsica would never have been invaded. The French saw the weakness of a distracted ministry, and were justified in treating you with contempt. They would probably have yielded in the first instance, rather than hazard a rupture with this country; but, being once engaged, they cannot retreat, without dishonour. Common sense foresees consequences which have escaped your Grace's penetration. Either we suffer the French to make an acquisition, the importance of which you have probably no conception of; or we oppose them by an underhand management, which only disgraces us in the eyes of Europe, without answering any purpose of policy or prudence. From secret, indirect assistance, a transition to some more open decisive measure becomes unavoidable; till at last we find ourselves principal in the war and are obliged to hazard every thing for an object which might have originally been obtained without expence or danger. I am not versed in the politics of the north; but this I believe is certain, that half the money you have distributed to carry the expulsion of Mr. Wilkes, or even your secretary's share in the last subscription, would have kept the Turks at your devotion. Was it economy, my Lord? or did the coy resistance you have constantly met with in the British senate, make you despair of corrupting the Divan? Your friends indeed have the first claim upon your bounty; but if five hundred pounds a-year can be spared in pension to Sir John Moore, it would not have disgraced you to have allowed something to the secret service of the public.

You will say, perhaps, that the situation of affairs at home demanded and engrossed the whole of your attention. Here, I confess, you have been active. An amiable, accomplished prince ascends the throne under the happiest of all auspices, the acclamations and united affections of his subjects. The first measures of his reign, and even the odium of a favourite, were not able to shake their attachment. Your services, my Lord, have been more successful. Since you were permitted to take the lead, we have seen the natural effects of a system of government at once both odious and contemptible. We have seen the laws sometimes scandalously relaxed, sometimes violently stretched beyond their tone. We have seen the person of the Sovereign insulted; and in profound peace, and with an undisputed title, the fidelity of his subjects brought by his own servants into public question. Without abilities, resolution, or interest, you have done more than Lord Bute could accomplish with all Scotland at his heels.

Your Grace, little anxious perhaps either for present or future reputation, will not desire to be handed down in these colours to posterity. You have reason to flatter yourself that the memory of your administration will survive even the forms of a constitution which our ancestors vainly hoped would be immortal: and, as for your personal character, I will not, for the honour of human nature, suppose that you can wish to have it remembered. The condition of the present times is desperate indeed: but there is a debt due to those who come after us; and it is the historian's office to punish, though he cannot correct. I do not give you to posterity as a pattern to imitate, but as an example to deter; and as your conduct comprehends every thing that a wise or honest minister should

SIR,   June 12. 1769.

THE Duke of Grafton's friends, not finding it convenient to enter into a contest with Junius, are now reduced to the last melancholy resource of defeated argument, the flat general charge of scurrility and falsehood. As for his style, I shall leave it to the critics. The truth of his facts is of more importance to the public. They are of such a nature, that I think a bare contradiction will have no weight with any man who judges for himself. Let us take them in the order in which they appear in his last letter.

1. Have not the first rights of the people, and the first principles of the constitution, been openly invaded, and the very name of an election made ridiculous, by the arbitary appointment of Mr. Luttrell?

2. Did not the Duke of Grafton frequently lead his mistress into public, and even place her at the head of his table, as if he had pulled down an ancient temple of Venus, and could bury all decency and shame under the ruins?—Is this the man who dares to talk of Mr. Wikes's morals?

3. Is not the character of his presumptive ancestors as strongly marked in him as if he had descended from them in a direct legitimate line? The idea of his death is only prophetic; and what is prophecy but a narrative preceding the fact?

4. Was not Lord Chatham the first who raised him to the rank and post of a minister, and the first whom he abandoned?

5. Did he not join with Lord Rockingham, and betray him?

6. Was he not the bosom friend of Mr. Wilkes, whom he now pursues to destruction?

7. Did he not take his degrees with credit at New-market, White's, and the opposition ?

8. After deserting Lord Chatham's principles, and sacrificing his friendship, is he not now closely united with a set of men, who, though they have occasionally joined with all parties, have in every different situation, and at all times, been equally and constantly detested by this country ?

9. Has not Sir John Moore a pension of five hundred pounds a-year ?—This may probably be an acquittance of favours upon the turf; but is it possible for a minister to offer a grosser outrage, to a nation, which has so very lately cleared away the beggary of the civil list at the expence of more than half a million ?

10. Is there any one mode of thinking or acting with respect to America, which the Duke of Grafton has not successively adopted and abandoned.

11. It there not a singular mark of shame set upon this man, who has so little delicacy and feeling as to submit to the opprobrium of marrying a near relation of one who had debauched his wife?—In the name of decency, how are these amiable cousins to meet at their uncle's table? —It will be a scene in OEdipus, without the distress.—Is it wealth, or wit, or beauty—or is the amorous youth in love ?

The rest is notorious. That Corsica has been sacrificed to the French ; that in some instances the laws have been scandalously relaxed, and in others daringly violated ; and that the King's subjects have been called upon to assure him of their fidelity, in spite of the measures of his servants.

A writer, who builds his arguments upon facts such as these, is not easily to be confuted. He is not to be answered by general assertions, or general reproaches. He may want eloquence to amuse and persuade : but, speaking truth, he must always convince.

PHILO JUNIUS.

LETTER XIV.

SIR,   June 22, 1769.

THE name of Old Noll is destined to be the ruin of the house of Stuart. There is an ominous fatality in it, which even the spurious descendants of the family cannot escape. Oliver Cromwell had the merit of conducting Charles the First to the block. Your correspondent Old Noll appears to have the same design upon the Duke of Grafton. His arguments consist better with the title he has assumed, than with the principles he professes; for, though he pretends to be an advocate for the Duke, he takes care to give us the best reasons why his patron should regularly follow the fate of his presumptive ancestor.—Through the whole course of the Duke of Grafton's life, I see a strange endeavour to unite contradictions, which cannot be reconciled. He marries, to be divorced; he keeps a mistress, to remind him of conjugal endearments: and he chooses such friends, as it is virtue in him to desert. If it were possible for the genius of that accomplished president who pronounced sentence upon Charles the First to be revived in some modern sycophant, his Grace, I doubt not, would by sympathy discover him among the dregs of mankind, and take him for a guide in those paths which naturally conduct a minister to the scaffold.

The assertion that two thirds of the nation approve of the acceptance of Mr. Luttrell (for even Old Noll is too modest to call it an election), can neither be maintained nor confuted by argument. It is a point of fact, on which every English gentleman will determine for himself. As to lawyers, their profession is supported by the indiscriminate defence of right and wrong; and I confess I have not that opinion of their knowledge or integrity, to think it necessary that they should decide for me upon a plain constitutional question. With respect to the appointment of Mr. Luttrell, the chancellor has never yet given any authentic opinion. Sir Fletcher Norton is indeed an honest, a very honest man; and the Attorney General is *ex officio* the guardian of liberty, to take care.

I presume, that it shall never break out into a criminal excess. Doctor Blackstone is Solicitor to the Queen. The
Doctor recollected that he had a place to preserve, though
he forgot that he had a reputation to lose. We have
now the good fortune to understand the Doctor's principles as well as writings. For the defence of truth, of law,
and reason, the Doctor's book may be safely consulted;
but whoever wishes to cheat a neighbour of his estate, or
to rob a country of its rights, need make no scruple of consulting the Doctor himself.

The example of the English nobility may, for aught I
know, sufficiently justify the Duke of Grafton, when he
indulges his genius in all the fashionable excesses of the
age; yet, considering his rank and station, I think it would
do him more honour to be able to deny the fact, than to
defend it by such authority. But if vice itself could be
excused, there is yet a certain display of it, a certain outrage to decency, and violation of public decorum, which,
for the benefit of society, should never be forgiven. It is
not that he kept a mistress at home, but that he constantly
attended her abroad. It is not the private indulgence, but
the public insult, of which I complain. The name of
Miss Parsons would hardly have been known, if the First
Lord of the Treasury had not led her in triumph through
the Opera House, even in the presence of the Queen.
When we see a man act in this manner, we may admit
the shameless depravity of his heart, but what are we to
think of his understanding?

His Grace, it seems, is now to be a regular domestic
man; and, as an omen of the future delicacy and correctness of his conduct, he marries a first cousin of the
man who had fixed that mark and title of infamy upon
him, which, at the same moment, makes a husband unhappy and ridiculous. The ties of consanguinity may
possibly preserve him from the same fate a second time;
and as to the distress of meeting, I take for granted the
venerable uncle of these common cousins has settled the
etiquette in such a manner, that, if a mistake should happen, it may reach no farther than from *Madame ma femme*
to *Madame ma cousine*.

The Duke of Grafton has always some excellent reason for deserting his friends—The age and incapacity of

Lord Chatham, the debility of Lord Rockingham, or the infamy of Mr. Wilkes. There was a time, indeed, when he did not appear to be quite so well acquainted, or so violently offended, with the infirmities of his friends. But now, I confess, they are not ill exchanged for the youthful, vigorous virtue of the Duke of Bedford, the firmness of General Conway, the blunt, or if I may call it the awkward, integrity of Mr. Rigby, and the spotless morality of Lord Sandwich.

If a late pension to a broken gambler be an act worthy of commendation, the Duke of Grafton's connections will furnish him with many opportunities of doing praiseworthy actions; and, as he himself bears no part of the expence, the generosity of distributing the public money, for the support of virtuous families in distress, will be an unquestionable proof of his Grace's humanity.

As to the public affairs, Old Noll is a little tender of descending to particulars. He does not deny that Corsica has been sacrificed to France; and he confesses, that with regard to America, his patron's measures have been subject to some variation; but then he promises wonders of stability and firmness for the future. These are mysteries of which we must not pretend to judge by experience; and, truly, I fear we shall perish in the Desert, before we arrive at the Land of Promise. In the regular course of things, the period of the Duke of Grafton's ministerial manhood should now be approaching. The imbecility of his infant-state was committed to Lord Chatham. Charles Townshend took some care of his education at that ambiguous age which lies between the follies of political-childhood and the vices of puberty. The empire of the passions soon succeeded. His earliest principles and connections were of course forgotten or despised. The company he has lately kept has been of no service to his morals; and, in the conduct of public affairs, we see the character of his time of life strongly distinguished. An obstinate ungovernable self-sufficiency plainly points out to us that state of imperfect maturity, at which the graceful levity of youth is lost, and the solidity of experience not yet acquired. It is possible the young man may in time grow wiser, and reform; but, if I understand his disposition, it is not of such corrigible stuff, that we should hope for any amendment in him before he has accomplished the destruction of this country. Like other rakes, he may perhaps live to see his error, but not until he has ruined his estate. PHILO JUNIUS,

LETTER XV.

TO HIS GRACE THE DUKE OF GRAFTON.

MY LORD,   July 8, 1769.

If nature had given you an understanding qualified to keep pace with the wishes and principles of your heart, she would have made you, perhaps the most formidable minister that ever was employed under a limited monarch, to accomplish the ruin of a free people. When neither the feelings of shame, the reproaches of conscience, nor the dread of punishment, form any bar to the designs of a minister, the people would have too much reason to lament their condition, if they did not find some resource in the weakness of his understanding. We owe it to the bounty of Providence, that the completest depravity of the heart is sometimes strangely united with a confusion of the mind, which counteracts the most favourite principles, and makes the same man treacherous without art, and a hypocrite without deceiving. The measures, for instance, in which your Grace's activity has been chiefly exerted, as they were adopted without skill, should have been conducted with more than common dexterity. But truly, my Lord, the execution has been as gross as the design. By one decisive step, you have defeated all the arts of writing. You have fairly confounded the intrigues of opposition, and silenced the clamours of faction. A dark ambiguous system might require and furnish the materials of ingenious illustration; and, in doubtful measures, the virulent exaggeration of party must be employed, to rouse and engage the passions of the people. You have now brought the merits of your administration to an issue, on which every Englishman, of the narrowest capacity, may determine for himself. It is not an alarm to the passions, but a calm appeal to the judgment of the people, upon their own most essential interests. A more experienced minister would not have hazarded a direct invasion of the first principles of the constitution, before he had made some progress in subduing the spirit of the people. With such a cause as yours, my Lord, it is not sufficient that you have the court at your devotion, unless you can find means to corrupt or intimidate the jury. The collective body of the people form that jury, and from their decision there is but one appeal.

Whether you have talents to support you at a crisis of such difficulty and danger, should long since have been considered. Judging truly of your disposition, you have perhaps mistaken the extent of your capacity. Good faith and folly have so long been received as synonymous terms, that the reverse proposition has grown into credit, and every villain fancies himself a man of abilities. It is the apprehension of your friends, my Lord, that you have drawn some hasty conclusion of this sort, and that a partial reliance upon your moral character has betrayed you beyond the depth of your understanding. You have now carried things too far to retreat. You have plainly declared to the people what they are to expect from the continuance of your administration. It is time for your Grace to consider what you also may expect in return from their spirit and their resentment.

Since the accession of our most gracious Sovereign to the throne, we have seen a system of government which may well be called a reign of experiments. Parties of all denominations have been employed and dismissed. The advice of the ablest men in this country has been repeatedly called for and rejected; and when the royal displeasure has been signified to a minister, the marks of it have usually been proportioned to his abilities and integrity. The spirit of the favourite had some apparent influence upon every administration; and every set of ministers preserved an appearance of duration as long as they submitted to that influence. But there were certain services to be performed for the favourite's security, or to gratify his resentments; which your predecessors in office had the wisdom or the virtue not to undertake. The moment this refractory spirit was discovered, their disgrace was determined. Lord Chatham, Mr. Grenville, and Lord Rockingham, have successively had the honour to be dismissed for preferring their duty, as servants of the public, to these compliances which were expected from their station. A submissive administration was at last gradually collected from the deserters of all parties, interests, and connections; and nothing remained but to find a leader for these gallant, well disciplined troops. Stand forth, my Lord, for thou art the man. Lord Bute found no resource o dependence or security in the proud imposing superiority of Lord Chatham's abilities, the shrewd inflexible judgment of Mr Grenville, nor in the mild but determined integrity of Lord Rockingham. His views and situation required a creature void of all these properties; and he was forced to go through every division, resolution, composition, and refinement, of political chemistry, before he happily arrived at the *caput mortuum* of vitriol in your Grace. Flat and insipid in your retired state, but, brought into action, you became vitriol again. Such are the extremes of alternate indolence or fury which have governed your whole administration. Your circumstances with regard to the people soon becoming desperate, like other honest servants you determined to involve the best of masters in the same difficulties with yourself. We owe it to your Grace's well-directed labours, that your Sovereign has been persuaded to doubt of the affections of his subjects, and the people to suspect the virtues of their Sovereign, at a time when both were unquestionable. You have degraded the Royal dignity into a base and dishonourable competition with Mr. Wilkes; nor had you abilities to carry even the last contemptible triumph over a private man, without the grossest violation of the fundamental laws of the constitution and rights of the people. But these are rights, my Lord, which you can no more annihilate, than you can the soil to which they are annexed. The question no longer turns upon points of national honour and security abroad, or on the degrees of expedience and propriety of measures at home. It was not inconsistent that you should abandon the cause of liberty in another country, which you had persecuted in your own; and in the common arts of domestic corruption, we miss no part of Sir Robert Walpole's system except his abilities. In this humble imitative line you might long have proceeded safe and contemptible. You might probably never have risen to the dignity of being hated and even have been despised with moderation. But it seems you meant to be distinguished; and, to a mind like yours, there was no other road to fame but by the destruction of a noble fabric, which you thought had been too long the admiration of mankind. The use you have made of the military force introduced an alarming change in the mode of executing the laws. The arbitrary appointment of Mr. Luttrell invades the foundation of the laws themselves, as it manifestly transfers the right of legislation from those whom the people have chosen, to those whom they have rejected. With a succession of such appointments, we may soon see a House of Commons collected, in the choice of which the other towns and counties of England will have as little share as the devoted county of Middlesex.

Yet I trust that your Grace will find that the people of this country are neither to be intimidated by violent measures, nor deceived by refinements. When they see Mr. Luttrell seated in the House of Commons by mere dint of power, and in direct opposition to the choice of a whole county, they will not listen to these subtleties by which every arbitrary exertion of authority is explained into the law and privilege of parliament. It requires no persuasion of argument, but simply the evidence of the senses, to convince them, that to transfer the right of election from the collective to the representative body of the people, contradicts all those ideas of a House of Commons, which they have received from their forefathers, and which they had already, though vainly perhaps, delivered to their children. The principles on which this violent measure has been defended, have added scorn to injury; and forced us to feel, that we are not only oppressed, but insulted.

With what force, my Lord, with what protection, are you prepared to meet the united detestation of the people of England? The city of London has given a generous example to the kingdom, in what manner a king of this country ought to be addressed; and I fancy, my Lord, it is not yet in your courage to stand between your Sovereign and the addresses of his subjects. The injuries you have done this country are such as demand not only redress, but vengeance. In vain shall you look for protection to that venal vote, which you have already paid for. —Another must be purchased; and, to save a minister, the House of Commons must declare themselves not only independent of their constituents, but the determined enemies of the constitution. Consider, my Lord, whether this be an extremity to which their fears will permit them to advance; or, if their protection should fail you, how far you are authorised to rely upon the sincerity of those smiles which a pious court lavishes without reluctance upon a libertine by profession. It is not indeed the least of the thousand contradictions which attend you, that a man, marked to the world by the grossest violation of all ceremony and decorum, should be the first servant of a court, in which prayers are morality, and kneeling is religion. Trust not too far to appearances, by which your predecessors have been deceived, though they have not been injured. Even the best of princes may at last discover, that this is a contention, in which every thing may be lost, but nothing can be gained; and as you became minister by accident, were adopted without choice, trusted without confidence, and continued without favour, be assured, that, whenever an occasion presses, you will be discarded without even the forms of regret. You will then have reason to be thankful, if you are permitted to retire to that seat of learning, which, in contemplation of the system of your life, the comparative purity of your manners with those of their high steward, and a thousand other recommending circumstances, has chosen you to encourage the growing virtue of their youth, and to preside over their education. Whenever the spirit of distributing prebends and bishopricks shall have departed from you, you will find that learned seminary perfectly recovered from the delirium of an installation, and, what in truth it ought to be, once more a peaceful scene of slumber and thoughtless meditation. The venerable tutors of the university will no longer distress your modesty, by proposing you for a pattern to their pupils. The learned dulness of declamation will be silent; and even the venal muse, though happiest in fiction, will forget your virtues. Yet, for the benefit of the succeeding age, I could wish that your retreat might be deferred, until your morals shall happily be ripened to that maturity of corruption, at which the worst examples cease to be contagious.   JUNIUS.

LETTER XVI.

TO THE PRINTER OF THE PUBLIC ADVERTISER.

SIR,   July 19 1769.

A GREAT deal of useless argument might have been saved in the political contest, which has arisen from the expulsion of Mr. Wilkes and the subsequent appointment of Mr. Luttrell, if the question had been once stated with precision, to the satisfaction of each party, and clearly understood by them both. But in this, as in almost every other dispute, it usually happens, that much time is lost in referring to a multitude of cases and precedents, which prove nothing to the purpose; or in maintaining propositions, which are either not disputed, or, whether they be admitted or denied, are entirely indifferent as to the matter in debate; until at last the mind, perplexed and confounded with the endless subtleties of controversy, loses sight of the main question, and never arrives at truth. Both parties in the dispute are apt enough to practise these dishonest artifices. The man who is conscious of the weakness of his cause, is interested in concealing it: and, on the other side, it is not uncommon to see a good cause mangled by advocates who do not know the real strength of it.

I should be glad to know, for instance, to what purpose, in the present case, so many precedents have been produced to prove, that the House of Commons have a right to expel one of their own members; that it belongs to them to judge of the validity of elections; or that the law of parliament is part of the law of the land? After all these propositions are admitted, Mr. Luttrell's right to his seat will continue to be just as disputable as it was before. Not one of them is at present in agitation. Let it be admitted that the House of Commons were authorised to expel Mr. Wilkes; that they are the proper court to judge of elections, and that the law of parliament is binding upon the people : still it remains to be inquired, whether the house, by their resolution in favour of Mr. Luttrell, have or have not truly declared that law. To facilitate this inquiry, I would have the question cleared of all foreign or indifferent matter. The following state of it will probably be thought a fair one by both parties; and then I imagine there is no gentleman in this country, who will not be capable of forming a judicious and true opinion upon it. I take the question to be strictly this: " Whether or not it be the known, established law of " parliament, that the expulsion of a member of the " House of Commons of itself creates in him such an in- " capacity to be re-elected, that, at a subsequent elec- " tion, any votes given to him are null and void; and " that any other candidate, who, except the person expel- " led, has the greatest number of votes, ought to be the " sitting member?"

To prove that the affirmative is the law of parliament, I apprehend it is not sufficient for the present House of Commons to declare it to be so. We may shut our eyes indeed to the dangerous consequences of suffering one branch of the Legislature to declare new laws, without argument or example, and it may perhaps be prudent enough to submit to authority; but a mere assertion will never convince, much less will it be thought reasonable to prove the right by the fact itself. The ministry have not yet pretended to such a tyranny over our minds. To support the affirmative fairly, it will either be necessary to produce some statute, in which that positive provision shall have been made, that specific disability clearly cre- ated, and the consequences of it declared; or, if there be no such statute, the custom of parliament must then be referred to; and some case or cases, strictly in point, must be produced, with the decision of the court upon them; for I readily admit, that the custom of parliament, once clearly proved, is equally binding with the common and statute law.

The consideration of what may be reasonable or unrea- sonable makes no part of this question. We are inquir- ing what the law is, not what it ought to be. Reason may be applied to show the impropriety or expedience of a law, but we must have either statute or precedent to prove the existence of it. At the same time I do not mean to admit that the late resolution of the House of Commons is defensible on general principles of reason, any more than in law. This is not the hinge on which the debate turns.

Supposing, therefore, that I have laid down an accurate state of the question, I will venture to affirm, 1st, That there is no statute existing, by which that specific disability which we speak of is created. If there be, let it be produced. The argument will then be at an end.

2dly, That there is no precedent, in all the proceedings of the House of Commons, which comes entirely home to the present case, viz. " where an expelled mem-" ber has been returned again, and another candidate, " with an inferior number of votes, has been declared " the sitting member." If there be such a precedent, let it be given to us plainly, and I am sure it will have more weight than all the cunning arguments which have been drawn from inference and probabilities.

The ministry in that laborious pamphlet, which I presume contains the whole strength of the party, have declared ˣ, " That Mr. Walpole's was the first and only in-" stance in which the electors of any county or borough " had returned a person expelled to serve in the same " parliament." It is not possible to conceive a case more exactly in point. Mr. Walpole was expelled; and, having a majority of votes at the next election, was returned again. The friends of Mr. Taylor, a candidate set up by the ministry, petitioned the House that he might be the siting member. Thus far the circumstances tally exactly, except that our House of Commons saved Mr. Luttrell the trouble of petitioning. The point of law, however, was the same. It came regularly before the House, and it was their business to determine upon it. They did determine it, for they declared Mr. Taylor not duly elected. If it be said that they meant this resolution as matter of favour and indulgence to the borough which had retorted Mr. Walpole upon them, in order that the burgesses, knowing what the law was, might correct their error, I answer,

I. That it is a strange way of arguing, to oppose a

supposition, which no man can prove, to a fact which proves itself.

II. That if this were the intention of the House of Commons, it must have defeated itself. The burgesses of Lynn could never have known their error, much less could they have corrected it by any instruction they received from the proceedings of the House of Commons. They might perhaps have foreseen, that, if they returned Mr. Walpole again, he would again be rejected; but they never could infer, from a resolution by which the candidate with the fewest votes was declared not duly elected, that, at a future election, and in similar circumstances, the House of Commons would reverse their resolution, and receive the same candidate as duly elected whom they had before rejected.

This indeed would have been a most extraordinary way of declaring the law of parliament, and what I presume no man, whose understanding is not at cross-purposes with itself, could possibly understand.

If, in a case of this importance, I thought myself at liberty to argue from suppositions rather than from facts, I think the probability, in this instance, is directly the reverse of what the ministry affirm; and that it is much more likely that the House of Commons at that time would rather have strained a point in favour of Mr. Taylor, than that they would have violated the law of parliament, and robbed Mr. Taylor of a right legally vested in him, to gratify a refractory borough, which, in defiance of them, had returned a person branded with the strongest mark of the displeasure of the House.

But really, Sir, this way of talking, for I cannot call it argument, is a mockery of the common understanding of the nation, too gross to be endured. Our dearest interests are at stake. An attempt has been made; not merely to rob a single county of its rights, but, by inevitable consequence, to alter the constitution of the House of Commons. This fatal attempt has succeeded, and stands as a precedent recorded for ever. If the ministry are unable to defend their cause by fair argument founded on facts, let them spare us at least the mortification of being amused and deluded like children. I believe there is yet a spirit of resistance in this country, which will not submit to be oppressed: but I am sure there is a fund of good sense in this country, which cannot be deceived.

JUNIUS.

LETTER XVII.

TO THE PRINTER OF THE PUBLIC ADVERTISER.

SIR,   Aug. 1. 1769.

It will not be necessary for Junius to take the trouble of answering your correspondent G. A. or the quotation from a speech without doors, published in your paper of the 28th of last month. The speech appeared before Junius's letter; and as the author seems to consider the great proposition, on which all his argument depends, viz. That Mr. Wilkes was under that known legal incapacity. of which Junius speaks, as a point granted, his speech is in no shape an answer to Junius, for this is the very question in debate.

As to G. A. I observe, first, that if he did not admit Junius's state of the question, he should have shown the fallacy of it, or given us a more exact one;—secondly, that considering the many hours and days which the ministry and their advocates have wasted in public debate, in compiling large quartos, and collecting innumerable precedents, expressly to prove that the late proceedings of the House of Commons are warranted by the law, custom, and practice of parliament, it is rather an extraordinary supposition, to be made by one of their own party, even for the sake of argument, " That no such statute, no such custom of parliament, " no such case in point, can be produced." G. A. may however make the supposition with safety. It contains nothing but literally the fact, except that there is a case exactly in point, with a decision of the House diametrically opposite to that which the present House of Commons came to in favour of Mr. Luttrell.

The ministry now begin to be ashamed of the weakness of their cause; and, as it usually happens with falsehood, are driven to the necessity of shifting their ground, and changing their whole defence. At first we were told, that nothing could be clearer than that the proceed-

ings of the House of Commons were justified by the known
law and uniform custom of parliament. But it now seems,
if there be no law, the House of Commons have a right
to make one; and if there be no precedent, they have a
right to create the first:—for this I presume is the amount
of the questions proposed to Junius. If your correspondent had been at all versed in the law of parliament, or
generally in the laws of this country, he would have seen
that his defence is as weak and false as the former.

The privileges of either House of Parliament, it is true,
are indefinite, that is, they have not been described or
laid down in any one code or declaration whatsoever;
but whenever a question of privilege has arisen, it has invariably been disputed or maintained upon the footing of
precedents alone ᵞ. In the course of the proceedings upon
the Aylsbury election, the House of Lords resolved,
" That neither House of Parliament had any power, by
" any vote or declaration, to create to themselves any new
" privilege that was not warranted by the known laws
" and customs of parliament." And to this rule the
House of Commons, though otherwise they had acted in a
very arbitrary manner, gave their assent; for they affirmed
that they had guided themselves by it, in asserting their
privileges.—Now, Sir, if this be true with respect to
matters of privilege, in which the House of Commons, in-
dividually and as a body, are principally concerned, how
much more strongly will it hold against any pretended
power in that House to create or declare a new law, by
which not only the rights of the House over their own
member, and those of the member himself, are included,
but all those of a third and separate party, I mean the
freeholders of the kingdom? To do justice to the ministry, they have not yet pretended that any one, or any
two of the three estates have power to make a new law,
without the concurrence of the third. They know that
a man who maintains such a doctrine, is liable, by statute, to the heaviest penalties. They do not acknow
ledge that the House of Commons have assumed a new
privilege, or declared a new law. On the contrary, they
affirm that their proceedings have been strictly conformable to, and founded upon the ancient law and custom of
parliament. Thus, therefore, the question returns to the

E

point at which Junius had fixed it, viz. "Whether or not "this be the law of parliament? If it be not, the House of Commons had no legal authority to establish the precedent; and the precedent itself is a mere fact, without any proof of right whatsoever.

Your correspondent concludes with a question of the simplest nature, Must a thing be wrong, because it has never been done before? No. But admitting it were proper to be done, that alone does not convey any authority to do it. As to the present case, I hope I shall never see the time when not only a single person, but a whole country, and in effect the entire collective body of the people, may again be robbed of their birth right, by a vote of the House of Commons. But if, for reasons which I am unable to comprehend, it be necessary to trust that House with a power so exorbitant and so unconstitutional, at least let it be given to them by an act of the legislature.

PHILO JUNIUS.

LETTER XVIII.

TO SIR WILLIAM BLACKSTONE, SOLICITOR GENERAL TO HER MAJESTY.

SIR,   July 29. 1769.

I SHALL make you no apology for considering a certain pamphlet, in which your late conduct is defended, as written by yourself. The personal interests, the personal resentments, and, above all, that wounded spirit, unaccustomed to reproach, and I hope not frequently conscious of deserving it, are signals which betray the author to us as plainly as if your name were in the title-page. You appeal to the public in defence of your reputation. We hold it, Sir, that an injury offered to an individual, is interesting to society. On this principle, the people of England made common cause with Mr. Wilkes. On this principle, if you are injured, they will join in your resentment. I shall not follow you through the insipid form of a third person, but address myself to you directly.

You seem to think the channel of a pamphlet more respectable, and better suited to the dignity of your cause than that of a newspaper. Be it so. Yet if newspapers are scurrilous, you must confess they are impartial. They give us, without any apparent preference, the wit and argument of the ministry, as well as the abusive dulness of the opposition. The scales are equally poised. It is not the printer's fault, if the greater weight inclines the balance.

Your pamphlet then is divided into an attack upon Mr. Grenville's character, and a defence of your own. It would have been more consistent perhaps with your professed intention, to have confined yourself to the last. But anger has some claim to indulgence, and railing is usually a relief to the mind. I hope you have found benefit from the experiment. It is not my design to enter into a formal vindication of Mr. Grenville, upon his own principles. I have neither the honour of being personally known to him, nor do I pretend to be completely master of all the facts. I need not run the risk of doing an injustice to his opinions, or to his conduct, when your pamphlet alone carries upon the face of it a full vindication of both.

Your first reflection is, that Mr. Grenville * was, of all men, the person who should not have complained of inconsistence with regard to Mr. Wilkes. This, Sir, is either an unmeaning sneer, a peevish expression of resentment, or, if it means any thing, you plainly beg the question; for whether his parliamentary conduct with regard to Mr. Wilkes has or has not been inconsistent, remains yet to be proved. But it seems he received upon the spot a sufficient chastisement for exercising so unfairly his talents of misrepresentation. You are a lawyer, Sir, and know better than I do upon what particular occasions a talent for misrepresentation may be fairly exerted; but to punish a man a second time, when he has been once sufficiently chastised, is rather too severe. It is not in the laws of England; it is not in your own Commentaries; nor is it yet, I believe, in the new law you have revealed to the House of Commons. I hope this doctrine has no existence but in your own heart. After all, Sir, if you had consulted that sober discretion, which you seem to oppose with triumph to the honest jollity of a tavern, it might have occured to you, that, although you could have succeeded in fixing a charge of inconsistence upon Mr. Grenville, it would not have tended in any shape to exculpate yourself.

Your next insinuation, that Sir William Meredith had hastily adopted the false glosses of his new ally, is of the same sort with the first. It conveys a sneer as little worthy of the gravity of your character, as it is useless to your defence. It is of little moment to the public to inquire, by whom the charge was conceived, or by whom it was adopted. The only question we ask is, whether or no it be true? The remainder of your reflections upon Mr. Grenville's conduct destroy themselves. He could not possibly come prepared to traduce your integrity to the House. He could not foresee that you would even speak upon the question; much less would he foresee that you could maintain a direct contradiction of that doctrine, which you had solemnly, disinterestedly, and, upon soberest reflection, delivered to the public. He came armed indeed with what he thought a respectable authority, to support what he was convinced was the cause of truth; and I doubt not he intended to give you, in the course of the debate, an honourable and public testimony of his esteem. Thinking highly of his abilities, I cannot however allow him the gift of divination. As to what you are pleased to call a plan coolly formed to impose upon the House of Commons, and his producing it without provocation at midnight, I consider it as the language of pique and invective, therefore unworthy of regard. But, Sir, I am sensible I have followed your example too long, and wandered from the point.

The quotation from your Commentaries is matter of record. It can neither be altered by your friends, nor misrepresented by your enemies; and I am willing to take your own word for what you have said in the House of Commons. If there be a real difference between what you have written and what you have spoken, you confess that your book ought to be the standard. Now, Sir, if words mean any thing, I apprehend, that when a long enumeration of disqualifications (whether by statute or the custom of parliament) concludes with these general comprehensive words, " But, subject to these restrictions

"and disqualifications, every subject of the realm is eligible
" of common right," a reader of plain understanding must
of course rest satisfied that no species of disqualification
whatsoever had been omitted. The known character of
the author, and the apparent accuracy with which the whole
work is compiled, would confirm him in his opinion; nor
could he possibly form any other judgment, without looking
upon your Commentaries in the same light in which you
consider those penal laws which, though not repealed, are
fallen into disuse, and are now in effect A SNARE TO THE
UNWARY.

You tell us indeed, that it was not part of your plan to
specify any temporary incapacity; and that you could not,
without a spirit of prophecy, have specified the disability
of a private individual, subsequent to the period at which
you wrote. What your plan was, I know not; but what
it should have been, in order to complete the work you
have given us, is by no means difficult to determine. The
incapacity, which you call temporary, may continue seven
years; and though you might not have foreseen the particular case of Mr. Wilkes, you might, and should have
foreseen the possibility of such a case, and told us how far
the House of Commons were authorised to proceed in it
by the law and custom of parliament. The freeholders of
Middlesex would then have known what they had to trust
to, and would never have returned Mr. Wilkes, when
Colonel Luttrell was a candidate against him. They would
have chosen some indifferent person, rather than submit to
be represented by the object of their contempt and detestation.

Your attempt to distinguish between disabilities which
affect whole classes of men, and those which affect individuals only, is really unworthy of your understanding.
Your Commentaries had taught me, that although the instance in which a penal law is exerted be particular, the
laws themselves are general. They are made for the benefit and instruction of the public, though the penalty
falls only upon an individual. You cannot but know,
Sir, that what was Mr. Wilkes's case yesterday, may be
yours or mine to-morrow; and that, consequently, the
common right of every subject of the realm is invaded by
it. Professing; therefore, to treat of the constitution of the

D 2

House of Commons, and of the laws and customs relative to that constitution, you certainly were guilty of a most unpardonable omission in taking no notice of a right and privilege of the House, more extraordinary and more arbitrary than all the others they possess put-together. If the expulsion of a member, not under any legal disability, of itself creates in him an incapacity to be elected, I see a ready way marked out, by which the majority may at any time remove the honestest and ablest men who happen to be in opposition to them. To say that they will not make this extravagant use of their power, would be a language unfit for a man so learned in the laws as you are. By your doctrine, Sir, they have the power; and laws, you know, are intended to guard against what men may do, not to trust to what they will do.

Upon the whole, Sir, the charge against you is of a plain, simple nature: It appears even upon the face of your own pamphlet. On the contrary, your justification of yourself is full of subtlety and refinement, and in some places not very intelligible. If I were personally your enemy, I should dwell, with a malignant pleasure, upon those great and useful qualifications which you certainly possess, and by which you once acquired, though they could not preserve to you, the respect and esteem of your country. I should enumerate the honours you have lost, and the virtues you have disgraced: but having no private resentments to gratify, I think it sufficient to have given my opinion of your public conduct, leaving the punishment it deserves to your closet and to yourself.

JUNIUS.

LETTER XIX.

TO THE PRINTER OF THE PUBLIC ADVERTISER.

SIR,   August 14. 1769.

A CORRESPONDENT of the St. James's Evening Post first wilfully misunderstands Junius, then censures him for a bad reasoner. Junius does not say that it was incumbent upon Dr. Blackstone to foresee and state the crimes for which Mr. Wilkes was expelled. If, by a spirit of prophecy, he had even done so, it would have been nothing to the purpose. The question is, Not for what particular offences a person may be expelled, but generally whether by the law of parliament expulsion alone creates a disqualification? If the affirmative be the law of parliament, Doctor Blackstone might, and should have told us so. The question is not confined to this or that particular person, but forms one great general branch of disqualification, too important in itself, and too extensive in its consequences, to be omitted in an accurate work, expressly treating of the law of parliament.

The truth of the matter is evidently this :—Dr. Blackstone, while he was speaking in the House of Commons, never once thought of his Commentaries, until the contradiction was unexpectedly urged, and stared him in the face. Instead of defending himself upon the spot, he sunk under the charge in an agony of confusion and despair. It is well known that there was a pause of some minutes in the House, from a general expectation that the Doctor would say something in his own defence ; but it seems his faculties were too much overpowered to think of those subtleties and refinements which have since occurred to him. It was then Mr. Grenville received the severe chastisement which the Doctor mentions with so much triumph : ". I wish the honourable gentleman, instead of " shaking his head, would shake a good argument out " of it." If to the elegance, novelty, and bitterness of this ingenious sarcasm, we add the natural melody of Sir Fletcher Norton's pipe, we shall not be surprised that Mr. Grenville was unable to make him any reply.

As to the Doctor, I would recommend it to him to be quiet. If not, he may perhaps hear again from Junius himself.

'PHILO. JUNIUS:

Postscript to a pamphlet intituled, ' An Answer to the Question Stated.' Supposed to be written by Dr. Blackstone, Solicitor to the Queen, in answer to Junius's Letter.

SINCE these papers were sent to the press, a writer in the public papers, who subscribes himself Junius, has made a feint of bringing this question to a short issue. Though the foregoing observations contain, in my opinion, at least, a full refutation of all that this writer has offered, I shall, however, bestow a very few words upon him. It will cost me very little trouble to unravel and expose the sophistry of this argument.

' I take the question (says he) to be strictly this: Whe- ther or no it be the known established law of parliament, ' that the expulsion of a member of the House of Com- ' mons of itself creates in him such an incapacity to be ' re-elected, that, at a subsequent election, any votes giv- ' en to him are null and void; and that any other candi- ' date who, except the person expelled, has the greatest ' number of votes, ought to be the sitting member?

Waving for the present any objection I may have to this state of the question, I shall venture to meet our champion upon his own ground, and attempt to support the affirma- tive of it, in one of the two ways by which he says it can be alone fairly supported. ' If there be no statute ' (says he) in which the specific disability is clearly created, ' &c. (and we acknowledge there is none,) the custom of ' parliament must then be referred to, and some case, ' or cases, strictly in point, must be produced, with the ' decision of the court upon them.' Now I assert, that this has been done. Mr. Walpole's case is strictly in point, to prove that expulsion creates absolute incapacity of being re-elected. This was the clear decision of the House upon it; and was a full declaration, that incapacity was the necessary consequence of expulsion. The law was as clearly and firmly fixed by this resolution, and is as binding in every subsequent case of expulsion, as if it had been declared by an express statute, " that a member " expelled by a resolution of the House of Commons shall " be deemed incapable of being re-elected." Whatever doubt then there might have been of the law before Mr. Walpole's case, with respect to the full operation of a vote of expulsion, there can be none now. The decision of the House upon this case is strictly in point to prove, that expulsion creates absolute incapacity in law of being re- elected.

But incapacity in law, in this instance, must have the same operation and effect with incapacity in law in every other instance. Now, incapacity of being re-elected im- plies in its very terms, that any votes given to the incapable person, at a subsequent election, are null and void. This is its necessary operation, or it has no operation at all: It is *vox et praeterea nihil*. We can no more be called upon to prove this proposition, than we can to prove that a dead man is not alive, or that twice two are four. When the terms are understood, the proposition is self-evident.

Lastly, It is, in all cases of election, the known and established law of the land, grounded upon the clearest principles of reason and common sense, that if the votes given to one candidate are null and void, they cannot be opposed to the votes given to another candidate. They cannot affect the votes of such candidate at all. As they have on the one hand no positive quality to add or establish, so they have on the other hand no negative one, to subtract or destroy. They are, in a word, a mere nonentity. Such was the determination of the House of Commons in the Malden and Bedford elections; cases strictly in point to the present question, as far as they are meant to be in point. And to say, that they are not in point in all circumstances, in those particularly which are independent of the proposition which they are quoted to prove, is to say no more than that Malden is not Midlesex, nor Serjeant Comyns Mr. Wilkes.

Let us see then how our proof s'ands. Expulsion creates incapacity, incapacity annihilates any votes given to the incapable person; the votes given to the qualified candidate stand upon their own bottom, firm and untouched, and can alone have effect. This, one would think, would be sufficient. But we are stopped short, and told that none of our precedents come home to the present case; and are challenged to produce " a precedent in " all the proceedings of the House of Commons that does " come home to it, viz. "where an expelled member has " been returned again, and another candidate, with an " inferior number of votes, has been declared the sitting " member."

Instead of a precedent, I will beg leave to put a case; which, I fancy, will be quite as decisive to the present point. Suppose another Sacheverel (and every party must have its Sacheverel) should at some future election take it into his head to offer himself a candidate for the county of Middlesex. He is opposed by a candidate, whose coat is of a different colour ; but, however, of a very good colour. The divine has an indisputable majority ; nay, the poor layman is absolutely distanced. The sheriff, after having had his conscience well informed by the reverend casuist, returns him, as he supposes, duly elected. The whole House is in an uproar, at the apprehension of so strange an appearance amongst them. A motion, however, is at length made, that the person was incapable of being elected, that his election therefore is null and void, and that his competitor ought to have been returned. No, says a great orator ; first show me your law for this proceeding. " Either produce me a statute, in which the " specific disability of a clergyman is created ; or, produce " me a precedent where a clergyman has been returned, " and another candidate, with an inferior number of votes " has been declared the sitting member." No such statute, no such precedent to be found. What answer then is to be given to this demand ? The very same answer which I will give to that of Junius : . That there is no more than one precedent in the proceedings of the House —" where an incapable person has been returned, and " another candidate, with an inferior number of votes, " has been declared the sitting member ; and, that this is " the known and established law, in all cases of incapa-" city, from whatever cause it may arise."

I shall now therefore beg leave to make a slight amendment to Junius's state of the question ; the affirmative of which will then stand thus :

. " It is the known and established law of parliament, " that the expulsion of any member of the House of Com-" mons creates in him an incapacity of being re-elected ; " that any votes given to him at a subsequent election, " are in consequence of such incapacity, null and void ; " and that any other candidate, who except the person " rendered incapable, has the greatest number of votes, " ought to be the sitting member."

But our business is not yet quite finished. Mr. Walpole's case must have a rehearing. " It is not possible" (says this writer) " to conceive a case more exactly in point. " Mr. Walpole was expelled ; and, having a majority of " votes at the next election, was returned again. The

" friends of Mr. Taylor, a candidate set up by the minis-
" try, petitioned the House that he might be the sitting
" member. Thus far the circumstances tally exactly,
" except that our House of Commons saved Mr. Luttrell
" the trouble of petitioning. The point of law, however,
" was the same. It came regularly before the House,
" and it was their business to determine upon it. They
" did determine it ; for they declared Mr. Taylor not duly
" elected."

Instead of examining the justness of this representation,
I shall beg leave to oppose against it my own view of this
case, in as plain a manner, and as few words as I am able.

It was the known and established law of parliament,
when the charge against Mr. Walpole came before the
House of Commons, that they had power to expel, to dis-
able, and to render incapable, for offences. In virtue of
this power, they expelled him. Had they, in the very
vote of expulsion, adjudged him, in terms, to be incapable
of being re-elected, there must have been at once an end
with him. But though the right of the House, both to expel and to adjudge incapable, was clear and indubitable, it
does not appear to me, that the full operation and effect
of a vote of expulsion singly was so. The law in this case
had never been expressly declared. There had been, no
event to call up such a declaration. I trouble not myself
with the grammatical meaning of the word expulsion. I
regard only its legal meaning. This was not, as I think,
precisely fixed. The House thought proper to fix it, and
explicitly to declare the full consequences of their former
vote, before they suffered these consequences to take effect. And in this proceeding they acted upon the most
liberal and solid principles of equity, justice, and law.
What then did the burgesses of Lynn collect from the second vote? Their subsequent conduct will tell us: it
will with certainty, tell us, that they considered it as decisive against Mr. Walpole ; it will also with certainty, tell
us, that upon supposition that the law of election stood
then as it does now, and that they knew it to stand thus,
they inferred, " that at a future election, and in case of
" a similar return, the House would receive the same can-
" didate, as duly elected, whom they had before rejected."
They could infer nothing but this.

It is needless to repeat the circumstance of dissimilarity in the present case. It will be sufficient to observe, that as the law of parliament, upon which the House of Commons grounded every step of their proceedings, was clear beyond the reach of doubt, so neither could the freeholders of Middlesex be at a loss to foresee what must be the inevitable consequence of their proceedings in opposition to it. For upon every return of Mr. Wilkes, the House made inquiry whether any votes were given to any other candidate.

But I could venture, for the experiment's sake, even to give this writer the utmost he asks; to allow the most perfect similarity throughout in these two cases: to allow, that the law of expulsion was quite as clear to the burgesses of Lynn as to the freeholders of Middlesex. It will, I am confident, avail his cause but little. It will only prove, that the law of election at that time was different from the present law. It will prove, that, in all cases of an incapable candidate returned, the law then was, that the whole election should be void. But now we know that this is not law. The cases of Malden and Bedford were, as has been seen, determined upon other and more just principles. And these determinations are, I imagine, admitted on all sides to be law.

I would willingly draw a veil over the remaining part of this paper. It is astonishing, it is painful, to see men of parts and ability giving into the most unworthy artifices, and descending so much below their true line of character. But if they are not the dupes of their sophistry (which is hardly to be conceived), let them consider that they are something much worse.

The dearest interests of this country are its laws and its constitution. Against every attack upon these, there will, I hope, be always found amongst us the firmest spirit of resistance, superior to the united efforts of faction and ambition. For ambition, though it does not always take the lead of faction, will be sure in the end to make the most fatal advantage of it, and draw it to its own purpose. But, I trust, our day of trial is yet far off; and there is a fund of good sense in this country, which cannot long be deceived by the arts either of false reasoning or false patriotism.

LETTER XX.

SIR,   Aug. 8. 1769.

THE gentleman who has published an answer to Sir William Meredith's pamphlet, having honoured me with a postscript of six quarto pages, which he modestly calls bestowing a very few words upon me, I cannot, in common politeness, refuse him a reply. The form and magnitude of a quarto imposes upon the mind ; and men who are unequal to the labour of discussing an intricate argument, or wish to avoid it, are willing enough to suppose, that much has been proved, because much has been said. Mine, I confess, are humble labours. I do not presume to instruct the learned, but simply to inform the body of the people ; and I prefer that channel of conveyance which is likely to spread farthest among them. The advocates of the ministry seem to me to write for fame ; and to flatter themselves, that the size of their works will make them immortal. They pile up reluctant quarto upon solid folio, as if their labours, because they are gigantic, could contend with truth and heaven.

The writer of the volume in question meets me upon my own ground. He acknowledges there is no statute by which the specific disability we speak of is created : but he affirms, that the custom of parliament has been referred to ; and that a case strictly in point has been produced, with the decission of the court upon it.——I thank him for coming so fairly to the point. He asserts, that the case of Mr. Walpole is strictly in point, to prove that expulsion creates an absolute incapacity of being re-elected ; and for this purpose he refers generally to the first vote of the House upon that occasion, without venturing to recite the vote itself. The unfair, disingenuous artifice of adopting that part of a precedent which seems to suit his purpose, and omitting the remainder, deserves some pity, but cannot excite my resentment. He takes advantage eagerly of the first resolution, by which Mr. Walpole's incapacity is declared ; but as to the two following, by which the candidate with the fewest votes was declared " not duly " elected," and the election itself vacated, I dare say he

F

would be well satisfied if they were for ever blotted out of the journals of the House of Commons. In fair argument, no part of a precedent should be admitted, unless the whole of it be given to us together. The author has divided his precedent; for he knew, that, taken together, it produced a consequence directly the reverse of that which he endeavours to draw from a vote of expulsion. But what will this honest person say, if I take him at his word, and demonstrate to him, that the House of Commons never meant to found Mr. Walpole's incapacity upon his expulsion only? What subterfuge will then remain?

Let it be remembered that we are speaking of the intention of men who lived more than half a century ago, and that such intention can only be collected from their words and actions as they are delivered to us upon record. To prove their designs by a supposition of what they would have done, opposed to what they actually did, is mere trifling and impertinence. The vote, by which Mr. Walpole's incapacity was declared, is thus expressed: "That Robert Walpole, Esq. having been this session "of parliament committed a prisoner to the Tower, and ex- "pelled this House for a breach of trust in the execution "of his office, and notorious corruption when Secretary "at War, was and is incapable of being elected a mem- "ber to serve in this present parliament [b]." Now, Sir, to my understanding, no proposition of this kind can be more evident, than that the House of Commons, by this very vote, themselves understood, and meant to declare, that Mr. Walpole's incapacity arose from the crimes he had comitted, not from the punishment the House annexed to them. The high breach of trust, the notorious corruption, are stated in the strongest terms. They do not tell us that he was incapable because he was expelled, but because he had been guilty of such offences as justly rendered him unworthy of a seat in parliament: If they had intended to fix the disability upon his expulsion alone, the mention of his crimes in the same vote would have been highly improper. It could only perplex the minds of the electors, who, if they collected any thing from so confused a declaration of the law of parliament, must have concluded that their representative had been declared incapable, because he was highly guilty, not because he had been punished. But even admitting them to have understood it in the other sense, they must then, from the very terms of the vote, have united the idea of his being sent to the Tower with that of his expulsion, and considered his incapacity as the joint effect of both [c].

I do not mean to give an opinion upon the justice of the proceedings of the House of Commons with regard to Mr. Walpole; but certainly, if I admitted their censure to be well founded, I could no way avoid agreeing with them in the consequence they drew from it. I could never have a doubt in law or reason, that a man convicted of a high breach of trust, and of a notorious corruption, in the execution of a public office, was and ought to be incapable of sitting in the same parliament. Far from attempting to invalidate that vote, I should have wished that the incapacity declared by it could legally have been continued for ever.

Now, Sir, observe how forcibly the argument returns. The House of Commons, upon the face of their proceedings, had the strongest motives to declare Mr. Walpole incapable of being re-elected. They thought such a man unworthy to sit among them. To that point they proceeded, and no farther; for they respected the rights of the people, while they asserted their own. They did not infer, from Mr. Walpole's incapacity, that his opponent was duly elected; on the contrary, they declared Mr. Taylor " not duly elected," and the election itself void.

Such, however, is the precedent which my honest friend assures us is strictly in point to prove, that expulsion of itself creates an incapacity of being elected. If it had been so, the present House of Commons should at least have followed strictly the example before them, and should have stated to us in the same vote the crimes for which they expelled Mr. Wilkes; whereas they resolve simply, that, " having been expelled, he was, and is incapable." In this proceeding, I am authorized to affirm, they have neither statute, nor custom, nor reason, nor one single precedent to support them. On the other side there is indeed a precedent so strongly in point, that all the enchanted castles of ministerial magic fall before it. In the year 1698 (a period which the rankest Tory dare not except against), Mr. Wollaston was expelled, re-elected, and admitted to take his seat in the same parliament. The ministry have precluded themselves from all objections drawn from the cause of his expulsion; for they affirm absolutely, that expulsion of itself creates the disability. Now, Sir, Let sophistry evade, let falsehood assert, and impudence deny—here stands the precedent, a land-mark to direct us through a troubled sea of controversy, conspicuous and unremoved.

I have dwelt the longer upon the discussion of this point, because in my opinion, it comprehends the whole question. The rest is unworthy of notice. We are inquiring whether incapacity be or be not created by expulsion. In the cases of Bedford and Malden, the incapacity of the persons returned was matter of public notoriety, for it was created by act of parliament. But really, Sir, my honest friend's suppositions are as unfavourable to him as his facts. He well knows that the clergy, besides that they are represented in common with their fellow-subjects, have also a separate parliament of their own:——that their incapacity to sit in the House of Commons has been confirmed by repeated decisions of the House; and that the law of parliament declared by those decisions, has been for about two centuries notorious and undisputed. The author is certainly at liberty to fancy cases, and make whatever comparisons he thinks proper; his suppositions still continue as distant from fact as his wild discourses are from solid argument.

The conclusion of his book is candid to an extreme. He offers to grant me all I desire. He thinks he may safely admit that the case of Mr. Walpole makes directly against him, for it seems he has one grand solution *in petto* for all difficulties. " If," says he, " I were to allow all this, " it will only prove, that the law of election was differ- " ent in Queen Anne's time from what it is at present."

This indeed is more than I expected. The principle, I know, has been maintained in fact; but I never expected to see it so formally declared. What can he mean? Does he assume this language to satisfy the doubts of the people? or does he mean to rouse their indignation? Are the ministry daring enough to affirm, that the House of Commons have a right to make and unmake the law of parliament at their pleasure?—Does the law of parliament, which we are so often told is the law of the land;—does the common right of every subject of the realm, depend upon an arbitrary capricious vote of one branch of the legislature? The voice of truth and reason must be silent.

The ministry tell us plainly, that this is no longer a question of right, but of power and force alone. What was law yesterday is not law to-day: and now it seems we have no better rule to live by, than the temporary discretion and fluctuating integrity of the House of Commons.

Professions of patriotism are become stale and ridiculous. For my own part, I claim no merit from endeavouring to do a service to my fellow-subjects. I have done it to the best of my understanding; and without looking for the approbation of other men, my conscience is satisfied. What remains to be done concerns the collective body of the people. They are now to determine for themselves, whether they will firmly and constisutionally assert their rights: or make an humble, slavish surrender of them at the feet of the ministry. To a generous mind, there cannot be a doubt. We owe it to our ancestors, to preserve entire those rights which they have delivered to our care: we owe it to our posterity, not to suffer their dearest inheritance to be destroyed. But if it were possible for us to be insensible of these sacred claims, there is yet an obligation binding upon ourselves, from which nothing can acquit us;—a personal interest, which we cannot surrender. To alienate even our own rights, would be a crime as much more enormous than suicide, as a life of civil security and freedom is superior to a bare existence; and if life be the bounty of heaven, we scornfully reject the noblest part of the gift, if we consent to surrender that certain rule of living, without which the condition of human nature is not only miserable, but contemptible.

JUNIUS.

LETTER XXI.

TO THE PRINTER OF THE PUBLIC ADVERTISER.

SIR,   Aug. 22. 1769.

I MUST beg of you to print a few lines, in explanation of some passages in my last letter, which I see have been misunderstood.

When I said, that the House of Commons never meant to found Mr. Walpole's incapacity on his expulsion only, I meant no more than to deny the general proposition, that expulsion alone creates the incapacity. If there be any thing ambiguous in the expression, I beg leave to explain it by saying, that, in my opinion, expulsion neither creates, nor in any part contributes to create the incapacity in question.

2. I carefully avoided entering into the merits of Mr. Walpole's case. I did not inquire, whether the House of Commons acted justly, or whether they truly declared the law of parliament. My remarks went only to their apparent meaning and intention, as it stands declared in their own resolution.

3. I never meant to affirm, that a commitment to the Tower created a disqualification. On the contrary, I considered that idea as an absurdity, into which the ministry must inevitably fall, if they reasoned right upon their own principles.

The case of Mr. Wollaston speaks for itself. The ministry assert that expulsion alone creates an absolute complete incapacity to be re-elected to sit in the same parliament. This proposition they have uniformly maintained, without any condition or modification whatsoever. Mr. Wollaston was expelled, re-elected, and admitted to take his seat in the same parliament.—I leave it to the public to determine, whether this be a plain matter of fact, or mere nonsense or declamation.

                                            JUNIUS.

LETTER XXII.

SIR,   Sept. 4. 1769.

ARGUMENT against FACT; or, A new system of political
Logic, by which the ministry have demonstrated to the
satisfaction of their friends, that expulsion alone creates
a complete incapacity to be re-elected; *alias*, that a
subject of this realm may be robbed of his common
right by a vote of the House of Commons.

FIRST FACT.

Mr. Wollaston, in 1698, was expelled, re-elected, and
admitted to take his seat.

ARGUMENT.

As this cannot conveniently be reconciled with our general proposition, it may be necessary to shift our ground,
and look back to the cause of Mr. Wollaston's expulsion.
From thence it will appear clearly, that, " although he
" was expelled, he had not rendered himself a culprit
" too ignominious to sit in parliament; and that having
" resigned his employment, he was no longer incapacitated
" by law." *Vide Serious Considerations*, page 23. Or
thus, " The House, somewhat innaccurately, used the
" word EXPELLED; they should have called it A MO-
" TION." *Vide Mungo's Case considered*, page 11. Or in
short, if these arguments should be thought insufficient,
we may fairly deny the fact. For example : " I affirm that
" he was not re-elected. The same Mr. Wollaston, who
" was expelled, was not again elected. The same indi-
" vidual, if you please, walked into the house, and took
" his seat there; but the same person in law was not ad-
" mitted a member of that parliament, from which he
" had been discarded." *Vide Letter to Junius*, page 12,

SECOND FACT.

Mr. Walpole having been committed to the Tower,
and expelled for a high breach of trust, and notorious corruption in a public office, was declared incapable, &c.

ARGUMENT.

From the terms of this vote, nothing can be more ev
dent, than that the House of Commons meant to fix the
incapacity upon the punishment, and not upon the crime;
but lest it should appear in a different light to weak, un-
informed persons, it may be advisable to gut the resolution, and give it to the public, with all possible solemnity,
in the following terms:— viz. " Resolved, that Robert
" Walpole, Esq. having been that session of parliament
" expelled the House, was and is incapable of being
" elected member to serve in that present parliament."
Vide Mungo on the use of Quotations, page 11,

N. B. The author of the answer to Sir William Meredith seems to have made use of Mungo's quotation;
for in page 18, he assures us, " That the declaratory
" vote of the 17th of February, 1769, was, indeed, a lite-
" ral copy of the résolution of the House in Mr. Wal-
" pole's case."

THIRD FACT.

His opponent, Mr. Taylor, having the smallest number
of votes at the next election, was declared NOT. DULY
ELECTED.

ARGUMENT.

This fact we consider as directly in point to prove that
Mr. Luttrell ought to be the sitting member, for the fol
lowing reasons: " The burgesses of Lynn could draw
" no other inference from this resolution but this that at
" a future election, and in case of s similar return, the
" House would receive the same candidate as duly elect-
" ed, whom they had before rejected." *Vide Postcript*
" *to Junius*, page 37. Or thus: " This their resolution
" leaves no room to doubt what part they would have
" taken, if, upon a subsequent re-election of Mr. Wal-
" pole, there had been any other candidate in competi
" tion with him. For, by their vote, they could have
" no other intention than to admit such other candidate."
Vide Mungo's Case considered, p. 39. Or, take it in this
light :—The burgesses of Lynn having, in defiance of the
House, retorted upon them a person, whom they had

branded with the most ignominious marks of their displeasure, were thereby so well entitled to favour. and indulgence, that the House could do no less than rob Mr. Taylor of a right legally vested in him, in order that tho burgesses might be apprised of the law of parliament; which law the House took a very direct way of explaining to them, by resolving that the candidate with the fewest votes was not duly elected :—" And was not this much " more equitable, more in the spirit of that equal and " substantial justice, which is the end of all law, than " if they had violently adhered to the strict maxims of " law ?" *Vide Serious Considerations*, p. 33 and 34. " And " if the present House of Commons had chosen to follow " the spirit of this resolution, they would have received " and established the candidate with the fewest votes." *Vide Answer to Sir W. M.* p. 18.

Permit me now, Sir, to show you, that the worthy Dr. Blackstone sometimes contradicts the ministry as well as himself. The Speech without Doors asserts, p. 9. " That the legal effect of an incapacity, founded on a " judicial determination of a complete court, is precisely " the same as that of an incapacity created by an act of par- " liament." Now for the Doctor.—" The law and the " opinion of the judge are not always convertible terms, " or one and the same thing ; since it sometimes may " happen that the judge may mistake the law." *Commentaries*, Vol. I. p. 71.

The Answer to Sir W. M. asserts, p. 23. " That the " returning officer is not a judicial, but a purely mini- " sterial officer. His return is no judicial act."—At 'em again, Doctor, " The sheriff, in his judicial capacity, is " to hear and determine causes of forty shillings value " and under in his county court. He has also a judicial " power in divers other civil cases. He is likewise to " decide the elections of Knights of the shire (subject to " the controul of the House of Commons,) to judge of " the qualification of voters, and to return such as he " shall DETERMINE to be duly elected." *Vide Commentaries*, Vol. I. page 332.

What conclusion shall we draw from such facts, and such arguments, such contradictions ? I cannot express my opinion of the present ministry more exactly than in

the words of Sir Richard Steele: "That we are govern-
"ed by a set of drivellers, whose folly takes away all
"dignity from distress, and makes even calamity ridicu-
"lous."

PHILO JUNIUS.

LETTER XXIII.

TO HIS GRACE THE DUKE OF BEDFORD.

MY LORD,   Sept. 19. 1769.

You are so little accustomed to receive any
marks of respect or esteem from the public, that if, in
the following lines, a compliment or expression of applause
should escape me, I fear you would consider it as a mockery of your established character, and perhaps an insult
to your understanding. You have nice feelings, my
Lord, if we may judge from your resentments. Cautious therefore, of giving offence, where you have so little
deserved it, I shall leave the illustration of your virtues to
other hands. Your friends have a privilege to play upon
the easiness of your temper, or possibly they are better
acquainted with your good qualities than I am. You
have done good by stealth. The rest is upon record. You
have still left ample room for speculation, when panegyric
is exhausted.

You are indeed a very considerable man. The highest
rank ;—a splendid fortune;—and a name, glorious till it
was yours,—were sufficient to have supported you with
meaner abilities than I think you possess. From the first,
you derive a constitutional claim to respect; from the second a natural extensive authority ;—the last created a
partial expectation of hereditary virtues. The use you have
made of these uncommon advantages, might have been
more honourable to yourself, but could not have been more
instructive to mankind. We may trace it in the venera-
tion of your country, the choice of your friends, and in
the accomplishment of every sanguine hope which the
public might have conceived from the illustrious name of
Russel.

The eminence of your station gave you a commanding
prospect of your duty. The road which led to honour,

was open to your view. You could not lose it by mistake, and you had no temptation to depart from it by design. Compare the natural dignity and importance of the richest peer of England;—the noble independence which he might have maintained in parliament, and the real interest and respect which he might have acquired, not only in parliament, but through the whole kingdom:—compare these glorious distinctions with the ambition of holding a share in government, the emoluments of a place, the sale of a borough, or the purchase of a corporation; and though you may not regret the virtues which create respect, you may see with anguish how much real importance and authority you have lost. Consider the character of an independent virtuous Duke of Bedford; imagine what he might be in this country, then reflect one moment upon what you are. If it be possible for me to withdraw my attention from the fact, I will tell you in the theory what such a man might be.

Conscious of his own weight and importance, his conduct in parliament would be directed by nothing but the constitutional duty of a peer. He would consider himself as a guardian of the laws. Willing to support the just measures of government, but determined to observe the conduct of the minister with suspicion, he would oppose the violence of faction with as much firmness as the encroachments of prerogative. He would be as little capable of bargaining with the minister for places for himself or his dependents, as of descending to mix himself in the intrigues of opposition. Whenever an important question called for his opinion in parliament, he would be heard by the most profligate minister with deference and respect. His authority would either sanctify or disgrace the measures of government.—The people would look up to him as their protector; and a virtuous prince would have one honest man in his dominions, in whose integrity and judgment he might safely confide. If it should be the will of Providence to afflict him with a domestic misfortune d, he would submit to the stroke with feeling, but not without dignity. He would consider the people as his children, and receive a generous heart-felt consolation in the sympathising tears and blessings of his country.

Your Grace may probably discover something more intelligible in the negative part of this illustrious character. The man I have described would never prostitute his dignity in parliament by an indecent violence, either in opposing or defending a minister. He would not at one moment rancorously persecute, at another basely cringe to the favourite of his Sovereign. After outraging the royal dignity with peremptory conditions, little short of menace and hostility, he would never descend to the humility of soliciting an interview[e] with the favourite, and of offering to recover at any price the honour of his friendship. Though deceived perhaps in his youth, he would not, through the course of a long life, have invariably chosen his friends from among the most profligate of mankind. His own honour would have forbidden him from mixing his private pleasures or conversation with jockeys, gamesters, blasphemers, gladiators or buffoons. He would then have never felt, much less would he have submitted to the dishonest necessity of engaging in the interests and intrigues of his dependents; of supplying their vices, or relieving their beggary at the expence of his country. He would not have betrayed such ignorance, or such contempt of the constitution, as openly to avow, in a court of a justice, the[f] purchase and sale of a borough. He would not have thought it consistent with his rank in the state, or even with his personal importance, to be the little tyrant of a little corporation.[g] He would never have been insulted with virtues which he had laboured to extinguish ; nor suffered the disgrace of a mortifying defeat, which has made him ridiculous and contemptible, even to the few by whom he was not detested. —I reverence the afflictions of a good man ;—his sorrows are sacred. But how can we take part in the distresses of a man whom we can neither love nor esteem ; or feel for a calamity of which he himself is insensible? Where was the father's heart, when he could look for, or find an immediate consolation for the loss of an only son, in consultations and bargains for a place at court, and even in the misery of ballotting at the India House!

Admitting then that you have mistaken or deserted those honourable principles which ought to have directed your conduct ; admitting that you have as little claim to private affection as to public esteem; let us see with what abilities, with what degree of judgment, you have carried your own system into execution. A great man, in the success, and even in the magnitude of his crimes, finds a rescue from contempt. Your Grace is every way unfortunate. Yet I will not look back to those ridiculous scenes by which in your earlier days you thought it an honour to be distinguished [h];—the recorded stripes, the public infamy, your own sufferings, or Mr Rigby's fortitude: These events undoubtedly left an impression, though not upon your mind. To such a mind it may, perhaps, be a pleasure to reflect, that there is hardly a corner of any of his Majesty's kingdoms, except France, in which, at one time or other, your valuable life has not been in danger. Amiable man! we see and acknowledge the protection of Providence, by which you have so often escaped the personal detestation of your fellow-subjects, and are still reserved for the public justice of your country.

Your history begins to be important at that auspicious period, at which you were deputed to represent the Earl of Bute at the court of Versailles. It was an honourable office, and executed with the same spirit with which it was accepted. Your patrons wanted an ambassador who would submit to make concessions, without daring to insist upon any honourable condition for his sovereign. Their business required a man who had as little feeling for his own dignity as for the welfare of his country; and they found him in the first rank of the nobility. Belleisle, Goree, Guadaloupe, St. Lucia, Martinique, the Fishery, and the Havannah, are glorious monuments of your Grace's talents for negotiation. My Lord, we are too well acquainted with your pecuniary character, to think it possible that so many public sacrifices should have been made without some private compensations. Your conduct carries with it an internal evidence, beyond all the proofs of a court of justice. Even the callous pride of Lord Egremont was alarmed [i]. He saw and felt his own dishonour in corresponding with you: and there certainly was a moment at which he meant to have resisted, had not a fatal lethargy prevailed over his faculties, and carried all sense and memory away with it.

I will not pretend to specify the secret terms on which you were invited to support [k] an administration which Lord

Bute pretended to leave in full possession of their ministerial authority, and perfectly masters of themselves. He was not of a temper to relinquish power, though he retired from employment. Stipulations were certainly made between your Grace and him, and certainly violated. After two years' submission, you thought you had collected strength sufficient to controul his influence, and that it was your turn to be a tyrant, because you had been a slave. When you found yourself mistaken in your opinion of your gracious Master's firmness, disappointment got the better of all your humble discretion, and carried you to an excess of outrage to his person, as distant from true spirit as from all decency and respect [l]. After robbing him of the rights of a King, you would not permit him to preserve the honour of a gentleman. It was then Lord Weymouth was nominated to Ireland, and dispatched (we well remember with what indecent hurry) to plunder the treasury of the first fruits of an employment, which you well knew he was never to execute [m].

This sudden declaration of war against the favourite, might have given you a momentary merit with the public, if it had either been adopted upon principle, or maintained with resolution. Without looking back to all your former servility, we need only observe your subsequent conduct, to see upon what motives you acted. Apparently united with Mr. Grenville, you waited until Lord Rockingham's feeble administration should dissolve in its own weakness. The moment their dismission was suspected, the moment you perceived that another system was adopted in the closet, you thought it no disgrace to return to your former dependence, and solicit once more the friendship of Lord Bute. You begged an interview, at which he had spirit enough to treat you with contempt.

It would now be of little use to point out by what a train of weak, injudicious measures, it became necessary, or was thought so, to call you back to a share in the administration [n]. The friends, whom you did not in the last instance desert, were not of a character to add strength or credit to government: and at that time your alliance with the Duke of Grafton was, I presume, hardly foreseen. We must look for other stipulations, to account for that sudden resolution of the closet, by which three of your dependents ° (whose characters, I think, cannot be less respected than they are) were advanced to offices, through which you might again control the minister, and probably engross the whole direction of affairs.

The possession of absolute power is now once more within your reach. The measures you have taken to obtain and confirm it, are too gross to escape the eyes of a discerning judicious prince. His palace is besieged; the lines of circumvallation are drawing round him; and, unless he finds a resource in his own activity, or in the attachment of the real friends of his family, the best of princes must submit to the confinement of a state-prisoner, until your Grace's death, or some less fortunate event, shall raise the siege. For the present, you may safely resume that style of insult and menace, which even a private gentleman cannot submit to hear without being contemptible. Mr. Mackenzie's history is not yet forgotten; and you may find precedents enough of the mode in which an imperious subject may signify his pleasure to his sovereign. Where will this gracious monarch look for assistance, when the wretched Grafton could forget his obligations to his master, and desert him for a hollow alliance with such a man as the Duke of Bedford!

Let us consider you then as arrived at the summit of wordly greatness; let us suppose that all your plans of avarice and ambition are accomplished, and your most sanguine wishes gratified, in the fear as well as the hatred of the people; can age itself forget that you are in the last act of life? Can gray hairs make folly venerable? And is there no period to be reserved for meditation and retirement? For shame! my Lord: let it not be recorded of you, that the latest moments of your life were dedicated to the same unworthy pursuits, the same busy agitations, in which your youth and manhood were exhausted. Consider, that although you cannot disgrace your former life, you are violating the character of age, and exposing the impotent imbecility, after you have lost the vigour of the passions.

Your friends will ask, perhaps, Whither shall this unhappy old man retire? Can he remain in the metropolis, where his life has been so often threatened, and his palace so often attacked? If he returns to Woburn, scorn and mockery await him. He must create a solitude round his estate, if he would avoid the face of reproach and derision. At Plymouth, his destruction would be more than probable: at Exeter, inevitable. No honest Englishman will ever forget his attachment, nor any honest Scotchman forgive his treachery, to Lord Bute. At every town he enters, he must change his liveries and name. Whichever way he flies, the hue and cry of the country pursues him.

In another kingdom, indeed, the blessings of his administration have been more sensibly felt; his virtues better understood; or at worst they will not, for him alone, forget their hospitality.—As well might Verres have returned to Sicily. You have twice escaped, my Lord; beware of a third experiment. The indignation of a whole people, plundered, insulted, and oppressed as they have been, will not always be disappointed.

It is in vain, therefore, to shift the scene. You can no more fly from your enemies than from yourself. Persecuted abroad, you look into your own heart for consolation, and find nothing but reproaches and despair. But, my Lord, you may quit the field of business, though not the field of danger; and though you cannot be safe, you may cease to be ridiculous. I fear you have listened too long to the advice of those pernicious friends, with whose interests you have sordidly united your own, and for whom you have sacrificed every thing that ought to be dear to a man of honour. They are still base enough to encourage the follies of your age, as they once did the vices of your youth. As little acquainted with the rules of decorum, as with the laws of morality, they will not suffer you to profit by experience, nor even to consult the propriety of a bad character. Even now they tell you, that life is no more than a dramatic scene, in which the hero should preserve his consistency to the last; and that as you lived without virtue, you should die without repentance.

JUNIUS.

LETTER XXIV.

TO JUNIUS.

SIR,   Sept. 14. 1769.

Having accidentally seen a republication of your Letters, wherein you have been pleased to assert that I had sold the companions of my success, I am again obliged to declare the said assertion to be a most infamous and malicious falshood; and I again call upon you to stand forth, avow yourself, and prove the charge. If you can make it out to the satisfaction of any one man in the kingdom, I will be content to be thought the worst man in it; if you do not, what must the nation think of you? Party has nothing to do in this affair: you have made a personal attack upon my honour, defamed me by a most vile calumny; which might possibly have sunk into oblivion, had not such uncommon pains been taken to renew and perpetuate this scandal, chiefly because it has been told in good language; for I give you full credit for your elegant diction, well-turned periods, and Attic wit: but wit is oftentimes false, though it may appear brilliant; which is exactly the case of your whole performance. But, Sir, I am obliged, in the most serious manner, to accuse you of being guilty of falsities. You have said the thing that is not. To support your story, you have recourse to the following irresistible argument: " You sold the companions of your victory, because, when " the 16th regiment was given to you, you was silent. " The conclusion is inevitable." I believe that such deep and acute reasoning could only come from such an extraordinary writer as Junius. But unfortunately for you, the premises as well as the conclusion are absolutely false. Many applications have been made to the ministry on the subject of the Manilla ransom since the time of my being colonel of that regiment. As I have for some years, quitted London, I was obliged to have recourse to the Honourable Colonel Monson and Sir Samuel Cornish to negotiate for me; in the last autumn, I personally delivered a memorial to the Earl of Shelburne, at his seat in Wiltshire. As you have told us of your importance, that you

G 2

are a person of rank and fortune, and above a common bribe, you may in all probability be not unknown to his Lordship, who can satisfy you of the truth of what I say. But I shall now take the liberty, Sir, to seize your battery, and turn it against yourself. If your puerile and tinsel logic could carry the least weight or conviction with it, how must you stand affected by the inevitable conclusion, as you are pleased to term it? According to Junius, silence is guilt. In many of the public papers, you have been called, in the most direct and offensive terms, a liar and a coward. When did you reply to these foul accusations? You have been quite silent, quite chop-fallen; therefore, because you was silent, the nation has a right to pronounce you both a liar and a coward from your own argument. But, Sir, I will give you fair play; I will afford you an opportunity to wipe off the first appellation, by desiring the proofs of your charge against me. Produce them! To wipe off the last, produce yourself. People cannot bear any longer your lion's skin, and the despicable imposture of the old Roman name which you have affected. For the future assume the name of some modern bravo and dark assassin: let your appellation have some affinity to your practice. But if I must perish, Junius, let me perish in the face of day; be for once a generous and open enemy. I allow that Gothic appeals to cold iron are no better proof of a man's honesty and veracity, than hot iron and burning plough-shares are of female chastity; but a soldier's honour is as delicate as a woman's; it must not be suspected: you have dared to throw more than a suspicion upon mine: you cannot but know the consequences, which even the meekness of Christianity would pardon me for, after the injury you have done me.

WILLIAM DRAPER.

LETTER XXV.

Hæret lateri lethalis arundo.

TO SIR WILLIAM DRAPER, K. B.

SIR,   Sept. 25. 1769.

AFTER so long an interval, I did not expect to see the debate revived between us. My answer to your last letter shall be short, for I write to you with reluctance, and I hope we shall now conclude our correspondence for ever.

Had you been originally, and without provocation, attacked by an annoymous writer, you would have some right to demand his name. But in this cause you are a volunteer. You engaged in it with the unpremeditated gallantry of a soldier. You were content to set your name in opposition to a man who would probably continue in concealment. You understood the terms upon which we were to correspond, and gave at least a tacit assent to them. After voluntarily attacking me under the character of Junius, what possible right have you to know me under any other? Will you forgive me if I insinuate to you, that you foresaw some honour in the apparent spirit of coming forward in person, and that you were not quite indifferent to the display of your literary qualifications?

You cannot but know that the republication of my letters was no more than a catchpenny contrivance of a printer, in which it was impossible I should be concerned, and for which I am no way answerable. At the same time I wish you to understand, that if I do not take the trouble of reprinting these papers, it is not from any fear of giving offence to Sir William Draper.

Your remarks upon a signature adopted merely for distinction, are unworthy of notice: but when you tell me I have submitted to be called a liar and a coward, I must ask you in my turn, Whether you seriously think it is any way incumbent upon me to take notice of the silly invectives of every simpleton who writes in a newspaper; and what opinion you would have conceived of my discretion, if I had suffered myself to be the dupe of so shallow an artifice?

Your appeal to the sword, though consistent enough with your late profession, will neither prove your innocence, nor clear you from suspicion.—Your complaints with regard to the Manilla ransom were for a considerable time a distress to government. You were appointed (greatly out of your turn) to the command of a regiment, and during that administration we heard no more of Sir William Draper. The facts of which I speak may indeed be variously accounted for, but they are too notorious to be denied: and I think you might have learnt at the university, that a false conclusion is an error in argument, not a breach of veracity. Your solicitations, I doubt not, were renewed under another administration. Admitting the fact, I fear an indifferent person would only infer from it, that experience had made you acquainted with the benefits of complaining. Remember, Sir, that you have yourself confessed, that, ' considering the critical situation of this country, the ministry are in the right to temporize with Spain.' This confession reduces you to an unfortunate dilemma. By renewing your solicitations, you must either mean to force your country into a war at a most unseasonable juncture; or, having no view or expectation of that kind, that you look for nothing but a private compensation to yourself.

As to me, it is by no means necessary that I should be exposed to the resentment of the worst and the most powerful men in this country, though I may be indifferent about yours. Though you would fight, there are others who would assasinate.

But after all, Sir, where is the injury? You assure me that my logic is puerile and tinsel; that it carries not the least weight or conviction, that my premises are false, and my conclusions absurd. If this be a just description of me, how is it possible for such a writer to disturb your peace of mind, or to injure a character so well established as yours? Take care, Sir William, how you indulge this unruly temper, lest the world should suspect that conscience has some share in your resentments. You have more to fear from the treachery of your own passions, than from any malevolence of mine.

I believe, Sir, you will never know me. A considerable time must certainly elapse before we are personally acquainted. You need not, however, regret the delay, or suffer an apprehension that any length of time can restore you to the Christian meekness of your temper, and disappoint your present indignation. If I understand your character, there is in your own breast a repository, in which your resentments may be safely laid up for future occasions, and preserved without the hazard of diminution. The *Odia in longum jaciens, quæ reconderet, auctaque promeret*, I thought had only belonged to the worst character of antiquity. The text is in Tacitus;—you know best where to look for the commentary.

JUNIUS.

LETTER XXVI.

A WORD AT PARTING TO JUNIUS.

SIR,   Oct. 7, 1769.

As you have not favoured me with either of the explanations demanded of you, I can have nothing more to say to you upon my own account. Your mercy to me, or tenderness for yourself, has been very great. The public will judge of your motives. If your excess of modesty forbids you to produce either the proofs or yourself, I will excuse it. Take courage; I have not the temper of Tiberius, any more than the rank or power. You, indeed, are a tyrant of another sort; and upon your political bed of torture can excruciate any subject, from a first minister down to such a grub or butterfly as myself: like another detested tyrant of antiquity, can make the wretched sufferer fit the bed, if the bed will not fit the sufferer, by disjointing or tearing the trembling limbs until they are stretched to its extremity. But courage, constancy, and patience, under torments, have sometimes caused the most hardened monsters to relent, and forgive the object of their cruelty. You, Sir, are determined to try all that human nature can endure, until she expires; else, was it possible that you could be the author of that most inhuman letter to the Duke of Bedford, I have read with astonishment and horror? Where, Sir, where were the feelings of your own heart, when you could upbraid a most affectionate father with the loss of his only and most amiable son? Read over again those cruel lines of yours, and let them wring your very soul. Cannot political questions be discussed without descending to the most odious personalties? Must you go wantonly out of your way to torment declining age, because the Duke of Bedford may have quarrelled with those whose cause and politics you espouse? For shame! for shame! As you have spoke daggers to him, you may justly dread the use of them against your own breast; did a want of courage, or of noble sentiments, stimulate him to such mean revenge. He is above it; he is brave. Do you fancy that your own base arts have infected our whole island? But your own reflections, your own conscience, must and will, if you have any spark of humanity remaining, give him most ample vengeance. Not all the power of words with which you are so graced, will ever wash out, or even palliate, this foul blot in your character. I have not time at present to dissect your letter so minutely as I could wish; but I will be bold enough to say, that it is (as to reason and argument) the most extraordinary piece of florid impotence that was ever imposed upon the eyes and ears of the too credulous and deluded mob. It accuses the Duke of Bedford of high treason. Upon what foundation? You tell us, "that the Duke's pecuniary charac- " ter makes it more than probable that he could not have " made such sacrifices at the peace, without some pri- " vate compensations: that his conduct carried with it an " interior evidence, beyond all the legal proofs of a court " of justice."

My academical education, Sir, bids me tell you, that it is necessary to establish the truth of your first proposition, before you presume to draw inferences from it. First prove the avarice, before you make the rash, hasty, and most wicked conclusion. This father, Junius, whom you call avaricious, allowed that son eight thousand pounds a year. Upon his most unfortunate death, which your usual good nature took care to remind him of, he greatly increased the jointure of the afflicted lady his widow. Is this avarice? Is this doing good by stealth? It is upon record.

If exact order, method, and true œconomy, as a master of a family; if splendour and just magnificence, without wild waste, and thoughtless extravagance, may constitute the character of an avaricious man, the Duke is guilty. But for a moment let us admit that an ambassador may love money too much, what proof do you give that he has taken any to betray his country? Is it hearsay, or the evidence of letters, or occular, or the evidence of those concerned in this black affair? Produce your authorities to the public. It is an impudent kind of sorcery to attempt to blind us with the smoke, without convincing us that the fire has existed. You first brand him with a vice that he is free from, to render him odious and suspected. Suspicion is the foul weapon with which you make all your chief attacks; with that you stab. But shall one of the first subjects of the realm be ruined in his fame? shall even his life be in constant danger, from a charge built upon such sandy foundations? Must his house be besieged by lawless ruffians, his journies impeded, and even the asylum of an altar be insecure from assertions so base and false? Potent as he is, the Duke is amenable to justice; if guilty, punishable. The parliament is the high and solemn tribunal for matters of such great moment. To that be they submitted. But I hope also that some notice will be taken of, and some punishment inflicted upon, false accusers; especially upon such, Junius, who are wilfully false. In any truth I will agree even with Junius; will agree with him that it is highly unbecoming the dignity of peers to tamper with burroughs. Aristocracy is as fatal as democracy. Our constitution admits of neither. It loves a King, Lords, and Commons, really chosen by the unbought suffrages of a free people. But if corruption only shifts hands; if the wealthy commoner gives the bribe, instead of the potent peer, is the state better served by this exchange? Is the real emancipation of the borough effected, because new parchment bonds may possibly supersede the old? To say the truth, wherever such practices prevail, they are equally criminal to, and destructive of, our freedom.

The rest of your declamation is scarce worth considering, except for the elegance of the language. Like Hamlet in the play, you produce two pictures: you tell us, that one is not like the Duke of Bedford; then you bring a most hideous caricatura; and tell us of the resemblance; but *multum abludit imago.*

All your long tedious accounts of the ministerial quarrels, and the intrigues of the cabinet, are reducible to a few short lines; and to convince you, Sir, that I do not mean to flatter any minister, either past or present, these are my thoughts: They seem to have acted like lovers, or children; have pouted, quarrelled, cried, kissed, and been friends again, as the objects of desire, the ministerial rattles, have been put into their hands. But such proceedings are very unworthy of the gravity and dignity of a great nation. We do not want men of abilities; but we have wanted steadiness; we want unanimity: your letters, Junius, will not contribute thereto. You may one day expire by a flame of your own kindling. But it is my humble opinion, that lenity and moderation, pardon and oblivion, will disappoint the efforts of all the seditious in the land, and extinguish their wide spreading fires. I have lived with this sentiment; with this I shall die.

WILLIAM DRAPER.

LETTER XXVII.

TO THE PRINTER OF THE PUBLIC ADVERTISER.

SIR,   Oct. 13 1769.

If Sir William Draper's bed be a bed of torture, he has made it for himself. I shall never interrupt his repose. Having changed the subject, there are parts of this last letter not undeserving of a reply: Leaving his private character and conduct out of the question, I shall consider him merely in the capacity of an author, whose labours certainly do no discredit to a newspaper.

We say, in common discourse, that a man may be his own enemy; and the frequency of the fact makes the expression intelligible. But that a man should be the bitterest enemy of his friends, implies a contradiction of a peculiar nature. There is something in it which cannot be conceived without a confusion of ideas, nor expressed without solecism in language. Sir William Draper is still that fatal friend Lord Granby found him. Yet I am

ready to do justice to his generosity; if indeed it be not
something more than generous, to be the voluntary advo- ·
cate of men who think themselves injured by his assistance,
and to consider nothing in the cause he adopts but the
difficulty of defending it. I thought however, he had been
better read in the history of the human heart than to compare or confound the tortures of the body with those of
the mind. He ought to have known, though perhaps it
might not be his interest to confess, that no outward tyranny can reach the mind. If conscience plays the tyrant, it would be greatly for the benefit of the world that
she were more arbitrary, and far less placable, than some
men find her.

But it seems I have outraged the feelings of a father's
heart.—Am I indeed so injudicious? Does Sir William
Draper think I would have hazarded my credit with a generous nation, by so gross a violation of the laws of humanity? Does he think I am so little acquainted with the
first and noblest characteristic of Englishmen? Or how
will he reconcile such folly with an understanding so full
of artifice as mine? Had he been a father, he would
have been but little offended with the severity of the reproach, or his mind would have been filled with the justice of it. He would have seen that I did not insult the
feelings of a father, but the father who felt nothing. He
would have trusted to the evidence of his own paternal
heart; and boldly denied the possibility of the fact, instead of defending it. Against whom then will his honest indignation be directed, when I assure him, that this
whole town beheld the Duke of Bedford's conduct, upon
the death of his son, with horror and astonishment? Sir
William Draper does himself but little honour in opposing the general sense of his country. The people are seldom wrong in their opinions,—in their sentiments they
are never mistaken. There may be a vanity perhaps in
a singular way of thinking; but a when man professes a
want of those feelings which do honour to the multitude,
he hazards something infinitely more important than the
character of his understanding. After all, as Sir William may possibly be in earnest in his anxiety for the Duke
of Bedford, I should be glad to relieve him from it. He may
rest assured that this worthy nobleman laughs, with equal

H

indifference, at my reproaches, and Sir William's distress about him. But here let it stop. Even the Duke of Bedford, insensible as he is, will consult the tranquility of his life, in not provoking the moderation of my temper. If, from the profoundest contempt, I should ever rise into anger, he should soon find, that all I have already said of him was lenity and compassion.

Out of a long catalogue, Sir William Draper has confined himself to the refutation of two charges only. The rest he had not time to discuss and indeed it would have been a laborious undertaking. To draw up a defence of such a series of enormities, would have required a life at least as long as that which has been uniformly employed in the practice of them. The public opinion of the Duke of Bedford's extreme œconomy is, it seems, entirely without foundation. Though not very prodigal abroad, in his own family at least he is regular and magnificent. He pays his debts, abhors a beggar, and makes a handsome provision for his son. His charity has improved upon the proverb, and ended where it began. Admitting the whole force of this single instance of his domestic generosity, (wonderful indeed, considering the narrowness of his fortune, and the little merit of his only son), the public may still perhaps be dissatisfied, and demand some other less equivocal proofs of his munificence. Sir William Draper should have entered boldly into the detail—of indigence relieved—of arts encouraged—of science patronised, men of learning protected, and works of genius rewarded;—in short, had there been a single instance, besides Mr. Rigby's, of blushing merit brought forward by the Duke for the service of the public, it should not have been omitted.

I wish it were possible to establish my inference with the same certainty on which I believe the principle is founded. My conclusion, however, was not drawn from the principle alone. I am not so unjust as to reason from one crime to another; though I think, that of all the vices, avarice is most apt to taint and corrupt the heart. I combined the known temper of the man with the extravagant concessions made by the ambassador; and though I doubt not sufficient care was taken to leave no document of any treasonable negociation, I still maintain that the conduct of this minister carries with it an internal and convincing

evidence against him. Sir William Draper seems not to
know the value or force of such a proof. He will not
permit us to judge of the motives of men, by the manifest
tendency of their actions, nor by the notorious character
of their minds. He calls for papers and witnesses, with
a triumphant security; as if nothing could be true but
what could be proved in a court of justice. Yet a religious
man might have remembered, upon what foundation
some truths, most interesting to mankind, have been
received and established. If it were not for the internal
evidence, which the purest of religions carries with it,
what would have become of his once well-quoted decalogue, and the meekness of his Christianity?

The generous warmth of his resentment makes him
confound the order of events. He forgets that the insults
and distresses which the Duke of Bedford has suffered,
and which Sir William has lamented with many delicate
touches of the true pathetic, were only recorded in my
letter to his Grace, not occasioned by it. It was a simple
candid narrative of facts; though, for aught I know, it
may carry with it something prophetic. His Grace undoubtedly has received several ominous hints; and I
think, in certain circumstances, a wise man would do well
to prepare himself for the event.

But I have a charge of a heavier nature against Sir
William Draper. He tells us that the Duke of Bedford is
amenable to justice; that parliament is a high and solemn tribunal; and that, if guilty, he may be punished
by due course of law; and all this he says with as much
gravity as if he believed one word of the matter. I hope,
indeed, the day of impeachments will arrive, before this
nobleman escapes out of life;—but to refer us to that mode
of proceeding now, with such a ministry, and such a House
of Commons as the present, what is it, but an indecent
mockery of the common sense of the nation? I think
he might have contented himself with defending the greatest
enemy, without insulting the distresses, of his country.

His concluding declaration of his opinion, with respect
to the present condition of affairs, is too loose and undetermined to be of any service to the public. How strange
is it that this gentleman should dedicate so much time and
argument to the defence of worthless or indifferent cha-

ractors, while he gives but seven solitary lines to the only
subject which can deserve his attention, or do credit to
his abilities?

JUNIUS.

LETTER XXVIII.

TO THE PRINTER OF THE PUBLIC ADVERTISER.

SIR,   Oct. 20. 1769.

I VERY sincerely applaud the spirit with which
a lady has paid the debt of gratitude to her benefactor.
Though I think she has mistaken the point, she shows a
virtue which makes her respectable. The question turned upon the personal generosity or avarice of a man,
whose private fortune is immense. The proofs of his munificence must be drawn from the uses to which he has
applied that fortune. I was not speaking of a Lord Lieutenant of Ireland, but of a rich English Duke, whose
wealth gave him the means of doing as much good in this
country, as he derived from his power in another. I am
far from wishing to lessen the merit of this single benevolent action;—perhaps it is the more conspicuous from
standing alone: All I mean to say is, that it proves nothing in the present argument.

JUNIUS.

LETTER XXIX.

TO THE PRINTER OF THE PUBLIC ADVERTISER.

SIR,   Oct. 19. 1769.

I AM well assured that Junius will never descend
to a dispute with such a writer as Modestus (whose letter
appeared in the Gazetteer of Monday), especially as the
dispute must be chiefly about words. Notwithstanding
the partiality of the public, it does not appear that Junius values himself upon any superior skill in composition; and I hope his time will always be more usefully
employed than in the trifling refinements of verbal criti-
cism. Modestus, however, shall have no reason to triumph
in the silence and moderation of Junius. If he knew as

much of the propriety of language, as I believe he does of the facts in question, he would have been as cautious of attacking Junius upon his composition, as he seems to be of entering into the subject of it; yet, after all, the last is the only article of any importance to the public.

I do not wonder at the unremitted rancour with which the Duke of Bedford and his adherents invariably speak of a nation which we well know has been too much injured to be easily forgiven. But why must Junius be an Irishman ?--" The absurdity of his writings betrays him. --Waving all consideration of the insult offered by Modestus to the declared judgment of the people (they may well bear this among the rest), let us follow the several instances, and try whether the charge be fairly supported.

First then--The leaving a man to enjoy such repose as he can find upon a bed of torture, is severe indeed; perhaps too much so, when applied to such a trifler as Sir William Draper; but there is nothing absurd either in the idea or expression. Modestus cannot distinguish between a sarcasm and a contradiction.

2. I affirm with Junius, that it is the frequency of the fact, which alone can make us comprehend how a man can be his own enemy. We should never arrive at the complex idea conveyed by those words, if we had only seen one or two instances of a man acting to his own prejudice. Offer the proposition to a child, or a man unused to compound his ideas, and you will soon see how little either of them understand you. It is not a simple idea, arising from a single fact; but a very complex idea, arising from many facts, well observed and accurately compared.

3. Modestus could not, without great affectation, mistake the meaning of Junius, when he speaks of a man who is the bitterest enemy of his friends. He could not but know, that Junius spoke, not of a false or hollow friendship, but of a real intention to serve, and that intention producing the worst effects of enmity. Whether the description be strictly applicable to Sir William Draper, is another question. Junius does not say that it is more criminal for a man to be the enemy of his friends than his own, though he might have affirmed it with truth. In a moral light, a man may certainly take greater

H 2

liberties with himself than with another. To sacrifice ourselves merely, is a weakness we may indulge in, if we think proper; for we do it at our own hazard and expence; but under the pretence of friendship, to sport with the reputation, or sacrifice the honour of another, is something worse than weakness; and if, in favour of the foolish intention, we do not call it a crime, we must allow at least that it arises from an overweening, busy, meddling impudence.—Junius says only, and he says truly, that it is more extraordinary, that it involves a greater contradiction, than the other; and is it not a maxim received in life, that in general we can determine more wisely for others than for ourselves? The reason of it is so clear in argument, that it hardly wants the confirmation of experience. Sir William Draper, I confess, is an exception to the general rule, though not much to his credit.

4. If this gentleman will go back to his ethicks, he may perhaps discover the truth of what Junius says, that no outward tyranny can reach the mind. The tortures of the body may be introduced by way of ornament or illustration to represent those of the mind, but strictly there is no similitude between them. They are totally different both in their cause and operation. The wretch who suffers upon the rack, is merely passive; but when the mind is tortured, it is not at the command of any outward power. It is the sense of guilt which constitutes the punishment, and creates that torture with which the guilty mind acts upon itself.

5. He misquotes what Junius says of conscience; and makes the sentence ridiculous, by making it his own.

So much for composition. Now for fact.—Junius, it seems, has mistaken the Duke of Bedford. His Grace had all the proper feelings of a father, though he took care to suppress the appearance of them. Yet it was an occasion, one would think, on which he need not have been ashamed of his grief; on which less fortitude would have done him more honour. I can conceive indeed a benevolent motive for his endeavouring to assume an air of tranquillity in his own family; and I wish I could discover any thing, in the rest of his character, to justify my assigning that motive to his behaviour. But is there no medium? Was, it necessary to appear abroad, to ballot at the India-house, and make a public display, though it were only of an apparent insensibility?—I know we are treading on tender ground; and Junius, I am convinced, does not wish to argue this question farther. Let the friends of the Duke of Bedford observe that humble silence which becomes their situation. They should recollect that there are still some facts in store, at which human nature would shudder. I shall be understood by those whom it concerns, when I say that these facts go farther than to the Duke ᵘ.

It is not inconsistent to suppose that a man may be quite indifferent about one part of a charge, yet severely stung with another; and though he feels no remorse, that he may wish to be revenged. The charge of insensibility carries a reproach indeed, but no danger with it. —Junius had said, " there are others who would assassi-" nate." Modestus, knowing his man, will not suffer the insinuation to be divided, but fixes it all upon the Duke of Bedford.

Without determining upon what evidence Junius would choose to be condemned, I will venture to maintain, in opposition to Modestus, or to Mr. Rigby (who is certainly not Modestus), or any other of the Bloomsberry gang, that the evidence against the Duke of Bedford is as strong as any presumptive evidence can be. It depends upon a combination of facts and reasoning, which require no confirmation from the anecdote of the Duke of Marlborough. This anecdote was referred to merely to show how ready a great man may be to receive a great bribe; and if Modestus could read the original, he would see that the expression, " only not accepted," was probably the only one in our language that exactly fitted the case. The bribe offered to the Duke of Marlborough was not refused.

I cannot conclude without taking notice of this honest gentleman's learning, and wishing he had given us a little more of it. When he accidentally found himself so near speaking truth, it was rather unfair of him to leave out the *non potuisse refelli*. As it stands, the *pudet hæc opprobria* may be divided equally between Mr. Rigby and the Duke of Bedford. Mr. Rigby, I take for granted, will assert his natural right to the modesty of the quotation, and leave all the opprobrium to his Grace.

PHILO JUNIUS.

LETTER XXX.

-TO THE PRINTER OF THE PUBLIC ADVERTISER.

SIR,   Oct. 17. 1769.

IT is not wonderful that the great cause in which this country is engaged should have roused and en-grossed the whole attention of the people. I rather admire the generous spirit with which they feel and assert their interest in this important question, than blame them for their indifference about any other. When the constitution is openly invaded, when the first original right of the people, from which all laws derive their authority, is directly attacked, inferior grievances naturally lose their force, and are suffered to pass by without punishment or obser-vation. The present ministry are as singularly marked by their fortune as by their crimes. Instead of atoning for their former conduct by any wise or popular measure, they have found, in the enormity of one fact, a cover and defence for a series of measures, which must have been fatal to any other administration. I fear we are too remiss in observing the whole of their proceedings. Struck with the principal figure, we do not sufficiently mark in what manner the canvass is filled up. Yet surely it is not a less crime, nor less fatal in its consequences, to en-courage a flagrant breach of the law by a military force, than to make use of the forms of parliament to destroy the constitution. The ministry seem determined to give us a choice of difficulties, and, if possible, to perplex us with the multitude of their offences. The expedient is worthy of the Duke of Grafton. But though he has preserved a gradation and variety in his measures, we should remember that the principle is uniform. Dictated by the same spirit, they deserve the same attention. The following fact, though of the most alarming nature, has not yet been clearly stated to the public; nor have the consequences of it been sufficiently understood. Had I taken it up at an earlier period, I should have been accused.

of an uncandid, malignant precipitation, as if I watched for an unfair advantage against the ministry, and would not allow them a reasonable time to do their duty. They now stand without excuse. Instead of employing the leisure they have had in a strict examination of the offence, and punishing the offenders, they seem to have considered that indulgence as a security to them; that, with a little time and management, the whole affair might be buried in silence, and utterly forgotten.

A major-general of the army is arrested by the sheriff's officers for a considerable debt. He persuades them to conduct him to the Tilt-yard in St. James's Park, under some pretence of business, which it imported him to settle before he was confined. He applies to a serjeant, not immediately on duty, to assist with some of his companions in favouring his escape. He attempts it. A bustle ensues. The bailiffs claim their prisoner. An officer of the guards, not then on duty, takes part in the affair, applies to the lieutenant commanding the Tilt-yard guard, and urges him to turn out his guard to relieve a general officer. The lieutenant declines interfering in person; but stands at a distance, and suffers the business to be done. The officer takes upon himself to order out the guard. In a moment they are in arms, quit their guard, march, rescue the general, and drive away the sheriff's officers; who in vain represent their right to the prisoner, and the nature of the arrest. The soldiers first conduct the general into the guard-room; then escort him to a place of safety, with bayonets fixed, and in all the forms of military triumph. I will not enlarge upon the various circumstances which attended this atrocious proceeding. The personal injury received by the officers of the law in the execution of their duty, may perhaps be atoned for by some private compensation. I consider nothing but the wound which has been given to the law itself, to which no remedy has been applied, no satisfaction made. Neither is it my design to dwell upon the misconduct of the parties concerned, any farther than is necessary to show the behaviour of the ministry in its true light. I would make every compassionate allowance for the infatuation of the prisoner, the false and criminal discretion of one officer, and the madness of another. I would leave the ignorant soldiers entirely out of the question. They are certainly the least guilty, though they are the only persons who have yet suffered, even in the appearance of punishment. The fact itself, however atrocious, is not the principal point to be considered. It might have happened under a more regular government, and with guards better disciplined than ours. The main question is, In what manner have the ministry acted on this extraordinary occasion? A general officer calls upon the King's own guard, then actually on duty, to rescue him from the laws of his country; yet at this moment he is in a situation no worse, than if he had not committed an offence, equally enormous in a civil and military view.—A lieutenant upon duty designedly quits his guard, and suffers it to be drawn out by another officer, for a purpose which he well knew (as we may collect from an appearance of caution, which only makes his behaviour the more criminal) to be in the highest degree illegal. Has this gentleman been called to a court-martial to answer for his conduct? No. Has it been censured? No. Has it been in any shape inquired into? No.—Another lieutenant, not upon duty, nor even in his regimentals, is daring enough to order out the King's guard, over which he had properly no command, and engages them in a violation of the laws of his country, perhaps the most singular and extravagant that ever was attempted.— What punishment has he suffered? Literary none. Supposing he should be prosecuted at common law for the rescue, will that circumstance, from which the ministry can derive no merit, excuse or justify their suffering so flagrant a breach of military discipline to pass by unpunished and unnoticed? Are they aware of the outrage offered to their Sovereign, when his own proper guard is ordered out to stop by main force the execution of his laws? What are we to conclude from so scandalous a neglect of their duty, but that they have other views which can only be answered by securing the attachment of the guards? The minister would hardly be so cautious of offending them, if he did not mean, in due time, to call for their assistance.

With respect to the parties themselves, let it be observed, that these gentlemen are neither young officers,

nor. very young men. 'Had they belonged to 'the un.-
fledged race of ensigns, who infest our streets, and dishonour our public places, it might perhaps be 'sufficient
to send them back to that discipline from' which their parents, judging lightly, from the maturity of their vices;
had removed them too soon. In this case, I am sorry to
see, not so much the folly of youth, as the spirit of the'
corps, and the connivance of government. I do not
question that there are many brave and worthy officers in
the regiment of guards. But considering them as a corps, I
fear it will be found that they are neither good soldiers
nor good subjects. Far be it from me to insinuate the
most distant reflection upon the army. On the contrary,
I honour and esteem the profession; and if these gentlemen were better soldiers, I am sure they would be better
subjects. It is not that there is any internal vice or defect in the profession itself, as regulated in this country,
but that it is the spirit of this particular corps to despise
their profession; and that, while they vainly assume the
lead of the army, they make it matter of impertinent
comparison, and triumph over the bravest troops in the
world (I mean our marching regiments), that they indeed
stand upon higher ground, and are priviledged to neglect
the laborious forms of military discipline and duty. Without dwelling longer upon a most invidious subject, I shall
leave it to military men, who have seen a service more
active than the parade, to determine whether or no I speak
truth.

How far this dangerous spirit has been encouraged by
government, and to what pernicious purposes it may be
applied hereafter, well deserves our most serious consideration. I know, indeed, that when this affair happened,
an affectation of alarm ran through the ministry. Something must be done to save appearances. The case was
too flagrant to be passed 'by' absolutely without notice.
But how have they acted? Instead of ordering the officers concerned (and who, strictly speaking, are alone
guilty) to be put under arrest, and brought to trial, they
would have it understood that they did their duty completely, in confining a serjeant and four private soldiers,
until they should be demanded by the civil power; so
that while the officers who ordered or permitted the

thing, to be done, escaped without censure, the poor men who obeyed these orders, who, in a military view, are no way responsible for what they did, and who for that reason have been discharged by the civil magistrates, are the only objects whom the ministry have thought proper to expose to punishment. They did not venture to bring even these men to a court-martial; because they knew their evidence would be fatal to some persons whom they were determined to protect. Otherwise, I doubt not, the lives of these unhappy friendless soldiers would long since have been sacrificed without scruple to the security of their guilty officers.

I have been accused of endeavouring to inflame the passions of the people.—Let me now appeal to their understanding. If there be any tool of administration daring enough to deny these facts, or shameless enough to defend the conduct of the ministry, let him come forward. I care not under what title he appears. He shall find me ready to maintain the truth of my narrative, and the justice of my observations upon it, at the hazard of my utmost credit with the public.

Under the most arbitrary governments, the common administration of justice is suffered to take its course. The subject, though robbed of his share in the legislature, is still protected by the laws. The political freedom of the English constitution was once the pride and honour of an Englishman. The civil equality of the laws preserved the property, and defended the safety of the subject. Are these glorious privileges the birthright of the people; or are we only tenants at the will of the ministry?—But that I know there is a spirit of resistance in the hearts of my countrymen; that they value life, not by its conveniencies, but by the independence and dignity of their condition; I should, at this moment, appeal only to their discretion. I should persuade them to banish from their minds all memory of what we were; I should tell them this is not a time to remember that we were Englishmen; and give it as my last advice, to make some early agreement with the minister, that, since it has pleased him to rob us of those political rights which once distinguished the inhabitants of a country where honour was happiness, he would leave us at least the humble obedient security, of citizens, and graciously condescend to protect us in our submission.

JUNIUS.

LETTER XXXI.

TO THE PRINTER OF THE PUBLIC ADVERTISER.

SIR,   Nov. 14. 1769.

THE variety of remarks which have been made upon the last letter of Junius, and my own opinion of, the writer, who whatever may be his faults, is certainly not a weak man, have induced me to examine, with some attention, the subject of that letter. I could not persuade myself, that, while he had plenty of important materials, he would have taken up a light or trifling occasion to attack the ministry; much less could I conceive that it was his intention to ruin the officers concerned in the rescue of General Gansel, or to injure the General himself. These are little objects, and can no way contribute to the great purposes he seems to have in view, by addressing himself to the public.—Without considering the ornamented style he has adopted, I determined to look farther into the matter, before I decided upon the merits of his letter. The first step I took, was to inquire into the truth of the facts; for if these were either false or misrepresented, the most artful exertion of his understanding, in reasoning upon them, would only be a disgrace to him.—Now Sir, I have found every circumstance stated by Junius to be literally true. General Gansel persuaded the bailiffs to conduct him to the parade, and certainly solicited a corporal and other soldiers to assist him in making his escape. Captain Dodd did certainly apply to Captain Garth for the assistance of his guard. Captain Garth declined appearing himself; but stood aloof, while the other took upon him to order out the King's Guard, and by main force rescued the General; It is also strictly true, that the General was escorted by a file of musqueteers to a place of security.—These are facts, Mr. Woodfall, which I promise you no gentleman in the guards will deny. If all or any of them are false, why are they not contradicted by the parties themselves? However secure against military censure, they have yet a character to lose; and surely, if they are innocent, it is not beneath them to pay some attention to the opinion of the public.

The force of Junius's observations upon these facts, cannot be better marked, than by stating and refuting the objections which have been made to them. One writer says, " Admitting the officers have offended, they " are punishable at common law; and will you have a " British subject punished twice for the same offence?" —I answer, that they have committed two offences, both very enormous, and violated two laws. The rescue is one offence, the flagrant breach of discipline another; and hitherto it does not appear that they have been punished, or even censured for either. Another gentleman lays much stress upon the calamity of the case; and instead of disproving facts, appeals at once to the compassion of the public. This idea, as well as the insinuation that " depriving the parties of their commissons would be " an injury to their creditors," can only refer to General Gansel. The other officers are in no distress, therefore have no claim to compassion; nor does it appear that their creditors, if they have any, are more likely to be satisfied by their continuing in the guards. But this sort of plea will not hold in any shape. Compassion to an offender, who has grossly violated the laws, is in effect a cruelty to the peaceable subject who has observed them; and, even admitting the force of any alleviating circumstance, it is nevertheless true, that, in this instance, the royal compassion has interposed too soon. The legal and proper mercy of a King of England may remit the punishment, but ought not to stop the trial.

Besides these particular objections, there has been a cry raised against Junius for his malice and injustice in attacking the ministry upon an event which they could neither hinder nor foresee. This, I must affirm, is a false representation of his argument. He lays no stress upon the event itself, as a ground of accusation against the ministry, but dwells entirely upon their subsequent conduct. He does not say that they are answerable for the offence; but for the scandalous neglect of their duty, in suffering an offence so flagrant to pass by without no-

tice or inquiry. Supposing them ever so regardless of
what they owe to the public and as indifferent about the
opinion as they are about the interests of their country,
what answer, as officers of the crown, will they give to
Junius, when he asks them, " Are they aware of the
" outrage offered to their sovereign, when his own pro-
" per guard is ordered out to stop by main force the exe-
" cution of his laws?—And when we see a ministry
giving such a strange unaccountable protection to the
officers of the guards, is it unfair to suspect that they
have some secret and unwarrantable motives for their
conduct? If they feel themselves injured by such a suspicion, why do they not immediately clear themselves
from it, by doing their duty? For the honour of the
guards, I cannot help expressing another suspicion, that,
if the commanding officer had not received a secret in-
junction to the contrary, he would, in the ordinary course
of his business, have applied for a court-martial to try
the two subalterns; the one for quitting his guard; the
other for taking upon him the command of the guard,
and employing it in the manner he did. I do not mean
to enter into, or defend the severity with which Junius
treats the guards. On the contrary, I will suppose, for
a moment, that they deserve a very different character.
If this be true, in what light will they consider the conduct of two subalterns, but as a general reproach and
disgrace to the whole corps? And will they not wish to
see them censured in a military way, if it were only for the
credit and discipline of the regiment?

Upon the whole, Sir, the ministry seem to me to have
taken a very improper advantage of the good nature of
the public, whose humanity, they found, considered nothing in this affair but the distress of General Gansel.
They would persuade us that it was only a common rescue by a few disorderly soldiers, and not the formal deliberate act of the King's guard, headed by an officer;
and the public has fallen into the deception. I think,
therefore, we are obliged to Junius for the care he has
taken to inquire into the facts, and for the just commentary with which he has given them to the world.—For
my own part, I am as unwilling as any man to load the
unfortunate; but really, Sir, the precedent with respect

to the guards, is of a most important nature, and alarming enough (considering the consequences with which it may be attended) to deserve a parliamentary inquiry ; when the guards are daring enough, not only to violate their own discipline, but publicly, and with the most atrocious violence, to stop the execution of the laws, and when such extraordinary offences pass with impunity, believe me, Sir, the precedent strikes deep.

PHILO-JUNIUS.

LETTER XXXII.

TO THE PRINTER OF THE PUBLIC ADVERTISER.

SIR,   Nov. 15. 1769.

I ADMIT the claim of a gentleman who publishes in the Gazetteer under the name of Modestus. He has some right to expect an answer from me ; though, I think, not so much from the merit or importance of his objections, as from my own voluntary engagement. I had a reason for not taking notice of him sooner, which, as he is a candid person, I believe he will think sufficient. In my first letter, I took for granted, from the time which had elapsed, that there was no intention to censure, nor even to try, the persons concerned in the rescue of General Gansel ; but Modestus having since either affirmed, or strongly insinuated, that the offenders might still be brought to a legal trial, any attempt to prejudice the cause, or to prejudice the minds of a jury or a court-martial, would be highly improper.

A man, more hostile to the ministry than I am, would not so often remind them of their duty. If the Duke of Grafton will not perform the duty of his station, why is he minister?—I will not descend to a scurrilous altercation with any man ; but this is a subject too important to be passed over with silent indifference. If the gentlemen, whose conduct is in question, are not brought to a trial, the Duke of Grafton shall hear from me again.

The motives on which I am supposed to have taken up this cause, are of little importance, compared with the facts themselves, and the observations I have made upon them. Without a vain profession of integrity, which in these times might justly be suspected, I shall show myself in effect a friend to the interests of my countrymen, and leave it to them to determine, whether I am moved by a personal malevolence to three private gentlemen, or merely by a hope of perplexing the ministry; or whether I am animated by a just and honourable purpose of obtaining a satisfaction to the laws of this country, equal, if possible, to the violation they have suffered.

JUNIUS.

LETTER XXXIII.

TO HIS GRACE THE DUKE OF GRAFTON.

MY LORD,　　　　　　　　　　　　Nov. 29. 1769.

THOUGH my opinion of your Grace's integrity was but little affected by the coyness with which you received Mr. Vaughan's proposals, I confess I give you some credit for your discretion. You had a fair opportunity of displaying a certain delicacy, of which you had not been suspected; and you were in the right to make use of it. By laying in. a moderate stock of reputation, you undoubtedly meant to provide for the future necessities of your character, that, with an honourable resistance upon record, you may safely indulge your genius, and yield to a favourite inclination with security. But you have discovered your purposes too soon; and, instead of the. modest reserve of virtue, have shown us the termagant chastity of a prude, who gratifies her passions with distinction, and prosecutes one lover for a rape, while she solicits the rude embraces of another.

Your cheek turns pale; for a guilty conscience tells you, you are undone.—Come forward, thou virtuous minister, and tell the world by what interest Mr. Hine has been recommended to so extraordinary a mark of his Majesty's favour; what was the price of the patent he has bought, and to what honourable purpose the purchase-money has been applied. Nothing less than many thousands could pay Colonel Burgoyne's expences at Preston. Do you dare to prosecute such a creature as Vaughan, while you are basely setting up the Royal Patronage to auction? Do you dare to complain of an attack upon your own honour, while you are selling the favours of the Crown, to raise a fund for corrupting the morals of the people? And, do you think it is possible such enormities should escape without impeachment? It is indeed highly your interest to maintain the present House of Commons. Having sold the nation to you in gross, they will undoubtedly protect you in the detail; for while they patronize your crimes, they feel for their own.

JUNIUS.

LETTER XXXIV[c].

TO HIS GRACE THE DUKE OF GRAFTON.

MY LORD,   Dec: 12. 1769.

I FIND with some surprise, that you are not supported as you deserve. Your most determined advocates have scruples about them, which you are unacquainted with; and though there be nothing too hazardous for your Grace to engage in, there are some things too infamous for the vilest prostitute of a newspaper to defend [a]. In what other manner shall we account for the profound, submissive silence, which you and your friends have observed upon a charge, which called immediately for the clearest refutation, and would have justified the severest measures of resentment? I did not attempt to blast your character by an indirect, ambiguous insinuation; but candidly stated to you a plain fact, which struck directly at the integrity of a privy counsellor, of a first commissioner of the treasury, and of a leading minister, who is supposed to enjoy the first share in his Majesty's confidence [b]. In every one of these capacities, I employed the most moderate terms to charge you with treachery to your sovereign, and breach of trust in your office. I accused you of having sold a patent place in the collection of the customs at Exeter, to one Mr. Hine; who, unable or unwilling to deposit the whole purchase money himself, raised part of it by contribution, and has now a certain Doctor Brook quartered upon the salary for one hundred pounds a-year.—No sale by the candle was ever conducted with greater formality.—I affirm, that the price at which the place was knocked down (and which, I have good reason to think, was not less than

three thousand five hundred pounds), was, with your connivance and consent, paid to Colonel Burgoyne, to reward
him, I presume, for the decency of his deportment at Preston; or to reimburse him, perhaps, for the fine of one
thousand pounds, which, for that very deportment, the
court of King's Bench thought proper to set upon him.—
It is not often that the chief justice and the prime minister
are so strangely at variance in their opinions of men and
things.

I thank God, there is not in human nature a degree of
impudence daring enough to deny the charge I have fixed
upon you. Your courteous secretary [c], your confidential
architect [d], are silent, as the grave. Even Mr. Rigby's
countenance fails him. He violates his second nature,
and blushes whenever he speaks of you.—Perhaps the
noble Colonel himself will relieve you. No man is more
tender of his reputation. He is not only nice, but perfectly sore in every thing that touches his honour. If any
man, for example, were to accuse him of taking his stand
at a gaming-table, and watching, with the soberest attention, for a fair opportunity of engaging a drunken young
nobleman at piquet, he would undoubtedly consider it as
an infamous aspersion upon his character, and resent it
like a man of honour.—Acquitting him, therefore, of drawing a regular and splendid subsistence from any unworthy
practices either in his own house or elsewhere, let me ask
your Grace, for what military merits you have been pleased to reward him with military government? He had a
regiment of dragoons, which one would imagine was at
least an equivalent for any services he ever performed.
Besides, he is but a young officer, considering his preferment, and, except in his activity at Preston, not very conspicuous in his profession. But it seems the sale of a civil
employment was not sufficient; and military governments,
which were intended for the support of worn-out veterans,
must be thrown into the scale, to defray the extensive bribery of a contested election. Are these the steps you take
to secure to your sovereign the attachment of his army!
With what countenance dare you appear in the royal presence, branded as you are with the infamy of a notorious
breach of trust? With what countenance can you take
your seat at the treasury-board or in council, when you

feel that every circulating whisper is at your expence alone, and stabs you to the heart? Have you a single friend in parliament so shameless, so thoroughly abandoned, as to undertake your defence? You know, my Lord, that there is not a man in either house, whose character, however flagitious, would not be ruined by mixing his reputation with yours; and does not your heart inform you, that you are degraded below the condition of a man, when you are obliged to bear these insults with submission, and even to thank me for my moderation?

We are told, by the highest judicial authority, that Mr. Vaughan's offer to purchase the reversion of a patent place in Jaimaica (which he was otherwise sufficiently entitled to) amounted to a high misdemeanor. Be it so; and if he deserves it, let him be punished. But the learned judge might have had a fairer opportunity of displaying the powers of his eloquence. Having delivered himself with so much energy upon the criminal nature, and dangerous consequences, of any attempt to corrupt a man in your Grace's station, what would he have said to the minister himself, to that very privy-counsellor, to that first commissioner of the treasury, who does not wait for, but impatiently solicits, the touch of corruption; who employs the meanest of his creatures in these honourable services, and, forgetting the genius and fidelity of his secretary, descends to apply to his house-builder for assistance?

This affair, my Lord, will do infinite credit to government, if, to clear your character, you should think proper to bring it into the House of Lords, or into the Court of King's Bench.——But, my Lord, you dare not do either.

JUNIUS.

LETTER XXXV.

TO THE PRINTER OF THE PUBLIC ADVERTISER.

Dec. 19. 1769.

When the complaints of a brave and powerful people are observed to increase in proportion to the wrongs they have suffered; when, instead of sinking into submission, they are roused to resistance; the time will soon arrive at which every inferior consideration must yield to the security of the sovereign, and to the general safety of the state. There is a moment of difficulty and danger, at which flattery and falsehood can no longer deceive, and simplicity itself can no longer be misled. Let us suppose it arrived. Let us suppose a gracious, well-intentioned prince, made sensible at last of the great duty he owes to his people, and of his own disgraceful situation; that he looks round him for assistance, and asks for no advice, but how to gratify the wishes and secure the happiness of his subjects. In these circumstances, it may be matter of curious SPECULATION to consider, if an honest man were permitted to approach a king, in what terms he would address himself to his sovereign. Let it be imagined, no matter how improbable, that the first prejudice against his character is removed; that the ceremonious difficulties of an audience are surmounted; that he feels himself animated by the purest and most honourable affection to his king and country, and that the great person whom he addresses has spirit enough to bid him speak freely, and understanding enough to listen to him with attention. Unacquainted with the vain impertinence of forms, he would deliver his sentiments with dignity and firmness, but not without respect.

SIR,

It is the misfortune of your life, and originally the cause of every reproach and distress which has attended your government, that you should never have been acquainted with the language of truth, until you heard it in the complaints of your people. It is not, however, too late to correct the error of your education. We are still inclined to make an indulgent allowance for the pernicious lessons you received in your youth, and to form the most sanguine hopes from the natural benevolence of your disposition [e]. We are far from thinking you capable of a direct, deliberate purpose to invade those original rights of your subjects, on which all their civil and political liberties depend. Had it been possible for us to entertain a suspicion so dishonourable to your character, we should long since have adopted a style of remonstrance very distant from the humility of complaint. The doctrine inculcated by our laws, " That the King can do no wrong," is admitted without reluctance. We separate the amiable, good-natured prince from the folly and treachery of his servants, and the private virtues of the man from the vices of his government. Were it not for this just distinction, I know not whether your Majesty's condition, or that of the English nation, would deserve most to be lamented. I would prepare your mind for a favourable reception of truth, by removing every painful, offensive idea of personal reproach. Your subjects, Sir, wish for nothing but that, as they are reasonable and affectionate enough to separate your person from your government, so you, in your turn, should distinguish between the conduct which becomes the permanent dignity of a King, and that which serves only to promote the temporary interest and miserable ambition of a minister.

You ascended the throne with a declared, and, I doubt not, a sincere resolution of giving universal satisfaction to your subjects. You found them pleased with the novelty of a young prince, whose countenance promised even more than his words; and loyal to you, not only from principle, but passion. It was not a cold profession of allegiance to the first magistrate; but a partial, animated attachment to a favourite prince, the native of their country. They did not wait to examine your conduct, nor to be determined by experience; but gave you a generous credit for the future blessings of your reign, and paid you in advance the dearest tribute of their affections. Such, Sir, was once the disposition of a people, who now surround your throne with reproaches and complaints. Do justice to yourself. Banish from your mind those unworthy opinions, with which some interested persons have laboured to possess you.—Distrust the men who tell you that the English are naturally light and inconstant—that they complain without a cause. Withdraw your confidence equally from all parties; from ministers, favourites, and relations; and let there be one moment in your life, in which you have consulted your own understanding.

When you affectedly renounced the name of Englishman, believe me, Sir, you were persuaded to pay a very ill-judged compliment to one part of your subjects at the expence of another. While the natives of Scotland are not in actual rebellion, they are undoubtedly entitled to protection; nor do I mean to condemn the policy of giving some encouragement to the novelty of their affections for the House of Hanover. I am ready to hope for every thing from their new born zeal, and from the future steadiness of their allegiance. But hitherto they have no claim to your favour. To honour them with a determined predilection and confidence, in exclusion of your English subjects, who placed your family, and in spite of treachery and rebellion, have supported it upon the throne, is a mistake too gross even for the unsuspecting generosity of youth. In this error we see a capital violation of the most obvious rules of policy and prudence. We trace it, however, to an original bias in your education, and are ready to allow for your inexperience.

To the same early influence we attribute it, that you have descended to take a share not only in the narrow views and interests of particular persons, but in the fatal malignity of their passions. At your accession to the throne, the whole system of government was altered, not from wisdom or deliberation, but because it had been adopted by your predecessor. A little personal motive of pique and resentment was sufficient to remove the ablest servants of the crown [f]; but it is not in this country, Sir, that such men can be dishonoured by the frowns of a King. They were dismissed, but could not be disgraced. Without entering into a minuter discussion of the merits of the peace, we may observe, in the imprudent hurry with which the first overtures from France were accepted, in the conduct of the negociation and terms of the treaty, the strongest marks of that precipitate spirit of concession, with which a certain party of your subjects have been at all times ready to purchase a peace with the natural enemies of this country. On your part we are satisfied that every thing was honourable and sincere; and if England was sold to France, we doubt not that your Majesty was equally betrayed. The conditions of the peace were matter of grief and surprise to your subjects, but not the immediate cause of their present discontent.

Hitherto, Sir, you had been sacrificed to the prejudices and passions of others. With what firmness will you bear the mention of your own?

A man, not very honourably distinguished in the world, commences a formal attack upon your favourite, considering nothing but how he might best expose his person and principles to detestation, and the national character of his countrymen to contempt. The natives of that country, Sir, are as much distinguished by a peculiar character, as by your Majesty's favour. Like another chosen people, they have been conducted into the land of plenty, where they find themselves effectually marked, and divided from mankind. There is hardly a period at which the most irregular character may not be redeemed. The mistakes of one sex find a retreat in patriotism; those of the other in devotion. Mr. Wilkes brought with him into politics the same liberal sentiments by which his private conduct had been directed; and seemed to think that, as there are few excesses in which an English gentleman may not be permitted to indulge, the same latitude was allowed him in the choice of his political principles, and in the spirit of maintaining them.—I mean to state, not entirely to defend, his conduct. In the earnestness of his zeal, he suffered some unwarrantable insinuations to escape him. He said more than moderate men would justify; but not enough to entitle him to the honor of your Majesty's personal resentment. The rays of Royal indignation, collected upon him, served only to illuminate, and could not consume. Animated by the favour of the people on the one side, and heated by persecution on the other, his views and sentiments changed with his situation. Hardly serious at first, he is now an enthusiast. The coldest bodies warm with opposition, the hardest sparkle in collision. There is a holy mistaken zeal in politics as well as religion. By persuading others, we convince ourselves. The passions are engaged, and create a maternal affection in the mind, which forces us to love the cause for which we suffer. Is this a contention worthy of a king? Are you not sensible how much the meanness of the cause gives an air of ridicule to the serious difficulties into which you have been betrayed? The destruction of one man has been now for many years the sole object of your government; and if there can be any thing still more disgraceful, we have seen, for such an object, the utmost influence of the executive power, and every ministerial artifice, exerted without success. Nor can you ever succeed, unless he should be imprudent enough to forfeit the protection of those laws to which you owe your crown, or unless your ministers should persuade you to make it a question of force alone, and try the whole strength of government in opposition to the people. The lessons he has received from experience, will probably guard him from such excess of folly; and in your Majesty's virtues we find an unquestionable assurance that no illegal violence will be attempted.

Far from suspecting you of so horrible a design, we would attribute the continual violation of the laws, and even this last enormous attack upon the vital principles of the constitution, to an ill-advised, unworthy, personal resentment. From one false step you have been betrayed into another; and as the cause was unworthy of you, your ministers were determined that the prudence of the execution should correspond with the wisdom and dignity of the design: They have reduced you to the necessity of choosing out of a variety of difficulties ;—to a situation so unhappy, that you can neither do wrong without ruin, nor right without affliction. These worthy servants have undoubtedly given you many singular proofs of their abilities: Not contented with making Mr. Wilkes a man of importance, they have judiciously transferred the question from the rights and interests of one man to the most important rights and interests of the people; and forced your subjects, from wishing well to the cause of an individual, to unite with him in their own. Let them proceed as they have begun, and your Majesty need not doubt that the catastrophe will do no dishonour to the conduct of the piece.

The circumstances to which you are reduced, will not admit of a compromise with the English nation. Undecisive qualifying measures will disgrace your government still more than open violence; and without satisfying the people, will excite their contempt. They have too much understanding and spirit to accept of an indirect satisfaction for a direct injury. Nothing less than a repeal, as formal as the resolution itself, can heal the wound which has been given to the constitution, nor will any thing less be accepted. I can readily believe that there is an influence sufficient to recal that pernicious vote. The House of Commons undoubtedly consider their duty to the crown as paramount to all other obligations. To us they are only indebted for an accidental existence, and have justly transferred their gratitude from their parents to their benefactors;--from those who gave them birth, to the minister from whose benevolence they derive the comforts and pleasures of their political life--who has taken the tenderest care of their infancy, and relieves their necessities without offending their delicacy. But if it were possible for their integrity to be degraded to a condition so vile and abject, that, compared with it, the present estimation they stand in is a state of honour and respect, consider, Sir, in what manner you will afterwards proceed. Can you conceive that the people of this country will long submit to be governed by so flexible a House of Commons? It is not in the nature of human society, that any form of government, in such circumstances, can long be preserved. In ours, the general contempt of the people is as fatal as their detestation. Such, I am persuaded, would be the necessary effect of any base concession made by the present House of Commons, and as a qualifying measure would not be accepted, it remains for you to decide whether you will, at any hazard, support a set of men who have reduced you to this unhappy dilemma, or whether you will gratify the united wishes of the whole people of England by dissolving the parliament.

Taking it for granted, as I do very sincerely, that you have personally no design against the constitution, or any view inconsistent with the good of your subjects, I think you cannot hesitate long upon the choice which it equally concerns your interest and your honour to adopt. On one side, you hazard the affections of all your English subjects, you relinquish every hope of repose to yourself, and you endanger the establishment of your family for ever. All this you venture for no object whatsoever, or for such an object as it would be an affront to you to name. Men of sense will examine your conduct with suspicion; while those who are incapable of comprehending to what degree they are injured, afflict you with clamours equally insolent and unmeaning. Supposing it possible that no fatal struggle should ensue, you determine at once to be un-happy, without the hope of a compensation either from interest or ambition. If an English king be hated or des-pised, he must be unhappy; and this perhaps is the only political truth which he ought to be convinced of without experiment. But if the English people should no longer confine their resentment to a submissive representation of their wrongs; if, following the glorious example of their ancestors, they should no longer appeal to the creature of the constitution, but to that high Being who gave them the rights of humanity, whose gifts it were sacrilege to surrender; let me ask you, Sir, upon what part of your subjects would you rely for assistance?'

The people of Ireland have been uniformly plundered and oppressed. In return they give you every day fresh marks of their resentment. They despise the miserable governor you have sent them [g], because he is the creature of Lord Bute; nor is it from any natural confusion in their ideas that they are so ready to confound the original of a king, with the disgraceful representation of him.

The distance of the colonies would make it impossible for them to take an active concern in your affairs, if they were as well affected to your government as they once pretended to be to your person. They were ready enough to distinguish between you and your ministers. They complained of an act of the legislature, but traced the origin of it no higher than to the servants of the crown: they pleased themselves with the hope that their sove-reign, if not favourable to their cause, at least was im-partial. The decisive personal part you took against them, has effectually banished that first distinction from their minds [h]. They consider you as united with your servants against America: and know how to distinguish the sovereign and a venal parliament on one side, from the real sentiments of the English people on the other. Looking forward to independence, they might possibly receive you for their king; but, if ever you retire to America, be assured they will give you such a covenant to digest, as the Presbytery of Scotland would have been ashamed to offer to Charles II. They left their native land in search of freedom, and found it in a desert: Di-vided as they are into a thousand forms of policy and religion, there is one point in which they all agree :—they equally detest the pageantry of a king, and the supercilious hypocrisy of a bishop.

It is not then from the alienated affections of Ireland or America that you can reasonably look for assistance; still less from the people of England, who are actually contending for their rights, and in this great question are parties against you. You are not, however, destitute of every appearance of support: You have all the Jacobites, Nonjurors, Roman Catholics, and Tories of this country, and all Scotland without exception. Considering from what family you are descended, the choice of your friends has been singularly directed; and truly Sir, if you had not lost the Whig interest of England, I should admire your dexterity in turning the hearts of your enemies. Is it possible for you to place any confidence in men, who, before they are faithful to you, must renounce every opinion, and betray every principle, both in church and state, which they inherit from their ancestors, and are confirmed in by their education? whose numbers are so inconsiderable, that they have long since been obliged to give up the principles and language which distinguish them as a party, and to fight under the banners of their enemies? Their zeal begins with hypocrisy, and must conclude in treachery. At first they deceive, at last they betray.

As to the Scotch, I must suppose your heart and understanding so biassed, from your earliest infancy, in their favour, that nothing less than your own misfortunes can undeceive you. You will not accept of the uniform experience of your ancestors; and, when once a man is determined to believe, the very absurdity of the doctrine confirms him in his faith. A bigotted understanding can draw a proof of attachment to the House of Hanover from a notorious zeal for the House of Stuart, and find an earnest of future loyalty in former rebellions. Appearances are, however, in their favour; so strongly indeed, that one would think they had forgotten that you are their lawful King, and had mistaken you for a pretender to the crown. Let it be admitted, then, that the Scotch are as sincere in their present professions as if you were in reality not an Englishman, but a Briton of the North. You would not be the first prince, of their native country, against whom they have rebelled, nor the first whom they have basely betrayed. Have you forgotten, Sir, or has your favourite concealed from you that part of our history, when the unhappy Charles (and he too had private virtues) fled from the open, avowed indignation of his English subjects, and surrendered himself at discretion to the good faith of his own countrymen. Without looking for support in their affections as subjects, he applied only to their honour as gentlemen for protection. They received him as they would your Majesty, with bows, and smiles, and falsehood, and kept him until they had settled their bargain with the English parliament; then basely sold their native king to the vengeance of his enemies. This, Sir, was not the act of a few traitors, but the deliberate treachery of a Scotch parliament, representing the nation. A wise prince might draw from it two lessons of equal utility to himself. On one side he might learn to dread the undisguised resentment of a generous people, who dare openly assert their rights, and who, in a just cause, are ready to meet their sovereign in the field. On the other side, he would be taught to apprehend something far more formidable;—a fawning treachery, against which no prudence can guard, no courage can defend. The insidious smile upon the cheek would warn him of the canker in the heart.

From the uses to which one part of the army had been too frequently applied, you have some reason to expect that there are no services they would refuse. Here too we trace the partiality of your understanding. You take the sense of the army from the conduct of the guards, with the same justice with which you collect the sense of the people from the representations of the ministry. Your marching regiments, Sir, will not make the guards their example either as soldiers or subjects. They feel and resent, as they ought to do, that invariable, undistinguishing favour, with which the guards are treated [i]; while those gallant troops, by whom every hazardous, every laborious service is performed, are left to perish in garrisons abroad, or pine in quarters at home, neglected and forgotten. If they had no sense of the great original duty they owe their country, their resentment would operate like patriotism, and leave your cause to be defended by those to whom you have lavished the rewards and honours of their profession. The Prætorian bands, enervated and debauched as they were, had still strength enough to awe the Roman populace; but when the distant legions took the alarm, they marched to Rome, and gave away the empire.

On this side, then, which ever way you turn your eyes, you see nothing but perplexity and distress. You may determine to support the very ministry who have reduced your affairs to this deplorable situation; you may shelter yourself under the forms of a parliament, and set your people at defiance; but be assured, Sir, that such a resolution would be as imprudent as it would be odious. If it did not immediately shake your establishment, it would rob you of your peace of mind for ever.

On the other, how different is the prospect! How easy, how safe and honourable, is the path before you! The English nation declare they are grossly injured by their representatives, and solicit your Majesty to exert your lawful prerogative, and give them an opportunity of recalling a trust which they find has been scandalously abused. You are not to be told that the power of the House of Commons is not original, but delegated to them for the welfare of the people, from whom they received it. A question of right arises between the constituent and the representative body. By what authority shall it be decided? Will your Majesty intefere in a question in which you have properly no immediate concern?—It would be a step equally odious and unnecessary. Shall the Lords be called upon to determine the rights and privileges of the Commons?—They cannot do it without a flagrant breach of the constitution. Or, will you refer it to the judges?—They have often told your ancestors that the law of parliament is above them. What part then remains, but to leave it to the people to determine for themselves? They alone are injured; and since there is no superior power to which the cause can be referred, they alone ought to determine.

I do not mean to perplex you with a tedious argument upon a subject already so discussed, that inspiration could hardly throw a new light upon it. There are, however, two points of view in which it particularly imports your

Majesty to consider the late proceedings of the House of Commons. By depriving a subject of his birthright, they have attributed to their own vote an authority equal to an act of the whole legislature; and, though perhaps not with the same motives, have strictly followed the example of the long parliament, which first declared the regal office useless, and soon after, with as little ceremony, dissolved the House of Lords. The same pretended power which robs an English subject of his birthright, may rob an English king of his crown. In another view, the resolution of the House of Commons, apparently not so dangerous to your Majesty, is still more alarming to your people. Not contented with divesting one man of his right, they have arbitrarily conveyed that right to another. They have set aside a return as illegal, without daring to censure those officers, who were particularly apprized of Mr. Wilkes incapacity, not only by the declaration of the House, but expressly by the writ directed to them, and who nevertheless returned him duly elected. They have rejected the majority of votes, the only criterion by which our laws judge of the sense of the people; they have transferred the right of election from the collective to the representative body; and by these acts, taken separately or together, they have essentially altered the constitution of the House of Commons. Versed, as your Majesty undoubtedly is, in the English history, it cannot easily escape you, how much it is your interest, as well as your duty, to prevent one of the three estates from encroaching upon the province of the other two, or assuming the authority of them all. When once they have departed from the great constitutional line, by which all their proceedings should be directed, who will answer for their future moderation? Or, what assurance will they give you, that, when they have trampled upon their equals, they will submit to a superior! Your Majesty may learn hereafter how nearly the slave and tyrant are allied.

Some of your council, more candid than the rest, admit the abandoned profligacy of the present House of Commons, but oppose their dissolution, upon an opinion, I confess, not very unwarrantable, that their successors would be equally at the disposal of the Treasury. I cannot persuade myself that the nation will have profited so little by experience. But if that opinion were well founded, you might then gratify our wishes at an easy rate, and appease the present clamour against your government; without offering any material injury to the favourite cause of corruption.

You have still an honourable part to act. The affections of your subjects may still be recovered. But before you subdue their hearts, you must gain a noble victory over your own. Discard those little personal resentments which have too long directed your public conduct. Pardon this man the remainder of his punishment; and if resentment still prevails, make it, what it should have been long since, an act, not of mercy, but of contempt. He will soon fall back into his natural station,—a silent senator, and hardly supporting the weekly eloquence of a newspaper. The gentle breath of peace would leave him on the surface, neglected and unremoved. It is only the tempest that lifts him from his place.

Without consulting your minister, call together your whole council. Let it appear to the public, that you can determine and act for yourself. Come forward to your people. Lay aside the wretched formalities of a king; and speak to your subjects with the spirit of a man, and in the language of a gentleman. Tell them you have been fatally deceived. The acknowledgement will be no disgrace, but rather an honour to your understanding. Tell them you are determined to remove every cause of complaint against your government; that you will give your confidence to no man who does not possess the confidence of your subjects; and leave it to themselves to determine, by their conduct at a future election, whether or no it be in reality the general sense of the nation, that their rights have been arbitrarily invaded by the present House of Commons, and the constitution betrayed. They will then do justice to their representatives, and to themselves.

These sentiments, Sir, and the style they are conveyed in, may be offensive perhaps, because they are new to you. Accustomed to the language of courtiers, you measure their affections by the vehemence of their expressions; and when they only praise you indirectly, you adaire their sincerity. But this is not a time to trifle with your fortune. They deceive you, Sir, who tell you that you have many friends whose affections are founded upon a principle of personal attachment. The first foundation of friendship, is not the power of conferring benefits, but the equality with which they are received, and may be returned. The fortune which made you a king, forbade you to have a friend. It is a law of nature which cannot be violated with impunity: The mistaken prince, who looks for friendship, will find a favourite, and in that favourite the ruin of his affairs.

The people of England are loyal to the House of Hanover, not from a vain preference of one family to another, but from a conviction that the establishment of that family was necessary to the support of their civil and religious liberties. This, Sir, is a principle of allegiance equally solid and rational;—fit for Englishmen to adopt, and well worthy of your Majesty's encouragement. We cannot be long deluded by nominal distinctions. The name of Stuart, of itself, is only contemptible;—armed with the sovereign authority, their principles are formidable. The prince who imitates their conduct, should be warned by their example; and, while he plumes himself upon the security of his title to the crown, should remember, that, as it was acquired by one revolution, it may be lost by another.

JUNIUS.

LETTER XXXVI.

TO HIS GRACE THE DUKE OF GRAFTON.

MY LORD,   Feb. 14. 1770.

If I were personally your enemy, I might pity and forgive you. You have every claim to compassion, that can arise from misery and distress. The condition you are reduced to, would disarm a private enemy of his resentment, and leave no consolation to the most vindictive spirit, but that such an object as you are, would disgrace the dignity of revenge. But in the relation you have borne to this country, you have no title to indulgence; and if I had followed the dictates of my own opinion, I should never have allowed you the respite of a moment. In your public character, you have injured every subject of the empire; and though an individual is not authorised to forgive the injuries done to society, he is called upon to assert his separate share in the public resentment. I submitted, however, to the judgment of men more moderate, perhaps more candid than myself. For my own part I do not pretend to understand those prudent forms of decorum, those gentle rules of discretion which some men endeavour to unite with the conduct of the greatest and most hazardous affairs. Engaged in the defence of an honourable cause, I would take a decisive part,—I should scorn to provide for a future retreat, or to keep terms with a man who preserves no measures with the public. Neither the abject submission of deserting his post in the hour of danger, nor even the ^{k} sacred shield of cowardice, should protect him. I would pursue him through life, and try the last exertion of my abilities to preserve the perishable infamy of his name, and make it immortal.

What, then, my Lord, is this the event of all the sacrifices you have made to Lord Bute's patronage, and to your own unfortunate ambition? Was it for this you abandoned your earliest friendships,—the warmest connections of your youth, and all those honourable engagements by which you once solicited, and might have acquired the esteem of your country? Have you secured no recompense for such a waste of honour?—Unhappy man! what party will receive the common deserter of all parties? Without a client to flatter, without a friend to console you, and with only one companion from the honest house of Bloomsbury, you must now retire into a dreadful solitude. At the most active period of life, you must quit the busy scene, and conceal yourself from the world, if you would hope to save the wretched remains of a ruined reputation. The vices operate like age ;— bring on disease before its time, and in the prime of youth leave the character broken and exhausted.

Yet your conduct has been mysterious, as well as contemptible. Where is now that firmness or obstinacy so long boasted of by your friends, and acknowledged by your enemies? We were taught to expect that you would not leave the ruin of this country to be completed by other hands, but were determined either to gain a decisive victory over the constitution, or to perish bravely at least behind the last dike of the prerogative. You knew the danger, and might have been provided for it. You took sufficient time to prepare for a meeting with your parliament, to confirm the mercenary fidelity of your dependents, and to suggest to your Sovereign a language suited to his dignity at least, if not to his benevolence and wisdom. Yet, while the whole kingdom was agitated with anxious expectation upon one great point, you meanly evaded the question, and, instead of the explicit firmness and decision of a king, gave us nothing but the misery of a ruined [1] grazier, and the whining piety of a Methodist. We had reason to expect that notice would have been taken of the petitions which the King had received from the English nation; and although I can conceive some personal motives for not yielding to them, I can find none, in common prudence or decency, for treating them with contempt. Be assured, my Lord, the English people will not tamely submit to this unworthy treatment:—they had a right to be heard; and their petitions, if not granted, deserved to be considered. Whatever be the real views and doctrine of a court, the Sovereign should be taught to preserve some forms of attention to his subjects; and, if he will not redress their grievances, not to make them a topic of jest and mockery among lords and ladies of the bedchamber. Injuries may be atoned for, and forgiven; but insults admit of no compensation. They degrade the mind in its own esteem, and force it to recover its level by revenge. This neglect of the petitions was, however a part of your original plan of government; nor will any consequences it has produced, account for your deserting your Sovereign, in the midst of that distress in which you and your [m] new friends had involved him. One would think, my Lord, you might have taken this spirited resolution before you had dissolved the last of those early connections, which once, even in your own opinion, did honour to your youth;—before you had obliged Lord Granby to quit a service he was attached to;—before you had discarded one chancellor, and killed another. To what an abject condition

have you laboured to reduce the best of princes, when
the unhappy man, who yields at last to such personal instance and solicitation as never can be fairly employed
against a subject, feels himself degraded by his compliance, and is unable to survive the disgraceful honours
which his gracious Sovereign had compelled him to accept. He was a man of spirit, for he had a quick sense
of shame, and death has redeemed his character. I know
your Grace too well to appeal to your feelings upon this
event; but there is another heart not yet, I hope, quite
callous to the touch of humanity, to which it ought to be a
dreadful lesson for ever [n].

Now, my Lord, let us consider the situation to which
you have conducted, and in which you have thought it
adviseable to abandon, your royal master. Whenever the
people have complained, and nothing better could be said
in defence of the measures of government, it has been
the fashion to answer us, though not very fairly, with
an appeal to the private virtues of your Sovereign: " Has
" he not, to relieve the people, surrendered a consider-
" able part of his revenue?—Has he not made the judges
" independent, by fixing them in their places for life?"
—My Lord, we acknowledge the gracious principle
which gave birth to these concessions, and have nothing
to regret but that it has never been adhered to. At the
end of seven years, we are loaded with a debt of above
five hundred thousand pounds upon the civil list; and
we now see the chancellor of Great Britain tyrannically
forced out of his office, not for want of abilities, not for
want of integrity, or of attention to his duty, but for delivering his honest opinion in parliament, upon the greatest constitutional question that has arisen since the Revolution.—We care not to whose private virtues you appeal: the theory of such a government is falsehood and
mockery; the practice is oppression. You have laboured
then (though I confess to no purpose) to rob your master
of the only plausible answer that ever was given in defence of his government,—of the opinion which the
people had conceived of his personal honour and integrity.
—The Duke of Bedford was more moderate than your
Grace. He only forced his master to violate a solemn
promise made to an individual [o]. But you, my Lord,

have successfully extended your advice to every political, every moral engagement, that could bind either the magistrate or the man. The condition of a king is often miserable, but it required your Grace's abilities to make it contemptible.—You will say, perhaps, that the faithful servants, in whose hands you have left him, are able to retrieve his honour, and to support his government. You have publicly declared, even since your resignation, that you approved of their measures, and admired their conduct, particularly that of the Earl of Sandwich. What a pity it is, that with all this appearance, you should think it necessary to separate yourself from such amiable companions! You forget, my Lord, that while you are lavish in the praise of men whom you desert, you are publicly opposing your conduct to your opinions, and depriving yourself of the only plausible pretence you had for leaving your Sovereign overwhelmed with distress. I call it plausible; for, in truth, there is no reason whatsoever, less than the frowns of your master, that could justify a man of spirit for abandoning his post at a moment so critical and important. It is in vain to evade the question. If you will not speak out the public have a right to judge from appearances. We are authorized to conclude, that you either differed from your colleagues, whose measures you still affect to defend, or that you thought the administration of the King's affairs no longer tenable. You are at liberty to choose between the hypocrite and the coward. Your best friends are in doubt which way they shall incline. Your country unites the characters, and gives you credit for them both. For my own part, I see nothing inconsistent in your conduct. You began with betraying the people,—you conclude with betraying the King.

In your treatment of particular persons, you have preserved the uniformity of your character. Even Mr. Bradshaw declares, that no man was ever so ill used as himself. As to the provision ᵖ you have made for his family, he was entitled to it by the house he lives in. The successor of one chancellor might well pretend to be the rival of another. It is the breach of private friendship which touches Mr. Bradshaw; and, to say the truth, when a man of his rank and abilities had taken so active a part in your affairs, he ought not to have been let down at last with a miserable pension of fifteen hundred pounds a-year. Colonel Luttrell, Mr. Onslow, and Governor Burgoyne, were equally engaged with you, and have rather more reason to complain than Mr. Bradshaw. These are men, my Lord, whose friendship you ought to have adhered to on the same principle on which you deserted Lord Rockingham, Lord Chatham, Lord Camden, and the Duke of Portland. We can easily account for your violating your engagements with men of honour, but why should you betray your natural connections? Why separate yourself from Lord Sandwich, Lord Gower, and Mr. Rigby, or leave the three worthy gentlemen above mentioned to shift for themselves? With all the fashionable indulgence of the times, this country does not abound in characters like theirs; and you may find it a very difficult matter to recruit the black catalogue of your friends.

The recollection of the royal patent you sold to Mr. Hine, obliges me to say a word in defence of a man whom you have taken the most dishonourable means to injure. I do not refer to the sham prosecution which you affected to carry on against him. On that ground, I doubt not, he is prepared to meet you with tenfold recrimination, and set you at defiance. The injury you have done him affects his moral character. You knew that the offer to purchase the reversion of a place, which has heretofore been sold under a decree of the Court of Chancery, however imprudent in his situation, would no way tend to cover him with that sort of guilt which you wished to fix upon him in the eyes of the world. You laboured then, by every species of false suggestion, and even by publishing counterfeit letters, to have it understood that he had proposed terms of accommodation to you, and had offered to abandon his principles, his party, and his friends. You consulted your own breast for a character of consummate treachery, and gave it to the public for that of Mr. Vaughan. I think myself obliged to do this justice to an injured man, because I was deceived by the appearances thrown out by your Grace, and have frequently spoken of his conduct with indignation. If he really be what I think him, honest, though mistaken, he will be happy in recovering his reputation, though at the expence of his understanding. Here, I see, the matter is likely to rest. Your Grace is afraid to carry on the prosecution. Mr. Hine keeps quiet possession of his purchase; and Governor Burgoyne, relieved from the apprehension of refunding the money, sits down, for the remainder of his life, INFAMOUS AND CONTENTED.

I believe, my Lord, I may now take my leave of you for ever. You are no longer that resolute minister, who had spirit to support the most violent measures; who compensated for the want of good and great qualities, by a brave determination (which some people admired and relied on) to maintain himself without them. The reputation of obstinacy and perseverance might have supplied the place of all the absent virtues. You have now added the last negative to your character, and meanly confessed that you are destitute of the common spirit of a man. Retire, then, my Lord, and hide your blushes from the world; for, with such a load of shame, even BLACK may change its colour. A mind such as yours, in the solitary hours of domestic enjoyment, may still find topics of consolation. You may find it in the memory of violated friendship; in the afflictions of an accomplished prince, whom you have disgraced and deserted; and in the agitations of a great country, driven, by your counsels, to the brink of destruction.

The palm of ministerial firmness is now transferred to Lord North. He tells us so himself, with the plenitude of the *ore rotundo*⁹; and I am ready enough to believe, that, while he can keep his place, he will not easily be persuaded to resign it. Your Grace was the firm minister of yesterday: Lord North is the firm minister of to-day. To-morrow, perhaps, his Majesty, in his wisdom, may give us a rival for you both. You are too well acquainted with the temper of your late allies, to think it possible that Lord North should be permitted to govern this country. If we may believe common fame, they have shown him their superiority already. His Majesty is indeed too gracious to insult his subjects, by choosing his first minister from among the domestics of the Duke of Bedford. That would have been too gross an outrage to the three kingdoms. Their purpose, however, is equally answered by pushing forward this unhappy figure, and

forcing it to bear the odium of measures which they in
reality direct. Without immediately appearing to govern,
they possess the power and distribute the emoluments of
government as they think proper. They still adhere to
the spirit of that calculation, which made Mr. Luttrell
representative of Middlesex. Far from regretting your
retreat, they assure us very gravely, that it increases the
real strength of the ministry. According to this way of
reasoning, they will probably grow stronger, and more
flourishing, every hour they exist; for I think there is
hardly a day passes in which some one or other of his
Majesty's servants does not leave them to improve by the
loss of his assistance. But, alas! their countenances speak
a different language. When the members drop off, the
main body cannot be insensible of its approaching dissolution. Even the violence of their proceedings is a signal
of despair. Like broken tenants, who have had warning to quit the premises, they curse their landlord, destroy the fixtures, throw every thing into confusion, and
care not what mischief they do to the estate.

JUNIUS.

LETTER XXXVII.

TO THE PRINTER OF THE PUBLIC ADVERTISER.

SIR, March 19. 1770.

I BELIEVE there is no man, however indifferent
about the interests of this country, who will not readily
confess that the situation to which we are now reduced,
whether it has arisen from the violence of faction, or from
an arbitary system of government, justifies the most melancholy apprehensions, and calls for the exertion of
whatever wisdom or vigour is left among us. The king's
answer to the remonstrance of the city of London, and
the measures since adopted by the ministry, amount to a
plain declaration, that the principle, on which Mr. Luttrell was seated in the House of Commons, is to be supported in all its consequences, and carried to its utmost
extent. The same spirit which violated the freedom of
election, now invades the declaration and bill of rights,
and threatens to punish the subject for exercising a privi-

lege, hitherto undisputed, of petitioning the crown. The grievances of the people are aggravated by insults; their complaints not merely disregarded, but checked by authority; and every one of those acts, against which they remonstrated, confirmed by the King's decisive approbation. At such a moment, no honest man will remain silent or inactive. However distinguished by rank or property, in the rights of freedom we are all equal. As we are Englishmen, the least considerable man among us has an interest equal to the proudest nobleman, in the laws and constitution of his country, and is equally called upon to make a generous contribution in support of them;—whether it be the heart to conceive, the understanding to direct, or the hand to execute. It is a common cause, in which we are all interested, in which we should all be engaged. The man who deserts it at this alarming crisis, is an enemy to his country, and, what I think of infinitely less importance, a traitor to his sovereign. The subject who is truly loyal to the chief magistrate, will neither advise nor submit to arbitrary measures. The city of London have given an example, which, I doubt not, will be followed by the whole kingdom. The noble spirit of the metropolis is the life-blood of the state, collected at the heart: from that point it circulates, with health and vigour, through every artery of the constitution. The time is come, when the body of the English people must assert their own cause: conscious of their strength, and animated by a sense of their duty, they will not surrender their birthrights to ministers, parliaments, or kings.

The city of London have expressed their sentiments with freedom and firmness; they have spoken truth boldly; and, in whatever light their remonstrance may be represented by courtiers, I defy the most subtle lawyer in this country to point out a single instance in which they have exceeded the truth. Even that assertion, which we are told is most offensive to parliament, in the theory of the English constitution, is strictly true. If any part of the representative body be not chosen by the people, that part vitiates and corrupts the whole. If there be a defect in the representation of the people, that power, which alone is equal to the making of the laws in this country, is not complete, and the acts of parliament under that

L 2

circumstance are not the acts of a pure and entire legislature. I speak of the theory of our constitution; and whatever difficulties or inconveniences may attend the practice, I am ready to maintain, that as far as the fact deviates from the principle, so far the practice is vicious and corrupt. I have not heard a question raised upon any other part of the remonstrance. That the principle on which the Middlesex election was determined, is more pernicious in its effects than either the levying of ship-money by Charles the First, or the suspending power assumed by his son, will hardly be disputed by any man who understands or wishes well to the English constitution. It is not an act of open violence done by the King, or any direct or palpable breach of the laws attempted by his minister, that can ever endanger the liberties of this country. Against such a king or minister, the people would immediately take the alarm, and all the parties unite to oppose him. The laws may be grossly violated in particular instances, without any direct attack upon the whole system. Facts of that kind stand alone; they are attributed to necessity, not defended by principle. We can never be really in danger, until the forms of parliament are made use of to destroy the substance of our civil and political liberties;—until parliament itself betrays its trust, by contributing to establish new principles of government, and employing the very weapons committed to it by the collective body, to stab the constitution.

As for the terms of the remonstrance, I presume it will not be affirmed, by any person less polished than a gentleman-usher, that this is a season for compliments. Our gracious King, indeed, is abundantly civil to himself. Instead of an answer to a petition, his Majesty very graciously pronounces his own panegyric; and I confess, that, as far as his personal behaviour, or the royal purity of his intentions, is concerned, the truth of those declarations, which the minister has drawn up for his master, cannot decently be disputed. In every other respect, I affirm, that they are absolutely unsupported either in argument or fact. I must add too, that supposing the speech were otherwise unexceptionable, it is not a direct answer to the petition of the city. His Majesty is pleased to say, that he is always ready to receive the requests of his subjects: yet the sheriffs were twice sent back with an excuse, and it was certainly debated in council whether or no the magistrates of the city of London should be admitted to an audience. Whether the remonstrance be or be not injurious to parliament, is the very question between the parliament and the people; and such a question as cannot be decided by the assertion of a third party, however respectable. That the petitioning for a dissolution of parliament is irreconcilable with the principles of the constitution, is a new doctrine. His majesty perhaps has not been informed, that the house of Commons themselves have, by a formal resolution, admitted it to be the right of the subject. His Majesty proceeds to assure us, that he has made the laws the rule of his conduct.—Was it in ordering or permitting his ministers to apprehend Mr. Wilkes by a general warrant?—Was it in suffering his ministers to revive the obsolete maxim of *nullum tempus* to rob the Duke of Portland of his property, and thereby give a decisive turn to a county election?—Was it in erecting a chamber consultation of surgeons, with authority to examine into, and supersede the legal verdict of a jury? Or did his Majesty consult the laws of this country, when he permitted his secretary of state to declare, that, whenever the civil magistrate is trifled with, a military force must be sent for, without the delay of a moment, and effectually employed? Or was it in the barbarous exactness with which this illegal, inhuman, doctrine was carried into execution?—If his Majesty had recollected these facts, I think he would never have said, at least with any reference to the measures of his government, that he had made the laws the rule of his conduct. To talk of preserving the affections, or relying on the support of his subjects, while he continues to act upon these principles, is indeed paying a compliment to their loyalty, which I hope they have too much spirit and understanding to deserve.

His Majesty, we are told, is not only punctual in the performance of his own duty, but careful not to assume any of those powers which the constitution has placed in other hands. Admitting this last assertion to be strictly true, it is no way to the purpose. The city of London have not desired the King to assume a power placed in other hands. If they had, I should hope to see the person, who dared to present such a petition, immediately impeached. They solicit their sovereign to exert that constitutional authority, which the laws have vested in him, for the benefit of his subjects. They call upon him to make use of his lawful prerogative, in a case which our laws evidently supposed might happen, since they have provided for it by trusting the sovereign with a discretionary power to dissolve the parliament. This request will, I am confident, be supported by remonstrances from all parts of the kingdom. His Majesty will find at last, that this is the sense of his people ; and that it is not his interest to support either ministry or parliament, at the hazard of a breach with the collective body of his subjects. —That he is the king of a free people, is indeed his greatest glory. That he may long continue the king of a free people, is the second wish that animates my heart. The first is, THAT THE PEOPLE MAY BE FREE.

JUNIUS.

LETTER XXXVIII.

TO THE PRINTER OF THE PUBLIC ADVERTISER.

SIR, April 3. 1770.

IN my last letter, I offered you my opinion of the truth and propriety of his Majesty's answer to the city of London, considering it merely as the speech of a minister, drawn up in his own defence, and delivered, as usual, by the chief magistrate. I would separate as much as possible, the King's personal character and behaviour from the acts of the present government. I wish it to be understood that his Majesty had in effect no more concern in the substance of what he said, than Sir James Hodges had in the remonstrance ; and that as Sir James, in virtue of his office, was obliged to speak the sentiments of the people, his Majesty might think himself bound, by the same official obligation, to give a graceful utterance to the sentiments of his minister. The cold formality of a well repeated lesson is widely distant from the animated expression of the heart.

This distinction, however, is only true with respect to the measure itself. The consequences of it reach beyond the minister, and materially affect his Majesty's honour. In their own nature they are formidable enough to alarm a man of prudence, and disgraceful enough to afflict a man of spirit. A subject, whose sincere attachment to his Majesty's person and family is founded upon rational principles, will not, in the present conjuncture, be scrupulous of alarming, or even of afflicting his sovereign. I know there is, another sort of loyalty, of which his Majesty has had plentiful experience. When the loyalty of Tories, Jacobites, and Scotchmen, has once taken possession of an unhappy prince, it seldom leaves him without accomplishing his destruction. When the poison of their doctrines has tainted the natural benevolence of his disposition, when their insidious counsels have corrupted the stamina of his government, what antidote can restore him to his political health and honour, but the firm sincerity of his English subjects?

It has not been usual in this country, at least since the days of Charles the First, to see the sovereign personally at variance or engaged in a direct altercation with his subjects. Acts of grace and indulgence are wisely appropriated to him, and should constantly be performed by himself. He never should appear but in an amiable light to his subjects. Even in France, as long as any ideas of a limited monarchy were thought worth preserving, it was a maxim, that no man should leave the royal presence discontented. They have lost or renounced the moderate principles of their government; and now when their parliaments venture to remonstrate, the tyrant comes forward, and answers absolutely for himself. The spirit of their present constitution requires that the king should be feared; and the principle, I believe, is tolerably supported by the fact. But, in our political system, the theory is at variance with the practice; for the king should be beloved. Measures of great severity may, indeed, in some circumstances, be necessary; but the minister who advises, should take the execution and odium of them entirely upon himself. He not only betrays his master, but violates the spirit of the English constitution, when he exposes the chief magistrate to the personal hatred or contempt of his subjects. When we speak of the firmness of government, we mean an uniform system of measures, deliberately adopted, and resolutely maintained, by the servants of the Crown, not a peevish asperity in the language or behaviour of the Sovereign. The government of a weak irresolute monarch may be wise, moderate, and firm; that of an obstinate capricious prince, on the contrary, may be feeble, undetermined, and relaxed. The reputation of public measures depends upon the minister, who is responsible; not upon the king, whose private opinions are not supposed to have any weight against the advice of his council, and whose personal authority should therefore never be interposed in public affairs.—This I believe is true constitutional doctrine. But for a moment let us suppose it false. Let it be taken for granted, that an occasion may arise in which a King of England shall be compelled to take upon himself the ungrateful office of rejecting the petitions, and censuring the conduct of his subjects; and let the city remonstrance be supposed to have created so extraordinary an occasion. On this principle, which I presume no friend of administration will dispute, let the wisdom and spirit of the ministry be examined. They advise the king to hazard his dignity, by a positive declaration of his own sentiments.—They suggest to him a language full of severity and reproach. What follows? When his Majesty had taken so decisive a part in support of his ministry and parliament, he had a right to expect from them a reciprocal demonstration of firmness in their own cause, and of their zeal for his honour. He had reason to expect (and such, I doubt not, were the blustering promises of Lord North), that the persons whom he had been advised to charge with having failed in their respect to him, with having injured parliament and violated the principles of the constitution, should not have been permitted to escape without some severe marks of the displeasure and vengeance of parliament. As the matter stands, the minister, after placing his sovereign in the most unfavourable light to his subjects, and after attempting to fix the ridicule and odium of his own precipitate measures upon the royal character, leaves him a solitary figure upon the scene, to recal, if he can, or to compensate, by future compliances, for one unhappy demonstration of ill-supported firmness and ineffectual resentment. As a man of spirit, his Majesty cannot but be sensible, that the lofty terms in which he was persuaded to reprimand the city, when united with the silly conclusion of the business, resemble the pomp of a mock-tragedy, where the most pathetic sentiments, and even the sufferings of the hero, are calculated for derision.

Such has been the boasted firmness and consistency of a minister [s], whose appearance in the House of Commons was thought essential to the King's service ;—whose presence was to influence every division ;—who had a voice to persuade, an eye to penetrate, a gesture to command. The reputation of these great qualities has been fatal to his friends. The little dignity of Mr. Ellis has been committed. The mind was sunk ;—combustibles were provided; and Welbore Ellis, the Guy Faux of the fable, waited only for the signal of command. All of a sudden the country gentlemen discover how grossly they have been deceived :—the ministers's heart fails him ; the grand plot is defeated in a moment ; and poor Mr. Ellis and his motion taken into custody. From the event of Friday last, one would imagine that some fatality hung over this gentleman. Whether he makes or suppresses a motion, he is equally sure of his disgrace. But the complexion of the times will suffer no man to be vice-treasurer of Ireland with impunity [t].

I do not mean to express the smallest anxiety for the minister's reputation. He acts separately for himself, and the most shameful inconsistency may perhaps be no disgrace to him. But when the sovereign, who represents the majesty of the state, appears in person, his dignity should be supported. The occasion should be important ;—the plan well considered ;—the execution steady and consistent. My zeal for his Majesty's real honour compels me to assert, that it has been too much the system of the present reign to introduce him personally, either to act for, or to defend his servants. They persuade him to do what is properly their business, and desert him in the midst of it [u]. Yet this is an inconvenience to which he must for ever be exposed, while he adheres to a ministry divided among themselves, or unequal in credit and ability to the great task they have undertaken. Instead of reserving the interposition of the royal personage as the last resource of government, their weakness obliges them to apply it to every ordinary occasion, and to render it cheap and common in the opinion of the people. Instead of supporting their master, they look to him for support ; and, for the emoluments of remaining one day more in office, care not how much his sacred character is prostituted and dishonoured.

If I thought it possible for this paper to reach the closet, I would venture to appeal at once to his Majesty's judgment. I would ask him, but in the most repectful terms, " As you are a young man, Sir, who ought to have a life " of happiness in prospect;—as you are a husband ;—as " you are a father (your filial duties, I own, have been " religiously performed) ; is it *bona fide* for your interest or " your honour, to sacrifice your domestic tranquility, and " to live in a perpetual disagreement with your people, " merely to preserve such a chain of beings as North, Bar- " rington, Weymouth, Gower, Ellis, Onslow, Rigby, Jer- " ry Dyson, and Sandwich? Their very names are a satire " upon all government; and I defy the gravest of your " chaplains to read the catalogue without laughing."

For my own part, Sir, I have always considered addresses from parliament, as a fashonable unmeaning formality. Usurpers, idiots, and tyrants, have been successively complimented with almost the same professions of duty and affection. But let us suppose them to mean exactly what they profess. The consequences deserve to be considered. Either the sovereign is a man of high spirit and dangerous ambition, ready to take advantage of the treachery of his parliament, ready to accept the surrender they make him of the public liberty ;—or he is a mild, undesigning prince, who provided they indulge him with a little state and pageantry, would of himself intend no mischief. On the first supposition, it must soon be decided by the sword, whether the constitution should be lost or preserved. On the second, a prince no way qualified for the execution of a great and hazardous enterprise, and without any determined object in view, may nevertheless be driven into such desperate measures, as may lead directly to his ruin, or disgrace himself by a shameful fluctuation between the extremes of violence at one moment, and timidity at another. The minister, perhaps, may have reason to be satisfied with the success of the present hour, and with the profits of his employment.

He is the tenant of the day, and has no interest in the inheritance. The sovereign himself is bound by other obligations; and ought to look forward to a superior, a permanent interest. His paternal tenderness should remind him, how many hostages he has given to society. The ties of nature come powerfully in aid of oaths and protestations. The father, who considers his own precarious state of health, and the possible hazard of a long minority, will wish to see the family estate free and unencumbered [v]. What is the dignity of the crown, though it were really maintained;—what is the honour of parliament, supposing it could exist without any foundation of integrity and justice;—or what is, the vain reputation of firmness, even if the scheme of the government were uniform and consistent, compared with the heart-felt affections of the people, with the happiness and security of the Royal Family, or even with the grateful acclamations of the populace? Whatever style of contempt may be adopted by ministers or parliaments, no man sincerely despises the voice of the English nation. The house of Commons are only interpreters, whose duty it is to convey the sense of the people faithfully to the crown. If the interpretation be false or imperfect, the constituent powers are called upon to deliver their own sentiments. Their speech is rude, but intelligible;—their gestures fierce, but full of explanation. Perplexed by sophistries, their honest eloquence rises into action. Their first appeal was to the integrity of their representatives;—the second to the king's justice;—the last argument of the people, whenever they have recourse to it, will carry more perhaps than persuasion to parliament, or supplication to the throne.

JUNIUS.

LETTER XXXIX.

TO THE PRINTER OF THE PUBLIC ADVERTISER.

SIR, May 28. 1770.

WHILE parliament was sitting, it would neither have been safe, nor perhaps quite regular, to offer any opinion to the public, upon the justice or wisdom of their proceedings. To pronounce fairly upon their conduct,

M

it was necessary to wait until we could consider, in one view, the beginning, progress, and conclusion of their deliberations. The cause of the public was undertaken and supported by men, whose abilities and united authority, to say nothing of the advantageous ground they stood on, might well be thought sufficient to determine a popular question in favour of the people. Neither was the House of Commons so absolutely engaged in defence of the ministry, or even of their own resolutions, but that they might have paid some decent regard to the known disposition of their constituents : and, without any dishonour to their firmness, might have retracted an opinion too hastily adopted, when they saw the alarm it had created, and how strongly it was opposed by the general sense of the nation. The ministry too would have consulted their own immediate interest, in making some concession satisfactory to the moderate part of the people. Without touching the fact, they might have consented to guard against, or give up the dangerous principle on which it was established. In this state of things, I think it was highly improbable at the beginning of the session, that the complaints of the people, upon a matter which, in their apprehension at least, immediately affected the life of the constitution, would be treated with as much contempt by their own representatives, and by the House of Lords, as they had been by the other branch of the legislature. Desparing of their integrity, we had a right to expect something from their prudence, and something from their fears. The Duke of Grafton certainly did not foresee to what an extent the corruption of a parliament might be carried. He thought, perhaps, that there was still some portion of shame or virtue left in the majority of the House of Commons, or that there was a line in public prostitution beyond which they would scruple to proceed. Had the young man been but a little more practised in the world, or had he ventured to measure the characters of other men by his own, he would not have been so easily discouraged.

The prorogation of parliament naturally calls upon us to review their proceedings, and to consider the condition in which they left the kingdom. I do not question but they have done what is usually called the king's business, much to his Majesty's satisfaction. We have only to lament, that, in consequence of a system introduced or revived in the present reign, this kind of merit should be very consistent with the neglect of every duty they owe to the nation. The interval between the opening of the last and close of the former session was longer than usual. Whatever were the views of the minister in deferring the meeting of parliament, sufficient, time was certainly given to every member of the House of Commons, to look back upon the steps he had taken and the consequences they had produced. The zeal of party, the violence of personal animosities, and the heat of contention, had leisure to subside. From that period, whatever resolution they took was deliberate and prepense. In the preceding session, the dependants of the ministry had affected to believe, that the final determination of the question would have satisfied the nation, or at least put a stop to their complaints; as if the certainty of an evil could diminish the sense of it, or the nature of injustice could be altered by decision. But they found the people of England were in a temper very distant from submission; and although it was contended that the House of Commons could not themselves reverse a resolution, which had the force and effect of a judicial sentence, there were other constitutional expedients, which would have given a security against any similar attempts for the future. The general proposition, in which the whole country had an interest, might have been reduced to a particular fact, in which Mr. Wilkes and Mr. Luttrell would alone have been concerned. The House of Lords might interpose;—the King might dissolve the parliament; —or, if every other resource failed, there still lay a grand constitutional writ of error, in behalf of the people, from the decision of one court to the wisdom of the whole legislature. Every one of these remedies has been successively attempted. The people performed their part with dignity, spirit, and perseverance. For many months his Majesty heard nothing from his people but the language of complaint and resentment;—unhappily for the country, it was the triumph of his courtiers that he heard it with an indifference approaching to contempt.

The House of Commons having assumed a power un-

known to the constitution, were determined not merely
to support it in the single instance in question, but to
maintain the doctrine in its utmost extent, and to establish the fact as a precedent in law, to be applied in whatever manner his Majesty's servants should hereafter think
fit.   Their proceedings upon this occasion are a strong
proof that a decision, in the first instance illegal and unjust, can only be supported by a continuation of falsehood
and injustice.   To support their former resolutions, they
were obliged to violate some of the best known and established rules of the House.   In one instance, they went
so far as to declare, in open defiance of truth and common sense, that it was not the rule of the House to divide
a complicated question at the request of a member [w].
But after trampling upon the laws of the land, it was not
wonderful that they should treat the private regulations of
their own assembly with equal disregard.   The Speaker,
being young in office, began with pretended ignorance,
and ended with deciding for the ministry.   We were not
surprised at the decision; but he hesitated and blushed at
his own baseness, and every man was astonished [x].

The interest of the public was vigorously supported in
the House of Lords.   Their right to defend the constitution against an encroachment of the other estates, and
the necessity of exerting it at this period, was urged to
them with every argument that could be supposed to influence the heart or the understanding.   But it soon appeared that they had already taken their part, and were
determined to support the House of Commons, not only
at the expence of truth and decency, but even by a surrender of their own most important rights.   Instead of
performing that duty which the constitution expected
from them, in return for the dignity and independence
of their station, in return for the hereditary share it has
given them in the legislature, the majority of them made
common cause with the other House, in oppressing the
people, and established another doctrine as false in itelf,
and if possible more pernicious to the constitution, than
that on which the Middlesex election was determined.
By resolving, " that they had no right to impeach a judg-
" ment of the House of Commons in any case whatso-
" ever, where that House has a competent jurisdiction,"

they in effect gave up that constitutional check and reciprocal control of one branch of the legislature over the other; which is perhaps the greatest and most important object provided for by the division of the whole legislative power into three estates: and now, let the judicial decisions of the House of Commons be ever so extravagant, let their declarations of the law be ever so flagrantly false, arbitrary, and oppressive to the subject, the House of Lords have imposed a slavish silence upon themselves;—they cannot interpose,—they cannot protect the subject,—they cannot defend the laws of their country. A concession so extraordinary in itself, so contradictory to the principles of their own institution, cannot but alarm the most unsuspecting mind. We may well conclude that the Lords would hardly have yielded so much to the other house, without the certainty of a compensation, which can only be made to them at the expence of the people x: The arbitrary power they have assumed of imposing fines, and committing during pleasure, will now be exercised in its full extent. The House of Commons are too much in their debt to question or interrupt their proceedings. The Crown too, we may be well assured, will lose nothing in this new distribution of power, After declaring, that to petition for a dissolution of parliament, is irreconcileable with the principles of the constitution, his Majesty has reason to expect that some extraordinary compliment will be returned to the royal prerogative. The three branches of the legislature seem to treat their separate rights, and interests as the Roman Triumvirs did their friends. They reciprocally sacrifice them to the animosities of each other, and establish a detestable union among themselves, upon the ruin of the laws and liberty of the commonwealth.

Through the whole proceedings of the House of Commons, in this session, there is an apparent, a palpable consciousness of guilt, which has prevented their daring to assert their own dignity, where it has been immediately and grossly attacked. In the course of Dr. Musgrave's examination, he said every thing that can be conceived mortifying to individuals, or offensive to the House: They voted his information frivolous; but they were awed by his firmness and integrity, and sunk under it.

The terms in which the sale of a patent to Mr. Hine were communicated to the public, naturally called for a parliamentary inquiry. The integrity of the House of Commons was directly impeached; but they had not courage to move in their own vindication, because the inquiry would have been fatal to Colonel Burgoyne and the Duke of Grafton. When Sir George Saville branded them with the name of traitors to their constituents; when the Lord Mayor, the Sheriffs, and Mr. Trecothick, expressly avowed and maintained every part of the city remonstrance; why did they tamely submit to be insulted? Why did they not immediately expel those refractory members? Conscious of the motives on which they had acted, they prudently preferred infamy to danger; and were better prepared to meet the contempt, than to rouse the indignation of the whole people. Had they expelled those five members, the consequence of the new doctrine of incapacitation would have come immediately home to every man. The truth of it would then have been fairly tried, without any reference to Mr. Wilkes's private character, or the dignity of the House, or the obstinacy of one particular county. These topics, I know, have had their weight with men, who, affecting a character of moderation, in reality consult nothing but their own immediate ease;—who are weak enough to acquiesce under a flagrant violation of the laws, when it does not directly touch themselves; and care not what injustice is practised upon a man, whose moral character they piously think themselves obliged to condemn. In any other circumstances, the House of Commons must have forfeited all credit and dignity, if, after such gross provocation, they had permitted those five gentlemen to sit any longer among them. We should then have seen and felt the operation of a precedent, which is represented to be perfectly barren and harmless. But there is a set of men in this country, whose understandings measure the violation of law by the magnitude of the instance, not by the important consequences which flow directly from the principle; and the minister, I presume, did not think it safe to quicken their apprehensions too soon. Had Mr. Hampden reasoned and acted like the moderate men of these days, instead of hazarding his whole fortune in a lawsuit with the Crown, he would have quietedly paid the twenty shillings demanded of him;—the Stuart family would probably have continued upon the throne, and at this moment the imposition of ship-money would have been an acknowledged prerogative of the Crown.

What then has been the business of the session, after voting the supplies, and confirming the determination of the Middlesex election? The extraordinary prorogation of the Irish Parliament, and the just discontents of that kingdom, have been passed by without notice. Neither the general situation of our colonies, nor that particular distress which forced the inhabitants of Boston to take up arms in their defence, have been thought worthy of a moment's consideration. In the repeal of those acts which were most offensive to America, the parliament have done every thing but remove the offence. They have relinquished the revenue, but judiciously taken care to preserve the contention. It is not pretended that the continuation of the tea-duty, is to produce, any direct benefit whatsoever to the mother-country. What is it then but an odious unprofitable exertion of a speculative right, and fixing a badge of slavery upon the Americans, without service to their masters? But it has pleased God to give us a ministry and a parliament, who are neither to be persuaded by argument, nor instructed by experience.

Lord North, I presume, will not claim an extraordinary merit from any thing he has done this year in the improvement or application of the revenue. A great operation, directed to an important object, though it should fail of success, marks the genius, and elevates the character of a minister. A poor contracted understanding deals in little schemes, which dishonour him if they fail, and do him no credit when they succeed. Lord North had fortunately the means in his possession of reducing all the four *per cents* at once. The failure of his first enterprise in finance, is not half so disgraceful to his reputation as a minister, as the enterprise itself is injurious to the public. Instead of striking one decisive blow, which would have cleared the market at once, upon terms proportioned to the price of the four *per cents* six weeks ago, he has tampered with a pitiful portion of a commodity which ought never to have been touched but in gross:

—he has given notice to the holders of that stock, of a design formed by government to prevail upon them to surrender it by degrees, consequently has warned them to hold up and enhance the price :—so that the plan of reducing the four *per cents* must either be dropped entirely, or continued with an increasing disadvantage to the public. The minister's sagacity has served to raise the value of the thing he means to purchase, and to sink that of the three *per cents*, which it is his purpose to sell. In effect, he has contrived to make it the interest of the proprietor of four *per cents*, to sell out and buy three *per cents* in the market, rather than subscribe his stock upon any terms that can possibly be offered by government.

The state of the nation leads us naturally to consider the situation of the king. The prorogation of parliament has the effect of a temporary dissolution. The odium of measures adopted by the collective body, sits lightly upon the separate members who compose it. They retire into summer quarters, and rest from the disgraceful labours of the campaign. But as for the sovereign, it is not so with him. He has a permanent existence in this country ; he cannot withdraw himself from the complaints, the discontents, the reproaches of his subjects. They pursue him to his retirement, and invade his domestic happiness, when no address can be obtained from an obsequious parliament, to encourage or console him. In other times, the interest of the king and people of England was, as it ought to be, entirely the same. A new system has not only been adopted in fact, but professed upon principle. Ministers are no longer the public servants of the state, but the private domestics of the sovereign. One particular class of men are permitted to call themselves the king's friends a, as if the body of the people were the king's enemies ; or as if his Majesty looked for a resource or consolation in the attachment of a few favourites, against the general contempt and detestation of his subjects. Edward, and Richard the Second, made the same distinction between the collective body of the people, and a contemptible party who surrounded the throne. The event of their mistaken conduct might have been a warning to their successors. Yet the errors of those princes were not without excuse. They had as many false friends as our present gracious sovereign, and infinitely greater temptations to seduce them. They were neither sober, religious, nor demure. Intoxicated with pleasure, they wasted their inheritance in pursuit of it. Their lives were like a rapid torrent, brillaint in prospect, though useless or dangerous in its course. In the dull, unanimated existence of other princes, we see nothing but a sickly stagnant water, which taints the atmosphere without fertilizing the soil.—The morality of a king is not to be measured by vulgar rules. His situation is singular. There are faults which do him honour, and virtues that disgrace him. A faultless insipid equality in his character, is neither capable of vice nor virtue in the extreme; but it secures his submission to those persons whom he has been accustomed to respect, and makes him a dangerous instrument of their ambition. Secluded from the world, attached from his infancy to one set of persons, and one set of ideas, he can neither open his heart to new connections, nor his mind to better information. A character of this sort is the soil fittest to produce that obstinate bigotry in politics and religion, which begins with a meritorious sacrifice of the understanding; and finally conducts the monarch and the martyr to the block.

At any other period, I doubt not, the scandalous disorders which have been introduced into the government of all the dependencies in the empire, would have roused the attention of the public. The odious abuse and prostitution of the prerogative at home,—the unconstitutional employment of the military,—the arbitary fines and commitments by the House of Lords and Court of King's Bench;—the mercy of a chaste and pious prince extended cheerfully to a wilful murderer, because that murderer is the brother of a common prostitute [b], would, I think, at any other time, have excited universal indignation. But the daring attack upon the constitution, in the Middlesex election, makes us callous and indifferent to inferior grievances. No man regards an eruption upon the surface, when the noble parts are invaded, and he feels a mortification approaching to his heart. The free election of our representatives in parliament comprehends because it is, the source and security of every right and privilege of the English nation. The ministry have realized the compendious ideas of Caligula. They know that the liberty, the laws, and property of an Englishman, have in truth but one neck ; and that to violate the freedom of election, strikes deeply at them all.

JUNIUS,

LETTER XL.

TO LORD NORTH.

MY LORD, Aug. 22. 1770.

MR. LUTTRELL's services were the chief support and ornament of the Duke of Grafton's administration. The honour of rewarding them was reserved for your Lordship. The Duke it seems, had contracted an obligation he was ashamed to acknowledge, and unable to acquit. You, my Lord, had no scruples. You accepted the succession with all its encumbrances; and have paid Mr. Luttrell his legacy, at the hazard of ruining the estate.

When this accomplished youth declared himself the champion of government, the world was busy in inquiring what honours or emoluments could be a sufficient recompense to a young man of his rank and fortune, for submitting to mark his entrance into life with the universal contempt and detestation of his country.—His noble father had not been so precipitate.—To vacate his seat in parliament,—to intrude upon a country in which he had no interest or connection,—to possess himself of another man's right, and to maintain it in defiance of public shame as well as justice, bespoke a degree of zeal, or of depravity, which all the favour of a pious prince could hardly requite. I protest, my Lord, there is in this young man's conduct a strain of prostitution, which, for its singularity, I cannot but admire. He has discovered a new line in the human character ;—he has degraded even the name of Luttrell, and gratified his father's most sanguine expectations.

The Duke of Grafton, with every possible disposition to patronize this kind of merit, was contented with pronouncing Colonel Luttrell's paneygeric. The gallant spirit, the disinterested zeal of the young adventurer, were echoed through the House of Lords. His grace repeatedly pledged himself to the House, as an evidence of the purity of his friend Mr. Luttrell's intentions;—that he had engaged without any prospect of personal benefit, and that the idea of compensation would mortally offend him [c]. The noble Duke could hardly be in earnest; but he had lately quitted his employment, and began to think it necessary to take some care of his reputation. At that very moment the Irish negotiation was probably begun. —Come forward, thou worthy representative of Lord Bute, and tell this insulted country, who advised the king to appoint Mr. Luttrell ADJUTANT GENERAL to the army in Ireland? By what management was Colonel Cunninghame prevailed on to resign his employment, and the obsequious Gisborne to accept of a pension for the government of Kinsale [d]? Was it an original stipulation with the Princess of Wales, or does he owe his preferment to your Lordship's partiality, or to the Duke of Bedford's friendship? My Lord, though it may not be possible to trace this measure to its source, we can follow the stream, and warn the country of its approaching destruction. The English nation must be roused, and put upon its guard. Mr. Luttrell has already shown us how far he may be trusted, whenever an open attack is to be made upon the liberties of this country. I do not doubt but there is a deliberate plan formed.—Your Lordship best knows by whom;—the corruption of the legislative body on this side—a military force on the other—and then, farewell to England! It is impossible that any minister shall dare to advise the king to place such a man as Luttrell in the confidential post of Adjutant General, if there were not some secret purpose in view, which only such a man as Luttrell is fit to promote. The insult offered to the army in general is as gross as the outrage intended to the people of England. What! Lieutenant Colonel Luttrell Adjutant General of an army of sixteen thousand men! One would think his Majesty's campaigns at Blackheath and Wimbledon might have taught him better.—I cannot help wishing General Harvey joy of a colleague who does so much honour to the employment.—But, my Lord, this measure is too daring to pass unnoticed, too dangerous to be received with indifference or submission. You shall not have time to new-model the Irish army. They will not submit to be garbled by Colonel Luttrell. As a mischief to the English constitution (for he is not worth the name of enemy), they already detest him. As a boy, impudently thrust over their heads, they will receive him with indignation and contempt.—As for you, my Lord, who perhaps are no more than the blind unhappy instrument of Lord Bute and her Royal Highness the Princess of Wales, be assured that you shall be called upon to answer for the advice which has been given, and either discover your accomplices, or fall a sacrifice to their security.

JUNIUS.

LETTER XLI.

TO THE RIGHT HONOURABLE LORD MANSFIELD.

MY LORD,   Nov. 14. 1770.

THE appearance of this letter will attract the curiosity of the public, and command even your Lordship's attention. I am considerably in your debt; and shall endeavour, once for all, to balance the account. Accept of this address, my Lord, as a prologue to more important scenes, in which you will probably be called upon to act or suffer.

You will not question my veracity, when I assure you, that it has not been owing to any particular respect for your person that I have abstained from you so long. Besides the distress and danger with which the press is threatened, when your Lordship is party, and the party is to be judge, I confess I have been deterred by the difficulty of the task. Our language has no term of reproach, the mind has no idea of detestation, which has not already been happily applied to you, and exhausted.—Ample justice has been done by abler pens than mine to the separate merits of your life and character. Let it be my humble office to collect the scattered sweets, till their united virtue tortures the sense.

Permit me to begin with paying a just tribute to Scotch sincerity wherever I find it. I own I am not apt to confide in the professions of gentlemen of that country; and, when they smile, I feel an involuntary emotion to guard myself against mischief. With this general opinion of an ancient nation, I always thought it much to your Lordship's honour, that, in your earlier days, you were but little infected with the prudence of your country. You had some original attachments, which you took every proper opportunity to acknowledge. The liberal spirit of youth prevailed over your native discretion. Your zeal in the cause of an unhappy prince was expressed with the sincerity of wine, and some of the solemnities of religion[e]. This, I conceive, is the most amiable point of view in which your character has appeared. Like an honest man, you took that part in politics which might have been expected from your birth, education, country, and connections. There was something generous in your attachment to the banished House of Stuart. We lament the mistakes of a good man, and do not begin to detest him until he affects to renounce his principles. Why did you not adhere to that loyalty you once professed? Why did not you follow the example of your worthy brother[f]? With him you might have shared in the honour of the Pretender's confidence—with him you might have preserved the integrity of your character; and England, I think, might have spared you without regret. Your friends will say, perhaps, that although you deserted the fortune of your liege Lord, you have adhered firmly to the principles which drove his father from the throne;— that, without openly supporting the person, you have done essential service to the cause, and consoled yourself for the loss of a favourite family, by reviving and establishing the maxims of their government. This is the way in which a Scotchman's understanding corrects the errors of his heart. My Lord, I acknowledge the truth of the defence, and can trace it through all your conduct. I see through your whole life one uniform plan to enlarge the power of the crown, at the expence of the liberty of the subject. To this object, your thoughts, words, and actions, have been constantly directed. In contempt or ignorance of the common law of England, you have made it your study to introduce into the court where you preside, maxims of jurisprudence unknown to Englishmen.

The Roman code, the law of nations, and the opinion of foreign civilians, are our perpetual theme;—but who ever heard you mention Magna Charta, or the Bill of Rights, with approbation or respect? By such treacherous arts, the noble simplicity and free spirit of our Saxon laws were first corrupted. The Norman conquest was not complete, until Norman lawyers had introduced their laws, and reduced slavery to a system.—This one leading principle directs your interpretation of the laws, and accounts for your treatment of juries. It is not in political questions only (for there the courtier might be forgiven); but let the cause be what it may, your understanding is equally on the rack, either to contract the power of the jury, or to mislead their judgment. For the truth of this assertion, I appeal to the doctrine you delivered in Lord Grosvenor's cause. An action for criminal conversation being brought by a peer against a prince of the blood, you were daring enough to tell the jury, that, in fixing the damages, they were to pay no regard to the quality or fortune of the parties;—that it was a trial between A and B;—that they were to consider the offence in a moral light only, and give no greater damages to a peer of the realm than to the meanest mechanic. I shall not attempt to refute a doctrine which, if it was meant for law, carries falsehood and absurdity upon the face of it; but, if it was meant for a declaration of your political creed, is clear and consistent. Under an arbitrary government, all ranks and distinctions are confounded. The honour of a nobleman is no more considered than the reputation of a peasant; for, with different liveries, they are equally slaves.

Even in matters of private property, we see the same bias and inclination to depart from the decisions of your predecessors, which you certainly ought to receive as evidence of the common law. Instead of those certain positive rules by which the judgment of a court of law should invariably be determined, you have fondly introduced your own unsettled notions of equity and substantial justice. Decisions given upon such principles do not alarm the public so much as they ought, because the consequence and tendency of each particular instance is not observed or regarded. In the mean time, the practice gains ground;

the Court of King's Bench becomes a court of equity; and the judge, instead of consulting strictly the law of the land, refers only to the wisdom of the court, and to the purity of his own conscience. The name of Mr. Justice Yates will naturally revive in your mind some of those emotions of fear and detestation with which you always beheld him. That great lawyer, that honest man, saw your whole conduct in the light that I do. After years of ineffectual resistance to the pernicious principles introduced by your Lordship, and uniformly supported by your humble friends upon the bench, he determined to quit a court whose proceedings and decisions he could neither assent to with honour, nor oppose with success.

ᵍ The injustice done to an individual is sometimes of service to the public. Facts are apt to alarm us more than the most dangerous principles. The sufferings and firmness of a printer have roused the public attention. You knew and felt that your conduct would not bear a parliamentary inquiry; and you hoped to escape it by the meanest, the basest sacrifice of dignity and consistency, that ever was made by a great magistrate. Where was your firmness, where was that vindictive spirit, of which we have seen so many examples, when a man, so inconsiderable as Bingley, could force you to confess, in the face of this country, that, for two years together, you had illegally deprived an English subject of his liberty, and that he had triumphed over you at last? Yet I own, my Lord, that yours is not an uncommon character. Women, and men like women, are timid, vindictive, and irresolute. Their passions counteract each other; and make the same creature, at one moment hateful, at another contemptible. I fancy, my Lord some time will elapse before you venture to commit another Englishman for refusing to answer interrogatories ʰ.

The doctrine you have constantly delivered in cases of libel, is another powerful evidence of a settled plan to contract the legal power of juries, and to draw questions, inseparable from fact, within the *arbitrium* of the court. Here, my Lord, you have fortune on your side. When you invade the province of the jury in matter of libel, you in effect attack the liberty of the press, and with a single stroke wound two of your greatest enemies.—In some instances you have succeeded, because jurymen are too often ignorant of their own rights, and too apt to be awed by the authority of a chief-justice. In other criminal prosecutions, the malice of the design is confessedly as much the subject of consideration to a jury as the certainty of the fact. If a different doctrine prevails in the case of libels, why should it not extend to all criminal cases?—why not to capital offences? I see no reason (and I dare say you will agree with me, that there is no good one) why the life of the subject should be better protected against you, than his liberty or property. Why should you enjoy the full power of pillory, fine and imprisonment, and not be indulged with hanging or transportation? With your Lordship's fertile genius and merciful disposition, I can conceive such an exercise of the power you have, as could hardly be aggravated by that which you have not.

.. But, my Lord, since you have laboured (and not unsuccessfully) to destroy the substance of the trial, why should you suffer the form of the verdict to remain? Why force twelve honest men, in palpable violation of their oaths, to pronounce their fellow-subject a guilty man, when, almost at the same moment, you forbid their inquiring into the only circumstance which, in the eye of law and reason, constitutes guilt—the malignity or innocence of his intentions:—But I understand your Lordship.—If you could succeed in making the trial by jury useless and ridiculous, you might then with greater safety introduce a bill into parliament for enlarging the jurisdiction of the court, and extending your favourite trial by interrogatories to every question in which the life or liberty of an Englishman is concerned i.

Your charge to the jury, in the prosecution against Almon and Woodfall, contradicts the highest legal authorities, as well as the plainest dictates of reason. In Millar's cause, and still more expressly in that of Baldwin you have proceeded a step farther, and grossly contradicted yourself.—You may know perhaps, though I do not mean to insult you by an appeal to your experience, that the language of truth is uniform and consistent. To depart from it safely, requires memory and discretion. In the two last trials, your charge to the jury began as usual,

with assuring them that they had nothing to do with the
law,—that they were to find the bare fact, and not concern themselves about the legal inferences drawn from it,
or the degree of the defendant's guilt.—Thus far you
were consistent with your former practice.—But how
will you account for the conclusion? You told the jury,
that " if, after all, they would take upon themselves to
" determine the law, they might do it; but they must be
" very sure that they determined according to law, for it
" touched their consciences, and they acted at their peril."
—If I understand your first proposition, you meant to affirm, that the jury were not competent judges of the law
in the criminal case of a libel;—that it did not fall within
their jurisdiction; and that, with respect to them, the malice or innocence of the defendant's intentions would be a
question *coram non judice.*—But the second proposition
clears away your own difficulties, and restores the jury
to all their judicial capacities. *k* You make the compe-
tence of the court to depend upon the legality of the decision? In the first instance, you deny the power absolutely. In the second, you admit the power, provided it
be legally exercised. Now, my Lord, without pretending
to reconcile the distinctions of Westminsterhall with the
simple information of common sense, or the integrity of
fair argument, I shall be understood by your Lordship,
when I assert, that, if a jury, or any other court of judicature (for jurors are judges), have no right to enter into a
cause or question of law, it signifies nothing whether
their decision be or be not according to law: Their decision is in itself a mere nullity :—the parties are not bound
to submit to it : and, if the jury run any risk of punishment, it is not for pronouncing a corrupt or illegal verdict, but for the illegality of meddling with a point on
which they can have no legal authority to decide *l*.
I cannot quit this subject, without reminding your
Lordship of the name of Mr. Benson. Without offering
any legal objection, you ordered a special juryman to be
set aside in a cause where the King was prosecutor. The
novelty of the fact required explanation. Will you condescend to tell the world, by what law or custom you were
authorized to make a peremptory challenge of a juryman ?
The parties indeed have this power; and perhaps your

Lordship, having accustomed yourself to unite the characters of judge and party, may claim it in virtue of the new capacity you have assumed, and profit by your own wrong. The time, within which you might have been punished for this daring attempt to pack a jury, is, I fear, elapsed; but no length of time shall erase the record of it.

The mischiefs you have done this country are not confined to your interpretation of the laws. You are a minister, my Lord; and, as such, have long been consulted. Let us candidly examine what use you have made of your ministerial influence. I will not descend to little matters, but come at once to those important points on which your resolution was waited for, on which the expectation of your opinion kept a great part of the nation in suspence.—A constitutional question arises upon a declaration of the law of parliament, by which the freedom of election and the birthright of the subject were supposed to have been invaded.—The King's servants were accused of violating the constitution.—The nation is in a ferment.—The ablest men of all parties engage in the question, and exert their utmost abilities in the discussion of it.—What part has the honest Lord Mansfield acted? As an eminent judge of the law, his opinion would have been respected.—As a peer, he had a right to demand an audience of his sovereign, and inform him that his ministers were pursuing unconstitutional measures.—Upon other occasions, my Lord, you have no difficulty in finding your way into the closet. The pretended neutrality of belonging to no party, will not save your reputation. In questions merely political, an honest man may stand neuter. But the laws and constitution are the general property of the subject; not to defend is to relinquish; —and who is there so senseles as to renounce his share in a common benefit, unless he hopes to profit by a new division of the spoil. As a lord of parliament, you were repeatedly called upon to condemn or defend the new law declared by the House of Commons. You affected to have scruples, and every expedient was attempted to remove them.—The question was proposed and urged to you in a thousand different shapes.—Your prudence still supplied you with evasion; —your resolution was invincible. For my own part, I am not anxious to penetrate this solemn secret. I care not to whose wisdom it is intrusted, nor how soon you carry it with you to your grave ᵐ. You have betrayed your opinion by the very care you have taken to conceal it. It is not from Lord Mansfield that we expect any reserve in declaring his real sentiments in favour of government, or in opposition to the people; nor is it difficult to account for the motions of a timid, dishonest heart, which neither has virtue enough to acknowledge truth, nor courage to contradict it.—Yet you continue to support an administration which you know is universally odious, and which, on some occasions, you yourself speak of with contempt. You would fain be thought to take no share in government; while, in reality, you are the main spring of the machine.—Here too we trace the little, prudential policy of a Scotchman:—Instead of acting that open, generous part, which becomes your rank and station, you meanly skulk into the closet, and give your sovereign such advice as you have not spirit to avow or defend. You secretly engross the power, while you decline the title, of minister; and though you dare not be chancellor, you know how to secure the emoluments of the office.—Are the seals to be for ever in commission, that you may enjoy five thousand pounds a-year?—I beg pardon, my Lord; —your fears have interposed at last, and forced you to resign.—The odium of continuing speaker of the House of Lords, upon such terms, was too formidable to be resisted. What a multitude of bad passions are forced to submit to a constitutional infirmity! But though you have relinquished the salary, you still assume the rights of a minister.—Your conduct, it seems, must be defended in parliament:—For what other purpose is your wretched friend, that miserable serjeant, posted to the House of Commons? Is it in the abilities of Mr. Leigh to defend the great Lord Mansfield?—or is he only the punch of the puppet-show, to speak as he is prompted by the CHIEF JUGGLER behind the curtain.ⁿ.

In public affairs, my Lord, cunning, let it be ever so well wrought, will not conduct a man honourably through life. Like bad money, it may be current for a time; but it will soon be cried down. It cannot consist with a liberal spirit, though it be sometimes united with extraordinary qualifications. When I acknowledge your abilities, you may believe I am sincere. I feel for human nature, when I see a man, so gifted as you are, descend to such vile practices.—Yet do not suffer your vanity to console you too soon. Believe me, my good Lord, you are not admired in the same degree in which you are detested. It is only the partiality of your friends, that balances the defects of your heart with the superiority of your understanding. No learned man, even among your own tribe, thinks you qualified to preside in a court of common law. Yet it is confessed, that, under Justinian, you might have made an incomparable prætor.—It is remarkable enough, but I hope not ominous, that the laws you understand best, and the judges you affect to admire most, flourished in the decline of a great empire, and are supposed to have contributed to its fall.

Here, my Lord, it may be proper for us to pause together.—It is not for my own sake that I wish you to consider the delicacy of your situation. Beware how you indulge the first emotions of your resentment. This paper is delivered to the world, and cannot be recalled. The persecution of an innocent printer cannot alter facts, nor refute arguments.—Do not furnish me with farther materials against yourself.—An honest man, like the true religion, appeals to the understanding, or modestly confides in the internal evidence of his conscience. The impostor employs force instead of argument, imposes silence were he cannot convince, and propagates his character by the sword.

JUNIUS.

LETTER XLII.

SIR,   Jan. 30. 1771.

IF we recollect in what manner the King's friends have been constantly employed, we shall have no reason to be surprised at any condition of disgrace to which the once-respected name of Englishmen may be degraded. His Majesty has no cares, but such as concern the laws and constitution of this country. In his royal breast there is no room left for resentment, no place for hostile sentiments against the natural enemies of his crown. The system of government is uniform.— Violence and oppression at home can only be supported by treachery and submission abroad. When the civil rights of the people are daringly invaded on one side, what have we to expect, but that their political rights should be deserted and betrayed, in the same proportion, on the other? The plan of domestic policy which has been invariably pursued from the moment of his present Majesty's accession, engrosses all the attention of his servants. They know that the security of their places depends upon their maintaining, at any hazard, the secret system of the closet. A foreign war might embarrass, an unfavourable event might ruin the minister, and defeat the deep-laid scheme of policy to which he and his associates owe their employments. Rather than suffer the execution of that scheme to be delayed or interrupted, the King has been advised to make a public surrender, a solemn sacrifice, in the face of all Europe, not only of the interests of his subjects, but of his own personal reputation, and of the dignity of that crown which his predecessors have worn with honour. These are strong terms, Sir, but they are supported by fact and argument.

The King of Great Britain had been for some years in possession of an island, to which, as the ministry themselves have repeatedly asserted, the Spaniards had no claim of right. The importance of the place is not in question. If it were, a better judgment might be formed of it from the opinion of Lord Anson and Lord Egmont, and from the anxiety of the Spaniards, than from any fallacious insinuations thrown out by men whose interest it is to undervalue that property which they are determined to relinquish. The pretensions of Spain were a subject of negotiation between the two courts. They had been discussed, but not admitted. The King of Spain, in these circumstances, bids adieu to amicable negociation, and appeals directly to the sword. The expedition against Port-Egmont does not appear to have been a sudden ill-concerted enterprise. It seems to have been conducted not only with the usual military precautions, but in all the forms and ceremonies of war. A frigate was first employed to examine the strength of the place. A message was then sent, demanding immediate possession, in the Catholic King's name, and ordering our people to depart. At last a military force appears, and compels the garrison to surrender. A formal capitulation ensues; and his Majesty's ship, which might at least have been permitted to bring home his troops immediately, is detained in port twenty days, and her rudder forcibly taken away. This train of facts carries no appearance of the rashness or violence of a Spanish governor. On the contrary, the whole plan seems to have been formed and executed, in consequence of deliberate orders and a regular instruction from the Spanish court. Mr. Buccarelli is not a pirate, nor has he been treated as such by those who employed him. I feel for the honour of a gentleman, when I affirm, that our King owes him a signal reparation.—Where will the humiliation of this country end? A king of Great Britain, not contented with placing himself upon a level with a Spanish governor, descends so low as to do a notorious injustice to that governor. As a salvo for his own reputation, he has been advised to traduce the character of a brave officer, and to treat him as a common robber, when he knew with certainty that Mr. Buccarelli had acted in obedience to his orders, and had done no more than his duty. Thus it happens in private life, with a man who has no spirit nor sense of honour,—One of his equals orders a servant to strike him.—Instead of returning the blow to the master, his courage is contented with throwing an aspersion, equally false and public, upon the character of the servant.

This short recapitulation was necessary to introduce the consideration of his Majesty's speech of 13th November 1770, and the subsequent measures of government. The excessive caution with which the speech was drawn up, had impressed upon me an early conviction, that no serious resentment was thought of, and that the conclusion of the business, whenever it happened. must in some degree be dishonourable to England. There appears through the whole speech a guard and reserve in the choice of expression, which shows how careful the ministry were not to embarrass their future projects by any firm or spirited declaration from the throne. When all hopes of peace are lost, his Majesty tells his parliament, that he is preparing—not for a barbarous war, but (with all his mother's softness) for a different situation.—An open hostility, authorized by the Catholic King, is called an act of a governor. This act to avoid the mention of a regular siege and surrender, passes under the piratical description of seizing by force; and the thing taken is described, not as a part of the King's territory or proper dominion, but merely as a possession; a word expressly chosen in contradistinction to, and exclusion of, the idea of right, and to prepare us for a future surrender both of the right and of the possession. Yet this speech, Sir, cautious and equivocal as it is, cannot, by any sophistry, be accommodated to the measures which have since been adopted. It seemed to promise, that whatever might be given up by secret stipulation, some care would be taken to save appearances to the public. The event shows us, that to depart, in the minutest article, from the nicety and strictness of punctilio, is as dangerous to national honour as to female virtue. The woman who admits of one familiarity, seldom knows where to stop, or what to refuse; and when the councils of a great country give way in a single instance,—when they once are inclined to submission, every step accelerates the rapidity of the descent. The ministry themselves, when they framed the speech, did not foresee, that they should ever accede to such an accommodation as they have since advised their master to accept of.

The King says, " The honour of my crown and the " rights of my people are deeply affected." The Spaniard, in his reply, says, " I give you back possession; " but I adhere to my claim of prior right, reserving the " assertion of it for a more favourable opportunity."

The speech says, " I made an immediate demand of " satisfaction; and if that fails, I am prepared to do " myself justice." This immediate demand must have been sent to Madrid on the 12th of September, or in a few days after. It was certainly refused, or evaded, and the King has not done himself justice.—When the first magistrate speaks to the nation, some care should be taken of his apparent veracity.

The speech proceeds to say, I " shall not discontinue " my preparations until I have received proper repara-

" tion for the injury." If this assurance may be relied on, what an enormous expence is entailed, *sine die*, upon this unhappy country! Restitution of a possession, and reparation of an injury, are as different in substance as they are in language. The very act of restitution may contain, as in this instance it palpably does, a shameful aggravation of the injury. A man of spirit does not measure the degree of an injury by the mere positive damage he has sustained. He considers the principle on which it is founded; he resents the superiority asserted over him, and rejects with indignation the claim of right which his adversary endeavours to establish, and would force him to acknowledge.

The motives on which the Catholic King makes restitution are, if possible, more insolent and disgraceful to our sovereign than even the declaratory condition annexed to it. After taking four months to consider whether the expedition was undertaken by his own orders or not, he condescends to disavow the enterprize, and to restore the island;—not from any regard to justice,—not from any regard he bears to his Britannic Majesty, but merely " from the persuasion, in which he is, of the pacific " sentiments of the King of Great Britain."—At this rate, if our king had discovered the spirit of a man,—if he had made a peremptory demand of satisfaction, the King of Spain would have given him a peremptory refusal. But why this unseasonable, this ridiculous mention of the King of Great Britain's pacific intentions? Have they ever been in question? Was he the aggressor? Does he attack foreign powers without provocation? Does he even resist when he is insulted? No, Sir; if any ideas of strife or hostility have entered his royal mind, they have a very different direction. The enemies of England have nothing to fear from them.

After all, Sir, to what kind of disavowal has the King of Spain at last consented? Supposing it made in proper time, it should have been accompanied with instant restitution; and if Mr. Buccarelli acted without orders, he deserved death. Now, Sir, instead of immediate restitution, we have a four months negotiation; and the officer, whose act is disavowed, returns to court, and is loaded with honours.

If the actual situation of Europe be considered, the treachery of the King's servants, particularly of Lord North, who takes the whole upon himself, will appear in the strongest colours of aggravation. Our allies were masters of the Mediterranean. The King of France's present aversion from war, and the distraction of his affairs, are notorious. He is now in a state of war with his people. In vain did the Catholic King solicit him to take part in the quarrel against us. His finances were in the last disorder, and it was probable that his troops might find sufficient employment at home. In these circumstances, we might have dictated the law to Spain. There are no terms to which she might not have been compelled to submit. At the worst, a war with Spain alone carries the fairest promise of advantage. One good effect at least would have been immediately produced by it. The desertion of France would have irritated her ally, and in all probability have dissolved the family-compact. The scene is now fatally changed. The advantage is thrown away. The most favourable opportunity is lost.—Hereafter we shall know the value of it. When the French king is reconciled to his subjects; when Spain has completed her preparations; when the collected strength of the House of Bourbon attacks us at once, the King himself will be able to determine upon the wisdom or imprudence of his present conduct. As far as the probability of argument extends, we may safely pronounce, that a conjuncture, which threatens the very being of this country, has been wilfully prepared and forwarded by our own ministry. How far the people may be animated to resistance under the present administration, I know not; but this I know with certainty, that, under the present administration, or if any thing like it should continue, it is of very little moment whether we are a conquered nation or not °.

Having travelled thus far in the high road of matter of fact, I may now be permitted to wander a little into the field of imagination. Let us banish from our minds the persuasion that these events have really happened in the reign of the best of princes. Let us consider them as nothing more than the materials of a fable, in which we may conceive the sovereign of some other country to be concerned. I mean to violate all the laws of probability, when I suppose, that this imaginary king, after having voluntarily disgraced himself in the eyes of his subjects, might return to a sense of his dishonour;—that he might perceive the snare laid for him by his ministers, and feel a spark of shame kindling in his breast.—The part he must then be obliged to act, would overwhelm him with confusion. To his parliament he must say, " I called " you together to receive your advice, and have never " asked your opinion."—To the merchant,—" I have " distressed your commerce ; I have dragged your sea- " men out of your ships; I have loaded you with a grie- " vous weight of insurances."—To the landholder,— " I told you war was too probable, when I was determi- " ned to submit to any terms of accommodation; I ex- " torted new taxes from you before it was possible they " could be wanted, and am now unable to account for " the application of them."—To the public creditor,— " I have delivered up your fortunes a prey to foreign- " ers, and to the vilest of your fellow-subjects." Per- haps this repenting prince might conclude with one ge- neral acknowledgement to them all:—" I have involved " every rank of my subjects in anxiety and distress ; and " have nothing to offer you in return, but the certainty of " national dishonour, an armed truce, and peace without " security."

If these accounts were settled, there would still remain an apology to be made to his navy and to his army. To the first he would say, " You were once the terror of " the world. But go back to your harbours. A man dis- " honoured as I am, has no use for your service." It is not probable that he would appear again before his soldiers, even in the pacific ceremony of a review P. But where- ever he appeared, the humiliating confession would be ex- torted from him ; " I have received a blow—and had not " spirit to resent it. I demanded satisfaction; and have " accepted a declaration, in which the right to strike me " again is asserted and confirmed." His countenance at least would speak this language, and even his guards would blush for him.

But to return to our argument.—The ministry, it seems, are labouring to draw a line of distinction between the ho- nour of the Crown and the rights of the People. This

new idea has yet been only started in discourse ; for in effect both objects have been equally sacrificed. I neither
understand the distinction, nor what use the ministry propose to make of it. The King's honour is that of his
people. Their real honour and real interest are the same,
—I am not contending for a vain punctilio. A clear unblemished character comprehends, not only the integrity
that will not offer, but the spirit that will not submit to,
an injury ; and whether it belongs to an individual or to
a community, it is the foundation of peace, of independence, and of safety. Private credit is wealth ;—public
honour is security.—The feather that adorns the royal bird
supports his flight. Strip him of his plumage, and you
fix him to the earth.

JUNIUS.

LETTER XLIII:

SIR,   Feb. 6. 1771.

I HOPE your correspondent Junius is better employed than in answering or reading the criticisms of a
newspaper. This is a task from which, if he were inclined to submit to it, his friends ought to relieve him.
Upon this principle I shall undertake to answer Anti-Junius ; more I believe to his conviction than to his satisfaction. Not daring to attack the main body of Junius's
last letter, he triumphs in having, as he thinks, surprised an out-post, and cut off a detached argument, a mere
straggling proposition. But even in this petty warfare he
sha l find himself defeated.

Junius does not speak of the Spanish nation as the natural enemies of England. He applies that description
with 'the strictest truth and justice, to the Spanish court.
From the moment when a prince of the House of Bourbon ascended that throne, their whole system of government was inverted, and became hostile to this country.
Unity of possession introduced a unity of politics ; and
Lewis the Fourteenth had reason when he said to his
grandson, " The Pyrenees are removed." The history

of the present century is one continued confirmation of the prophecy.

The assertion, " That violence and oppression at home " can only be supported by treachery and submission a- " broad," is applied to a free people whose rights are invaded, not to the government of a country where despotic or absolute power is confessedly vested in the prince ; and with this application, the assertion is true. An absolute monarch, having no points to carry at home, will naturally maintain the honour of his crown in all transactions with foreign powers : But if we could suppose the sovereign of a free nation, possessed with a design to make himself absolute, he would be inconsistent with himself if he suffered his projects to be interrupted or embarrassed by a foreign war, unless that war tended, as in some cases it might, to promote his principal design. Of the three exceptions to this general rule of conduct (quoted by Anti-Junius), that of Oliver Cromwell is the only one in point. Harry the Eighth, by the submission of his parliament, was as absolute a prince as Lewis the Fourteenth. Queen Elizabeth's government was not oppressive to the people ; and as to her foreign wars, it ought to be considered that they were unavoidable. The national honour was not in question : She was compelled to fight in defence of her own person and of her title to the crown. In the common cause of selfish policy, Oliver Cromwell should have cultivated the friendsip of foreign powers, or at least have avoided disputes with them, the better to establish his tyranny at home. Had he been only a bad man, he would have sacrificed the honour of the nation to the success of his domestic policy. But, with all his crimes, he had the spirit of an Englishman. The conduct of such a man must always be an exception to vulgar rules. He had abilities sufficient to reconcile contradictions, and to make a great nation at the same moment unhappy and formidable. If it were not for the respect I bear the minister, I could name a man, who, without one grain of understanding, can do half as much as Oliver Cromwell.

Whether or no there be a secret system in the closet, and what may be the object of it, are questions which can only be determined by appearances, and on which every man must decide for himself.

The whole plan of Junius's letter proves, that he himself makes no distinction between the real honour of the crown, and the real interest of the people. In the climax to which your correspondent objects, Junius adopts the language of the court, and by that conformity gives strength to his argument. He says, " the king has not only sa- " crificed the interests of his people, but (what was like- " ly to touch him more nearly) his personal reputation and " the dignity of his crown."

The queries put by Anti-Junius can only be answered by the ministry. Abandoned as they are, I fancy they will not confess that they have, for so many years, maintained possession of another man's property. After admitting the assertion of the ministry—viz " that the Spaniards had " no rightful claim, " and after justifying them for saying so;—it is his business, not mine, to give us some good' rea- son for their " suffering the pretensions of Spain to be a " subject of negociation." He admits the facts ;—let him reconcile them if he can.

The last paragraph brings us back to the original que- stion, Whether the Spanish declaration contains such a satisfaction as the king of Great Britain ought to have accepted? This was the field upon which he ought to have encountered Junius openly and fairly. But here he leaves the argument, as no longer defensible. I shall therefore conclude with one general admonition to my fellow-subjects ;—that, when they hear these matters debated, they should not suffer themselves to be misled by general declamations upon the conveniences of peace, or the miseries of war. Between peace and war, abstractedly, there is not, there cannot be a question in the mind of a rational being. The real questions are, " Have we any " security, that the peace we have so dearly purchased " will last a twelvemonth?" and if not,—" Have we, or " have we not, sacrificed the fairest opportunity of making war with advantage?"

PHILO JUNIUS.

Q 2

LETTER XLIV.

TO THE PRINTER OF THE PUBLIC ADVERTISER.

SIR,   April 22. 1771.

To write for profit, without taxing the press;—
to write for fame, and to be unknown;—to support the
intrigues of faction, and to be disowned, as a dangerous
auxiliary, by every party in the kingdom; are contradictions which the minister must reconcile, before I forfeit
my credit with the public. I may quit the service, but it
would be absurd to suspect me of desertion. The reputation of these papers is an honourable pledge for my attachment to the people. To sacrifice a respected character, and to renounce the esteem of society, requires more
than Mr. Wedderburne's resolution; and though in him
it was rather a profession than a desertion of his principles,
(I speak tenderly of this gentleman; for when treachery
is in question, I think we should make allowances for a
Scotchman), yet we have seen him in the House of Commons overwhelmed with confusion, and almost bereft of
his faculties. But, in truth, Sir, I have left no room for
an accommodation with the piety of St. James's. My
offences are not to be redeemed by recantation or repentance. On one side, our warmest patriots would disclaim
me as a burden to their honest ambition. On the other,
the vilest prostitution, if Junius could descend to it, would
lose its natural merit and influence in the cabinet, and
treachery be no longer a recommendation to the royal
favour.

The persons who, till within these few years, have been
most distinguished by their zeal for high-church and prerogative, are now, it seems the great assertors of the privileges of the House of Commous. This sudden alteration of their sentiments or language carries with it a suspicious appearance. When I hear the undefined privileges
of the popular branch of the legislature exalted by Tories
and Jacobites, at the expence of those strict rights, which
are known to the subject and limited by the laws, I cannot but suspect, that some mischievous scheme is in agitation, to destroy both law and privilege, by opposing them
to each other. They who have uniformly denied the

power of the whole legislature to alter the descent of the crown, and whose ancestors, in rebellion against his Majesty's family, have defended that doctrine at the hazard of their lives, now tell us, that privilege of parliament is the only rule of right, and the chief security of the public freedom.—I fear, Sir, that while forms remain there has been some material change in the substance of our constitution. The opinions of these men were too absurd to be so easily renounced.: Liberal minds are open to conviction.— Liberal doctrines are capable of improvement.—There are proselytes from atheism, but none from superstition. If their present professions were sincere, I think they could, not but be highly offended at seeing a question, concerning parliamentary privilege, unnecessarily started at a season so unfavourable to the House of Commons, and by so very mean and insignificant a person as the minor Onslow. They knew, that the present House of Commons, having commenced hostilities with the people, and degraded the authority of the laws by their own example, were likely enough to be resisted *per fas et nefas*. If they were really friends to privilege, they would have thought the question of right too dangerous to be hazarded at this season, and, without the formality of a convention, would have left it undecided.

I have been silent hitherto ; though not from that shameful indifference about the interests of society which too many of us profess, and call moderation. I confess, Sir, that I felt the prejudices of my education, in favour of a House of Commons, still hanging about me. I thought that: a question between law and privilege, could never be brought to a formal decision, without inconvenience to the public service, or a manifest diminution of legal liberty ;—that it ought therefore to be carefully avoided.: and when I saw that the violence of the House of Commons had carried them too far to retreat, I determined not to deliver a hasty opinion upon a matter of so much delicacy and importance.

The state of things is much altered in this country since it was necessary to protect our representatives against the direct power of the crown. We have nothing to apprehend from prerogative, but every thing from undue influence. Formerly it was the interest of the people, that the privileges of parliament should be left unlimited and undefined. At present, it is not only their interest, but I hold it to be essentially necessary to the preservation of the constitution, that the privileges of parliament should be strictly ascertained, and confined within the narrowest bounds the nature of their institution will admit of. Upon the same principle on which I would have resisted prerogative in the last century, I now resist privilege. It is indifferent to me, whether the crown, by its own immediate act, imposes new, and dispenses with old laws; or whether the same arbitrary power produces the same effects through the medium of the House of Commons. We trusted our representatives with privileges for their own defence and ours. We cannot hinder their desertion, but we can prevent their carrying over their arms to the service of the enemy. It will be said, that I began with endeavouring to reduce the argument concerning privilege to a mere question of convenience;—that I deny at one moment what I would allow at another; and that to resist the power of a prostituted House of Commons, may establish a precedent injurious to all future parliaments.— To this, I answer generally, that human affairs are in no instance governed by strict positive right. If change of circumstances were to have no weight in directing our conduct and opinions, the mutual intercourse of mankind would be nothing more than a contention between positive and equitable right. Society would be a state of war, and law itself would be injustice. On this general ground, it is highly reasonable that the degree of our submission to privileges which have never been defined by any positive law, should be considered as a question of convenience, and proportioned to the confidence we repose in the integrity of our representatives. As to the injury we may do to any future and more respectable House of Commons, I own I am not now sanguine enough to expect a more plentiful harvest of parliamentary virtue in one year than another. Our political climate is severely altered; and without dwelling upon the depravity of modern times, I think no reasonable man will expect, that, as human nature is constituted, the enormous influence of the crown should cease to prevail over the virtue of individuals. The mischief lies too deep to be cured by any remedy less than some great convulsion, which may either carry back the constitution to its original principles, or utterly destroy it. I do not doubt, that in the first session after the next election, some popular measures may be adopted. The present House of Commons have injured themselves by a too early and public profession of their principles ; and, if a strain of prostitution, which had no example, were within the reach of emulation, it might be imprudent to hazard the experiment too soon. But, after all, Sir, it is very immaterial whether a House of Commons shall preserve their virtue for a week, a month, or a year. The influence, which makes a septennial parliament dependent upon the pleasure of the crown, has a permanent operation, and cannot fail of success.—My premises, I know, will be denied in argument ; but every man's conscience tells him they are true. It remains then to be considered, whether it be for the interest of the people, that privilege of parliament (which ?, in respect to the purposes for which it has hitherto been acquiesced under, is merely nominal) should be contracted within some certain limits ? or, whether the subject shall be left at the mercy of a power, arbitary upon the face of it, and notoriously under the direction of the crown ?

I do not mean to decline the question of right : on the contrary, Sir, I join issue with the advocates for privilege ; and affirm, that " excepting the cases wherein the House of " Commons are a court of judicature (to which from the " nature of their office, a coercive power must belong), " and excepting such contempts as immediately interrupt " their proceedings, they have no legal authority to im- " prison any man for any supposed violation of privilege " whatsoever."—It is not pretended, that privilege, as now claimed, has ever been defined or confirmed by statute ; neither can it be said, with any colour of truth, to be a part of the common law of England, which had grown into prescription long before we knew any thing of the existence of a House of Commons. As for the law of parliament, it is only another name for the privilege in question ; and since the power of creating new privileges has been formally renounced by both Houses,—since there is no code in which we can study the law of parliament, we have but one way left to make ourselves acquainted with it,—that is, to compare the nature of the institution of a House of Commons with the facts upon record. To establish a claim of privilege in either House, and to distinguish original right from usurpation, it must appear, that it is indispensably necessary for the performance of the duty they are employed in, and also that it has been uniformly allowed. From the first part of this description, it follows clearly, that whatever privilege does of right belong to the present House of Commons, did equally belong to the first assembly of their predecessors; was as completely vested in them, and might have been exercised in the same extent. From the second, we must infer, that privileges, which for several centuries were not only never allowed, but never even claimed by the House of Commons, must be founded upon usurpation. The constitutional duties of a House of Commons are not very complicated nor mysterious. They are to propose or assent to wholesome laws for the benefit of the nation. They are to grant the necessary aids to the king; petition for the redress of grievances; and prosecute treason or high crimes against the state. If unlimited privilege be necessary to the performance of these duties, we have reason to conclude, that for many centuries after the institution of the House of Commons, they were never performed. I am not bound to prove a negative; but I appeal to the English history, when I affirm, that with the exceptions already stated, (which yet I might safely relinquish), there is no precedent from the year 1265 to the death of Queen Elizabeth, of the House of Commons having imprisoned any man (not a member of their House) for contempt or breach of privilege. In the most flagrant cases, and when their acknowledged privileges were most grossly violated, the poor Commons, as they then styled themselves, never took the power of punishment into their own hands. They either sought redress by petition to the king, or what is more remarkable, applied for justice to the House of Lords; and, when satisfaction was denied them or delayed, their only remedy was to refuse proceeding upon the king's business. So little conception had our ancestors of the monstrous doctrines now maintained concerning privilege, that in the reign of Elizabeth, even liberty of speech, the vital principle of a deliberative assembly, was restrained by the queen's authority to a simple aye or no; and this restriction, though imposed upon three successive parliaments [r], was never once disputed by the House of Commons.

I know there are many precedents of arbitrary commitments for contempt: but, besides that they are of too modern a date to warrant a presumption that such a power was originally vested in the House of Commons,—fact alone does not constitute right.—If it does, general warrants were lawful.—An ordinance of the two Houses has a force equal to law; and the criminal jurisdiction assumed by the Commons in 1621, in the case of Edward Loyd, is a good precedent to warrant the like proceedings against any man, who shall unadvisedly mention the folly of a king, or the ambition of a Princess.——The truth is, Sir, that the greatest and most exceptionable part of the privileges now contended for, were introduced and asserted by a House of Commons which abolished both monarchy and peerage, and whose proceedings, although they ended in one glorious act of substantial justice, could no way be reconciled to the forms of the consitution. Their successors profited by the example, and confirmed their power by a moderate or a proper use of it. Thus it grew by degrees, from a notorious innovation at one period, to be tacitly admitted as the privilege of parliament at another.

If, however, it could be proved, from considerations of necessity or convenience, that an unlimited power of commitment ought to be intrusted to the House of Commons, and that in fact they have exercised it without opposition, still, in contemplation of law, the presumption is strongly against them. It is a leading maxim of the laws of England (and without it all laws are nugatory,) that there is no right without a remedy, nor any legal power without a legal course to carry it into effect. Let the power now in question be tried by this rule. The Speaker issues his warrant of attachment. The party attached either resists force with force, or appeals to a magistrate, who declares the warrant illegal, and discharges the prisoner. Does the law provide no legal means for enforcing a legal warrant? Is there no regular proceeding pointed out in our law-books to assert and vindicate the authority of so high a court as the House of Commons? The question is answered directly by the fact. Their unlawful commands are resisted, and they have no remedy. The imprisonment of their own members is revenge indeed, but it is no assertion of the privilege they contend for [s]. Their whole proceeding stops; and there they stand, ashamed to retreat, and unable to advance. Sir, these ignorant men should be informed, that the execution of the laws of England is not left in this uncertain defenceless condition. If the process of the courts of Westminister-hall be resisted, they have a direct course sufficient to enforce submission. The court of King's Bench commands the sheriff to raise the *posse comitatus*. The Courts of Chancery and Exchequer issue a writ of rebellion; which must also be supported, if necessary, by the power of the county.— To whom will our honest representatives direct their writ of rebellion? The guards, I doubt not, are willing enough to be employed; but they know nothing of the doctrine of writs, and may think it necessary to wait for a letter from Lord Barrington.

It may now be objected to me, that my arguments prove too much: for that certainly there may be instances of contempt and insult to the House of Commons, which do not fall within my own exceptions; yet, in regard to the dignity of the House, ought not to pass unpunished. Be it so.—The courts of criminal jurisdiction are open to prosecutions, which the Attorney-General may commence by information or indictment. A libel, tending to asperse or vilify the House of Commons, or any of their members, may be as severely punished in the Court of King's Bench, as a libel upon the king. Mr. de Grey thought so, when he drew up the information upon my letter to his Majesty, or he had no meaning in charging it to be a scandalous libel upon the House of Commons. In my opinion, they would consult their real dignity much better, by appealing to the laws when they are offended, than by violating the first principle of natural justice, which forbids us to be judges when we are parties to the cause [t].

I do not mean to pursue them through the remainder of their proceedings. In their first resolutions, it is possible they might have been deceived by ill-considered precedents. For the rest, there is no colour of palliation or excuse. They have advised the king to resume a power of dispensing with the laws by royal proclamation [u]; and kings, we see, are ready enough to follow such advice.—By mere violence, and without the shadow of right, they have ex punged the record of a judicial proceeding [v]. Nothing re- mained, but to attribute to their own vote a power of stop- ping the whole distribution of criminal and civil justice.

The public virtues of the chief magistrate have long since ceased to be in question. But it is said, that he has private good qualities; and I myself have been ready to acknowledge them. They are now brought to the test. If he loves his people, he will dissolve a parliament which they can never confide in or respect.—If he has any re- gard for his own honour, he will disdain to be any longer connected with such abandoned prostitution. But, if it were conceivable, that a king of this country had lost all sense of personal honour, and all concern for the welfare of his subjects, I confess, Sir, I should be contented to re- nounce the forms of the constitution once more, if there were no other way to obtain substantial justice for the peo- ple [w].

JUNIUS.

LETTER XLV.

TO THE PRINTER OF THE PUBLIC ADVERTISER.

SIR,   May 1. 1771.

THEY who object to detached parts of Junius's last letter, either do not meet him fairly, or have not con- sidered the general scope and course of his argument.— There are degrees in all the private vices;—Why not in public prostitution?—The influence of the crown natural- ly makes a septennial parliament dependent.—Does it fol- low, that every House of Commons will plunge at once in- to the lowest depths of prostitution?—Junius supposes, that the present House of Commons, in going such enor- mous lengths, have been imprudent to themselves, as well as wicked to the public;—that their example is not with- in the reach of emulation;—and that, in the first session after the next election, some popular measures may probably be adopted. He does not expect that a dissolution of parliament will destroy corruption, but that at least it will be a check and terror to their successors, who will have seen that, in flagrant cases, their constituents can and will interpose with effect.—After all, Sir, will you not endeavour to remove or alleviate the most dangerous symptoms, because you cannot eradicate the disease? Will you not punish treason or parricide, because the sight of a gibbet does not prevent highway robberies?—When the main argument of Junius is admitted to be unanswerable, I think it would become the minor critic, who hunts for blemishes, to be a little more distrustful of his own sagacity.—The other objection is hardly worth an answer. When Junius observes, that kings are ready enough to follow such advice, he does not mean to insinuate, that, if the advice of parliament were good, the king would be so ready to follow it.

PHILO JUNIUS.

LETTER XLVI.

TO THE PRINTER OF THE PUBLIC ADVERTISER.

SIR,   May 22. 1771.

VERY early in the debate upon the decision of the Middlesex election; it was well observed by Junius, that the House of Commons had not only exceeded their boasted precedent of the expulsion and subsequent incapacitation of Mr. Walpole, but that they had not even adhered to it strictly as far as it went. After convicting Mr. Dyson of giving a false quotation from the Journals, and having explained the purpose which that contemptible fraud was intended to answer, he proceeds to state the vote itself by which Mr. Walpole's supposed incapacity was declared,—viz. " Resolved, That Robert Walpole, " Esq. having been this session of parliament committed " a prisoner to the Tower, and expelled this house for a " high breach of trust in the execution of his office, and " notorious corruption when Secretary at War, was, and " is, incapable of being elected a member to serve in this " present parliament:"—And then observes, that, from the terms of the vote, we have no right to annex the incapacitation to the expulsion only; for that, as the proposition stands, it must arise equally from the expulsion and the commitment to the Tower. I believe, Sir, no man, who knows any thing of dialectics, or who understands English, will dispute the truth and fairness of this construction. But Junius has a great authority to support him; which, to speak with the Duke of Grafton, I accidentally met with this morning in the course of my reading. It contains an admonition, which cannot be repeated too often. Lord Sommers, in his excellent tract upon the Rights of the people, after reciting the votes of the convention of the 28th of January 1689, viz.—" That " King James the second, having endeavoured to subvert " the constitution of this kingdom, by breaking the ori- " ginal contract between king and people; and, by the " advice of Jesuits and other wicked persons, having vio- " lated the laws, and having withdrawn himself out of " this kingdom, hath abdicated the government," &c.— makes this observation upon it: " The word abdicated " relates to all the clauses aforegoing, as well as to his " deserting the kingdom, or else they would have been " wholly in vain." And, that there might be no pretence for confining the abdication merely to the withdrawing, Lord Sommers farther observes, " That King James, by " refusing to govern us according to that law by which he " held the crown, did implicitly renounce his title to it." If Junius's construction of the vote against Mr. Walpole be now admitted (and indeed I cannot comprehend how it can honestly be disputed), the advocates of the House of Commons must either give up their precedent entirely, or be reduced to the necessity of maintaining one of the grossest absurdities imaginable, viz: " That a com- " mitment to the Tower is a constituent part of, and con- " tributes half at least to, the incapacitation of the person " who suffers it." I need not make you any excuse for endeavouring to keep alive the attention of the public to the decision of the Middlesex election. The more I consider it, the more I am convinced that, as a fact, it is indeed highly injurious to the rights of the people; but that, as a precedent, it is one of the most dangerous that ever was established against those who are to come after us. Yet

vinced, that very little, if any regard, at all, ought to be paid to the resolutions of one branch of the legislature, declaratory of the law of the land, or even of what they call the law of parliament. It will appear that these resolutions have no one of the properties, by which, in this country particularly, law is distinguished from mere will and pleasure ; but that, on the contrary, they bear every mark of a power arbitrarily assumed, and capriciously applied ;—that they are usually made in times of contest, and to serve some unworthy purpose of passion or party ; —that the law is seldom declared, until after the fact by which it is supposed to be violated ;—that legislation and jurisdiction are united in the same persons, and exercised at the same moment ;—and that a court, from which there is no appeal, assumes an original jurisdiction in a criminal case : In short, Sir, to collect a thousand absurdities into one mass, " we have a law, which cannot be " known, because it is *ex post facto*, the party is both le- " gislator and judge, and the jurisdiction is without ap " peal." Well might the judges say, " The law of par " liament is above us."

You will not wonder, Sir, that, with these qualifications, the declaratory resolutions of the House of Commons should appear to be in perpetual contradiction, not only to common sense, and to the laws we are acquainted with (and which alone we can obey), but even to one another. I was lead to trouble you with these observations, by a passage which, to speak in lutestring, I met with this morning, in the course of my reading, and upon which I mean to put a question to the advocates for privilege.—On the 8th of March, 1704, (Vide Journals, Vol. XIV. p. 565.), the House thought proper to come to the following resolutions :—1. " That no commoner " of England, committed by the House of Commons for " breach of privilege, or contempt of that House, ought " to be, by any writ of *Habeas Corpus*, made to appear " in any other place, or before any other judicature, du- " ring that session of parliament wherein such person " was so committed."

2. " That the Sergeant at Arms, attending this House, " do make no return of, or yield any obedience to the " said writs of *Habeas Corpus* ; and, for such his refusal,

" that he have the protection of the House of Com-
" mons ˣ."

Welbore Ellis, What say you? Is this the law of
parliament, or is it not? I am a plain man, Sir, and
cannot follow you through the phlegmatic forms of an
oration. Speak out, Grildrig; say yes, or no.—If you
say yes, I shall then inquire by what authority Mr. De
Grey, the honest Lord Mansfield, and the Barons of the
Exchequer, dared to grant a writ of *Habeas Corpus* for
bringing the bodies of the Lord Mayor and Mr. Oliver
before them; and why the Lieutenant of the Tower made
any return to a writ, which the House of Commons had,
in a similar instance, declared to be unlawful.—If you say
no, take care you do not at once give up the cause, in support of which you have so long and so laboriously tortured
your understanding. Take care you do not confess that
there is no test by which we can distinguish,—no evidence
by which we can determine what is, and what is not the
law of parliament. The resolutions I have quoted stand
upon your Journals, uncontroverted and unrepealed;—
they contain a declaration of the law of parliament, by
a court competent to the question, and whose decision, as
you and Lord Mansfield say, must be law, because there
is no appeal from it: and they were made, not hastily,
but after long deliberation upon a constitutional question.
—What farther sanction or solemnity will you annex to
any resolution of the present House of Commons, beyond
what appears upon the face of those two resolutions, the
legality of which you now deny? If you say that parliaments are not infallible; and that Queen Anne, in
consequence of the violent proceedings of that House of
Commons, was obliged to prorogue and dissolve them; I
shall agree with you very heartily, and think that the
precedent ought to be followed immediately. But you,
Mr. Ellis, who hold this language, are inconsistent with
your own principles. You have hitherto maintained, that
the House of Commons are the sole judges of their own
privileges, and that their declaration does *ipso facto* constitute the law of parliament: yet now you confess that
parliaments are fallible, and that their resolutions may be
illegal; consequently, that their resolutions do not constitute the law of parliament. When the king was urged

to dissolve the present parliament; you advised him to tell his subjects, that " he was careful not to assume any of " those powers which the constitution has placed in other " hands," &c. Yet Queen Anne, it seems, was justified in exerting her prerogative to stop a House of Commons, whose proceedings, compared with those of the assembly of which you are a most worthy member, were the perfection of justice and reason.

In what a labyrinth of nonsense does a man involve himself, who labours to maintain falsehood by argument ? How much better would it become the dignity of the House of Commons to speak plainly to the people, and tell us at once, " that their will must be obeyed, not because " it is lawful and reasonable, but because it is their will ?" Their constituents would have a better opinion of their candour, and, I promise you, not a worse opinion of their integrity.

Philo Junius.

LETTER XLIX.

TO HIS GRACE THE DUKE OF GRAFTON.

MY LORD, June 22. 1771.

The profound respect I bear to the gracious prince who governs this country with no less honour to himself than satisfaction to his subjects, and who restores you to your rank under his standard, will save you from a multitude of reproaches. The attention I should have paid to your failings is involuntarily attracted to the hand that rewards them ; and though I am not so partial to the royal judgment, as to affirm, that the favour of a king can remove mountains of infamy, it serves to lesson at least, for undoubtedly it divides, the burden. While I remember how much is due to his sacred character, I cannot, with any decent appearance of propriety, call you the meanest and the basest fellow in the kingdom. I protest, my Lord, I do not think you so. You will have a dangerous rival in that kind of fame to which you have hitherto so happily directed your ambition, as long as there is one man living who thinks you worthy of his confidence, and fit to be trusted with any share in his government. I confess you have great intrinsic merit; but take care you do not value it too highly. Consider how much of it would have been lost to the world, if the King had not graciously affixed his stamp, and given it currency among his subjects. If it be true that a virtuous man, struggling with adversity, be a scene worthy of the gods, the glorious contention between you and the best of Princes, deserves a circle equally attentive and respectable. I think I already see other gods rising from the earth to behold it.

- But this language is too mild for the occasion. The King is determined that our abilities shall not be lost to society. The perpetration and description of new crimes will find employment for us both. My Lord, if the persons who had been loudest in their professions of patriotism, had done their duty to the public with the same zeal and perseverance that I did, I will not assert that government would have recovered its dignity, but at least our gracious sovereign must have spared his subjects this last insult ᵞ; which, if there be any feeling left among us, they will resent more than even the real injuries they received from every measure of your Grace's administration. In vain would he have looked round him for another character so consummate as yours. Lord Mansfield shrinks from his principles;—his ideas of government perhaps go farther than your own; but his heart disgraces the theory of his understanding.—Charles Fox is yet in blossom; and as for Mr. Wedderburne, there is something about him which even treachery cannot trust. For the present, therefore, the best of princes must have contented himself with Lord Sandwich.—You would long since have received your final dismission and reward; and I, my Lord, who do not esteem you the more for the high office you possess, would willingly have followed you to your retirement. There is surely something singularly benevolent in the character of our sovereign. From the moment he ascended the throne, there is no crime, of which human nature is capable (and I call upon the Recorder to witness it), that has not appeared venial in his sight. With any other prince, the shameful desertion of him in the midst of that distress which you alone had created,—in the very crisis of danger, when he fancied he

saw the throne already surrounded by men of virtue and
abilities, would have outweighed the memory of your
former services. But his Majesty is full of justice, and
understands the doctrine of compensations. He remem-
bers with gratitude how soon you had accommodated your
morals to the necessity of his service;—how cheerfully you
had abandoned the engagements of private friendship, and
renounced the most solemn professions to the public. The
sacrifice of Lord Chatham was not lost upon him. Even
the cowardice and perfidy of deserting him may have done
you no disservice in his esteem. The instance was painful,
but the principle might please.

You did not neglect the magistrate while you flattered
the man. The expulsion of Mr. Wilkes, predetermined
in the cabinet;—the power of depriving the subject of
his birthright, attributed to a resolution of one branch of
the legislature;—the constitution impudently invaded by
the House of Commons;—the right of defending it treacherously renounced by the House of Lords:—these are the
strokes, my Lord, which, in the present reign, recommend to office, and constitute a minister. They would
have determined your sovereign's judgment, if they had
made no impression upon his heart. We need not look
for any other species of merit to account for his taking
the earliest opportunity to recall you to his counsels. Yet
you have other merit in abundance.——Mr. Hine,—the
Duke of Portland,—and Mr. Yorke:—breach of trust,
robbery, and murder. You would think it a compliment
to your gallantry, if I added rape to the catalogue;—but
the style of your amours secures you from resistance. I
know how well these several charges have been defended.
In the first instance, the breach of trust is supposed to have
been its own reward. Mr. Bradshaw affirms upon his honour, (and so may the gift of smiling never depart from
him!) that you reserved no part of Mr. Hine's purchase
money for your own use, but that every shilling of it was
scrupulously paid to Governor Burgoyne.—Make haste, my
Lord;—another patent, applied in time, may keep the
Oaks ² in the family.—If not, Birnham-Wood, I fear, must
come to the Macaroni.

The Duke of Portland was in life your earliest friend.
In defence of his property he had nothing to plead, but

equity against Sir James Lowther, and prescription against the crown. You felt for your friend; " but the law " must take its course." Posterity will scarce believe that Lord Bute's son-in-law had barely interest enough at the treasury to get his grant completed before the general election.[a].

Enough has been said of that detestable transaction which ended in the death of Mr Yorke.—I cannot speak of it without horror and compassion. To excuse yourself, you publicly impeach your accomplice; and to his mind perhaps the accusation may be flattery. But in murder you are both principals. It was once a question of emulation; and, if the event had not disappointed the immediate schemes of the closet, it might still have been a hopeful subject of jest and merriment between you.

This letter, my Lord, is only a preface to my future correspondence. The remainder of the summer shall be dedicated to your amusement. I mean now and then to relieve the severity of your morning studies, and to prepare you for the business of the day. Without pretending to more than Mr Bradshaw's sincerity, you may rely upon my attachment as long as you are in office.

Will your Grace forgive me, if I venture to express some anxiety for a man whom I know you do not love? My Lord Weymouth has cowardice to plead, and a desertion of a later date than your own. You know the privy seal was intended for him; and, if you consider the dignity of the post he deserted, you will hardly think it decent to quarter him on Mr Rigby. Yet he must have bread, my Lord;—or rather he must have wine. If you deny him the cup, there will be no keeping him within the pale of the ministry.

JUNIUS.

LETTER L.

TO HIS GRACE THE DUKE OF GRAFTON.

MY LORD, July 9. 1771.

THE influence of your Grace's fortune still seems to preside over the treasury. The genius of Mr. Bradshaw inspires Mr. Robinson[b]. How remarkable it is (and I speak of it not as matter of reproach, but as something peculiar to your character), that you have never yet formed a friendship which has not been fatal to the object of it; nor adopted a cause, to which, one way or other, you have not done mischief! Your attachment is infamy while it lasts; and, whichever way it turns, leaves ruin and disgrace behind it. The deluded girl who yields to such a profligate, even while he is constant, forfeits her reputation as well as her innocence, and finds herself abandoned at last to misery and shame.—Thus it happened with the best of princes. Poor Dingley too!—I protest I hardly know which of them we ought most to lament?—the unhappy man who sinks under the sense of his dishonour, or him who survives it? Characters, so finished, are placed beyond the reach of panegyric. Death has fixed his seal upon Dingley; and you, my Lord, have set your mark upon the other.

The only letter I ever addressed to the King was so unkindly received, that I believe I shall never presume to trouble his Majesty in that way again. But my zeal for his service is superior to neglect; and, like Mr. Wilkes's patriotism, thrives by persecution. Yet his Majesty is much addicted to useful reading; and, if I am not ill informed, has honoured the Public Advertiser with particular attention. I have endeavoured, therefore, and not without success (as perhaps you may remember), to furnish it with such interesting and edifying intelligence, as probably would not reach him through any other channel. The services you have done the nation,—your integrity in office, and signal fidelity to your approved good master, have been faithfully recorded. Nor have his own virtues been entirely neglected. These letters, my Lord, are read in other countries, and in other languages; and I think I may affirm without vanity, that the gracious character of the best of Princes, is by this time not only perfectly known to his subjects, but tolerably well understood by the rest of Europe. In this respect alone I have the advantage of Mr. Whitehead. His plan, I think, is too narrow. He seems to manufacture his verses for the sole use of the hero who is supposed to be the subject of them; and, that his meaning may not be exported in foreign bottoms, sets all translation at defiance.

Your Grace's reappointment to a seat in the cabinet, was announced to the public by the ominous return of Lord Bute to this country. When that noxious planet approaches England, he never fails to bring plague and pestilence along with him. The King already feels the malignant effect of your influence over his counsels. Your former administration made Mr. Wilkes an alderman of London, and representative of Middlesex. Your next appearance in office is marked with his election to the shrievalty. In whatever measure you are concerned, you are not only disappointed of success, but always contrive to make the government of the best of princes contemptible in his own eyes, and ridiculous to the whole world. Making all due allowance for the effect of the minister's declared interposition, Mr. Robinson's activity, and Mr. Horne's new zeal in support of administration, we still want the genius of the Duke of Grafton to account for committing the whole interest of government in the city to the conduct of Mr. Harley. I will not bear hard upon your faithful friend and emissary Mr. Touchit; for I know the difficulties of his situation, and that a few lottery-tickets are of use to his œconomy. There is a proverb concerning persons in the predicament of this gentleman, which, however, cannot be strictly applied to him: They commence dupes, and finish knaves. Now Mr. Touchit's character is uniform. I am convinced that his sentiments never depended upon his circumstances, and that, in the most prosperous state of his fortune, he was always the very man he is at present.—But was there no other person of rank and consequence in the city, whom government could confide in, but a notorious Jacobite? Did you imagine that the whole body of the Dissenters, that the whole Whig interest of London, would attend at the levee, and submit to the directions of a notorious Jacobite? Was there no Whig magistrate in the city, to whom the servants of George the Third could intrust the management of a business so very interesting to their master as the election of sheriffs? Is there no room at St. James's but for Scotchmen and Jacobites? My Lord, I do not mean to question the sincerity of Mr. Harley's attachment to his Majesty's government. Since

Q

the commencement of the present reign, I have seen still greater contradictions reconciled. The principles of these worthy Jacobites are not so absurd as they have been represented. Their ideas of divine right are not so much annexed to the person or family, as to the political character of the sovereign. Had there ever been an honest man among the Stuarts, his Majesty's present friends would have been Whigs upon principle. But the conversion of the best of princes has removed their scruples. They have forgiven him the sins of his Hanoverian ancestors, and acknowledge the hand of Providence in the descent of the crown upon the head of a true Stuart. In you, my Lord, they also behold, with a kind of predilection, which borders upon loyalty, the natural representative of that illustrious family. The mode of your descent from Charles the Second is only a bar to your pretensions to the crown, and no way interrupts the regularity of your succession to all the virtues of the Stuarts.

The unfortunate success of the Reverend Mr. Horne's endeavours in support of the ministerial nomination of sheriffs, will, I fear, obstruct his preferment. Permit me to recommend him to your Grace's protection. You will find him copiously gifted with those qualities of the heart, which usually direct you in the choice of your friendships. He too was Mr. Wilkes's friend, and as incapable as you are of the liberal resentment of a gentleman. No, my Lord,—it was the solitary vindictive malice of a monk, brooding over the infirmities of his friend, until he thought they quickened into public life; and feasting with a rancorous rapture upon the sordid catalogue of his distresses. Now let him go back to his cloister. The church is a proper retreat for him. In his principles he is already a bishop.

The mention of this man has moved me from my natural moderation. Let me return to your Grace. You are the pillow upon which I am determined to rest all my resentments. What idea can the best of sovereigns form to himself of his own government?—In what repute can he conceive that he stands with his people, when he sees, beyond the possibility of a doubt, that, whatever be the office, the suspicion of his favour is fatal to the candidate; and that when the party he wishes well to has the fairest prospect of success, if his royal inclination should unfortunately be discovered, it drops like an acid, and turns the election?

This event, among others, may perhaps contribute to open his Majesty's eyes to his real honour and interest. In spite of all your Grace's intgenuity, he may at last perceive the inconvenience of selecting, with such a curious felicity, every villain in the nation to fill the various departments of his government. Yet I should be sorry to confine him in the choice either of his footmen or his friends.

JUNIUS.

LETTER LI.
FROM THE REVEREND MR. HORNE TO JUNIUS.

SIR,   July. 13. 1771.

FARCE, Comedy, and Tragedy—Wilkes, Foote, and Junius, united at the same time against one poor Parson, are fearful odds. The two former are only labouring in their vocation; and may equally plead in excuse, that their aim is a livelihood. I admit the plea for the second; his is an honest calling, and my clothes were lawful game; but I cannot so readily approve Mr Wilkes or commend him for making patriotism a trade, and a fraudulent trade. But what shall I say to Junius? the grave, the solemn, the didactic! Ridicule indeed has been ridiculously called the test of truth; but surely, to confess that you lose your natural moderation when mention is made of the man, does not promise much truth or justice when you speak of him yourself.

You charge me with " a new zeal in support of administration," and with " endeavours in support of the " ministerial nomination of sheriffs." The reputation which your talents have deservedly gained to the signature of Junius, draws from me a reply, which I disdained to give to the anonymous lies of Mr. Wilkes. You make frequent use of the word Gentleman; I only call myself a man, and desire no other distinction; if you are either, you are bound to make good your charges, or to confess that you have done me a hasty injustice upon no authority.

I put the matter fairly to issue.—I say, that, so far from "any " new zeal in support of administration, " I am possessed with the utmost abhorence of their measures; and that I have ever shown myself, and am still ready, in any rational manner, to lay down all I have—my life, in opposition to those measures. I say, that I have not, and never have had, any communication or connection of any kind, directly or indirectly, with any courtier or ministerial man, or any of their adherents; that I never have received, or solicited, or expected, or desired, or do now hope for, any reward of any sort, from any party or set of men in administration or opposition. I say, that I never used any " endeavours in support of the ministerial no-" mination of sheriffs;" that I did not solicit any one liveryman for his vote for any one of the candidates, nor employ any other person to solicit; and that I did not write one single line or word in favour of Messrs. Plumbe and Kirkman, whom I understand to have been supported by the ministry.

You are bound to refute what I here advance, or to lose your credit for veracity. You must produce facts: surmise and general abuse, in however elegant language, ought not to pass for proofs. You have every advantage; and I have every disadvantage: you are unknown; I give my name. All parties, both in and out of administration, have their reasons (which I shall relate hereafter) for uniting in their wishes against me; and the popular prejudice is as strongly in your favour as it is violent against the Parson.

Singular as my present situation is, it is neither painful, nor was it unforeseen. He is not fit for public business, who does not even at his entrance, prepare his mind for such an event. Health, fortune, tranquillity, and private connections, I have sacrificed upon the altar of the public; and the only return I receive, because I will not concur to dupe and mislead a senseless multitude, is barely, that they have not yet torn me in pieces. That this has been the only return is my pride, and a source of more real satisfaction than honours or prosperity. I can practise, before I am old, the lessons I learned in my youth ; nor shall I ever forget the words of my ancient Monitor :

> " 'Tis the last key-stone
> That makes the arch : the rest that there were put
> Are nothing, till that comes to bind and shut :
> Then stands it a triumphal mark ! then men
> Observe the strength, the height, the why and when
> It was erected; and still, walking under,
> Meet some new matter to look up and wonder!"

I am, Sir, your humble servant,

JOHN HORNE.

LETTER LII.

TO THE REVEREND MR. HORNE.

SIR,   July 24. 1771

I CANNOT descend to an altercation with you in the newspapers ; but, since I have attacked your character, and you complain of injustice, I think you have some right to an explanation. You defy me to prove that you ever solicited a vote, or wrote a word, in support of the ministerial aldermen. Sir, I did never suspect you of such gross folly. It would have been impossible for Mr. Horne to have solicited votes, and very difficult to have written for the newspapers in defence of that cause, without being detected and brought to shame. Neither do I pretend to any intelligence concerning you, or to know more of your conduct than you yourself have thought proper to communicate to the public. It is from your own letters I conclude that you have sold yourself to the ministry : or, if that charge be too severe, and supposing it possible to be deceived by appearances so very strongly against you, what are your friends to say in your defence ? Must they not confess, that, to gratify your personal hatred of Mr. Wilkes, you sacrificed, as far as depended on your interest and abilities, the cause of the country ? I can make allowance for the violence of the passions ; and if ever I should be convinced that you had no motive but to destroy Wilkes, I shall then be ready to do justice to your character, and to declare to the world that I despise you somewhat less than I do at present. But as a public man, I must for ever condemn you. You cannot but know,—nay, you dare not pretend to be ignorant, that the highest gratification of which the most detestable * * in this nation is capable, would have been the defeat of Wilkes. I know that man much better than any of you. Nature intended him only for a good-humoured fool. A systematical education, with long practice, has made him a consummate hypocrite. Yet this man, to say nothing of his worthy ministers, you have most assiduously laboured to gratify. To exclude Wilkes, it was not necessary you should solicit votes for his opponents. We incline the balance as effectually by lessening the weight in one scale, as by increasing it in the other.

The mode of your attack upon Wilkes (though I am far from thinking meanly of your abilities) convinces me, that you either want judgment extremely, or that you are blinded by your resentment. You ought to have foreseen, that the charges you urged against Wilkes could never do him any mischief. After all, when we expected discoveries highly interesting to the community, what a pitiful detail did it end in!—Some old clothes, a Welsh poney, a French footman, and a hamper of claret. Indeed, Mr. Horne, the public should, and will forgive him his claret and his footman, and even the ambition of making his brother chamberlain of London, as long as he stands forth against a ministry and parliament who are doing every thing they can to enslave the country, and as long as he is a thorn in the king's side. You will not suspect me as setting up Wilkes for a perfect character. The question to the public is, Where shall we find a man, who, with purer principles, will go the lengths and run the hazards that he has done? The season calls for such a man, and he ought to be supported. What would have been the triumph of that odious hypocrite and his minions, if Wilkes had been defeated? It was not your fault, reverend Sir, that he did not enjoy it completely.—But now, I promise you, you have so little power to do mischief, that I much question whether the ministry will adhere to the promises they have made you. It will be in vain to say that I am a partizan of Mr. Wilkes, or personally your enemy. You will convince no man, for you do not believe it yourself. Yet, I confess, I am a little offended at the low rate, at which you seem to value my understanding. I beg, Mr. Horne, you will hereafter believe, that I measure the integrity of men by their conduct, not by their professions. Such tales may entertain Mr. Oliver, or your grandmother; but, trust me, they are thrown away upon Junius.

You say you are a man. Was it generous; was it manly, repeatedly to introduce into a newspaper the name of a young lady, with whom you must heretofore have lived on terms of politeness and good humour?—But I have done with you. In my opinion your credit is irrecoverably ruined. Mr. Townshend, I think, is nearly in the same predicament. Poor Oliver has been shamefully duped by you. You have made him sacrifice all the honour he got by his imprisonment. As for Mr. Sawbridge, whose character I really respect, I am astonished he does not see through your duplicity. Never was so base a design so poorly conducted.—This letter, you see, is not intended for the public ; but, if you think it will do you any service, you are at liberty to publish it.

JUNIUS.

P. S. This letter was transmitted privately by the printer to Mr. Horne, by Junius's request. Mr. Horne returned it to the printer, with directions to publish it.

LETTER LIII.

FROM THE REVEREND MR. HORNE TO JUNIUS.

SIR,   July 31. 1771.

You have disappointed me. When I told you, that surmise and general abuse, in however elegant language, ought not pass for proofs, I evidently hinted at the reply which I expected: but you have dropped your usual elegance, and seem willingly to try what will be the effect of surmise and general abuse in very course language. Your answer to my letter (which I hope was cool, and temperate, and modest) has convinced me, that my idea of a man is much superior to yours of a gentleman. Of your former letters I have always said, *Materiem superabat opus ;* I do not think so of the present ; the principles are more detestable than the expressions are mean and illiberal. I am contented, that all those who adopt the one should for ever load me with the other.

I appeal to the common sense of the public, to which I have ever directed myself: I believe they have it, though I am sometimes half inclined to suspect that Mr. Wilkes has formed a truer judgment of mankind than I have. However, of this I am sure, that there is nothing else upon which to place a steady reliance. Trick, and low cunning, and addressing their prejudices and passions, may be the fittest means to carry a particular point; but if they have not common sense, there is no prospect of gaining for them any real permanent good. The same passions which have been artfully used by an honest man for their advantage, may be more artfully employed by a dishonest man for their destruction. I desire them to apply their common sense to this letter of Junius; not for my sake, but their own: it concerns them most nearly; for the principles it contains lead to disgrace and ruin, and are inconsistent with every notion of civil society.

The charges which Junius has brought against me, are made ridiculous by his own inconsistency and self contradiction. He charges me positively with "a new zeal in " support of administration;" and with " endeavours in " support of the ministerial nomination of sheriffs." And he assigns two inconsistent motives for my conduct: either that I have " sold myself to the ministry," or am instigated " by the solitary vindictive malice of a monk;" either that I am influenced by a sordid desire of gain, or am hurried on by " personal hatred, and blinded by resent- " ment." In his letter to the Duke of Grafton, he supposes me actuated by both: in his letter to me, he at first doubts which of the two, whether interest or revenge, is my motive. However, at last he determines for the former, and again positively asserts, that " the ministry " have made me promises:" yet he produces no instance of corruption, nor pretends to have any intelligence of a ministerial connection. He mentions no cause of a personal hatred to Mr. Wilkes, nor any reason for my resentment or revenge; nor has Mr. Wilkes himself ever hinted any, though repeatedly pressed. When Junius is called upon to justify his accusation, he answers, " He " cannot descend to an altercation with me in the news-

" papers." Junius, who exists only in the newspapers, who acknowledges " he has attacked my character there, " and thinks I have some right to an explanation ;" 'yet this Junius " cannot descend to an altercation in the " newspapers !" And because he; cannot descend to an altercation with me in the newspapers, he sends a letter of abuse by the printer, which he finishes with telling, me—" I am at liberty to publish it." This, to be sure, is a most excellent method to avoid an altercation in the news-papers!

The proofs of his positive charges are as extraordinary : " He does not pretend to any intelligence concerning me, " or to know more of my conduct than I myself have " thought proper to communicate to the public." He does not suspect me of such gross folly as to have soli-cited votes, or to have written anonymously in the news-papers ; because it is impossible to do either of these with-out being detected and brought to shame.—Junius says this !—who yet imagines that he has himself written two years under that signature (and more under others), with-out being detected !—his warmest admirers will not here-after add, without being brought to shame. But though he never did suspect me of such gross folly as to run the hazard of being detected and brought to shame by anony-mous writing, he insists, that I have been guilty of a much grosser folly, of incurring the certainty of shame and de-tection, by writings signed with my name ! But this is a small flight for the towering Junius : HE IS FAR from " thinking meanly of my abilities," though he is, " con-" vinced that I want judgment extremely ;" and can " really respect Mr. Sawbridge's character," though he declares him c to be so poor a creature, as not to " see " through the basest design conducted in the poorest " manner !" And this most base design is conducted in the poorest manner, by a man whom he does not suspect of gross folly, and of whose abilities he is FAR from think-ing meanly !

Should we ask Junius to reconcile these contradictions, and explain this nonsense, the answer is ready ;—" He " cannot descend to an altercation in the newspapers." He feels no reluctance to attack the character of any man : the throne is not too high, nor the cottage too low : his mighty malice can grasp both extremes: he hints not his accusations as opinion, conjecture, or inference, but delivers them as positive assertions. Do the accused complain of injustice? He acknowledges they have some sort of right to an explanation: but if they ask for proofs and facts, he begs to be excused; and though he is no where else to be encountered—" he cannot descend to an altercation in the " newspapers."

And this, perhaps, Junius may think the " liberal re-" sentment of a gentleman:" This skulking assassination he may call courage. In all things, as in this, I hope we differ.

> I thought that fortitude had been a mean
> 'Twixt fear and rashness: not a lust obscene
> Or appetite of offending; but a skill
> And nice discernment between good and ill.
> Her ends are honesty and public good;
> And without these she is not understood.

Of two things, however, he has condescended to give proof. He very properly produces a young lady, to prove that I am not a man; and a good old woman, my grandmother, to prove Mr. Oliver a fool. Poor old soul! She read her Bible far otherwise than Junius! She often found there, that the sins of the fathers had been visited on the children; and therefore was cautious that herself, and her immediate descendants, should leave no reproach on her posterity: and they left none. How little could she foresee this reverse of Junius, who visits my political sins upon my grandmother! I do not charge this to the score of malice in him; it proceeded entirely from his propensity to blunder; that whilst he was reproaching me for introducing, in the most harmless manner, the name of one female, he might himself, at the same instant introduce two.

I am represented alternately, as it suits Junius's purpose, under the opposite characters of a gloomy monk, and a man of politeness and good humour. I am called " a solitary monk," in order to confirm the notion given of me in Mr. Wilkes's anonymous paragraphs, that I never laugh. And the terms of politeness and good humour, on which I am said to have lived heretofore with the young lady, are intended to confirm other paragraphs of Mr. Wilkes, in which he is supposed to have offended me by refusing his daughter. Ridiculous! Yet I cannot deny but that Junius has proved me unmanly and ungenerous, as clearly as he has shown me corrupt and vindictive. And I will tell him more; I have paid the present ministry as many visits and compliments as ever I paid to the young lady; and shall all my life treat them with the same politeness and good humour.

But Junius "begs me to believe, that he measures the " integrity of men by their conduct, not by their profes-" sions." Sure this Junius must imagine his readers as void of understanding as he is of modesty! Where shall we find the standard of his integrity? By what are we to measure the conduct of this lurking assassin?—And he says this to me, whose conduct, whereever I could personally appear, has been as direct, and open, and public as my words. I have not, like him, concealed myself in my chamber, to shoot my arrows out of the window; nor contented myself to view the battle from afar; but publicly mixed in the engagement, and shared the danger. To whom have I, like him, refused my name upon complaint of injury? What printer have I desired to conceal me? In the infinite variety of business in which I have been concerned, where it is not so easy to be faultless, which of my actions can he arraign? To what danger has any man been exposed, which I have not faced? information, action, imprisonment, or death? What labour have I refused? what expence have I declined? what pleasure have I not renounced?—But Junius, to whom no conduct belongs, " measures the integrity of men by their conduct, not by " their professions;" himself all the while being nothing but professions, and those too anonymous! The political ignorance or wilful falsehood of this declaimer is extreme. His own former letters justify both my conduct and those whom his last letter abuses: for the public measures which Junius has been all along defending, were ours whom he attacks; and the uniform opposer of those measures has been Mr. Wilkes, whose bad actions and intentions he endeavours to screen.

Let Junius now, if he pleases, change his abuse; and, quitting his loose hold of interest and revenge, accuse me of vanity, and call this defence boasting. I own I have pride to see statutes decreed, and the highest honours

conferred, for measures and actions which all men have approved; whilst those who counselled and caused them are execrated and insulted. The darkness in which Junius thinks himself shrouded, has not concealed him; nor the artifice of only attacking under that signature those he would pull down (whilst he recommends by other ways those he would have promoted), disguised from me whose partizan he is. When Lord Chatham can forgive the awkward situation in which, for the sake of the public, he was designedly placed by the thanks to him from the city; and when Wilkes's name ceases to be necessary to Lord Rockingham to keep up a clamour against the persons of the ministry, without obliging the different factions now in opposition to bind themselves before hand to some certain points, and to stipulate some precise advantages to the public; then, and not till then, may those whom he now abuses expect the approbation of Junius. The approbation of the public for our faithful attention to their interest, by endeavours for those stipulations, which have made us as obnoxious to the factions in opposition as to those in administration, is not perhaps to be expected till some years hence; when the public will look back, and see how shamefully they have been deluded, and by what arts they were made to lose the golden opportunity of preventing what they will surely experience,—a change of ministers, without a material change of measures, and without any security for a tottering constitution.

But what cares Junius for the security of the constitution? He has now unfolded to us his diabolical principles. As a public man, he must ever condemn any measure which may tend accidentally to gratify the sovereign; and Mr. Wilkes is to be supported and assisted in all his attempts (no matter how ridiculous and mischievous his projects), " as long as he continues to be a thorn in the " King's side!"—The cause of the country, it seems, in the opinion of Junius, is merely to vex the King; and any rascal is to be supported in any roguery, provided he can only thereby plant a thorn in the King's side.—This is the very extremity of faction, and the last degree of political wickedness. Because Lord Chatham has been ill treated by the King, and treacherously betrayed by the Duke of Grafton, the latter is to be " the pillow on

" which Junius will rest his resentment;" and the public are to oppose the measures of government from mere motives of personal enmity to the sovereign! These are the avowed principles of the man who, in the same letter, says, "If ever he should be convinced that I had no mo-" tive but to destroy Wilkes, he shall then be ready to " do justice to my character, and to declare to the world " that he despises me somewhat less than he does at pre-" sent!" Had I ever acted from personal affection or enmity to Mr. Wilkes, I should justly be despised; but what does he deserve, whose avowed motive is personal enmity to the sovereign? The contempt which I should otherwise feel for the absurdity and glaring inconsistency of Junius, is here swallowed up in my abhorrence of his principles. The right divine and sacredness of kings is to me a senseless jargon. It was thought a daring expression of Oliver Cromwell in the time of Charles the First, that if he found himself placed opposite to the King in battle, he would discharge his piece into his bosom as soon as into any other man's. I go farther: had I lived in those days, I would not have waited for chance to give me an opportunity, of doing my duty; I would have sought him through the ranks, and, without the least personal enmity, have discharged my piece into his bosom rather than into any other man's. The king whose actions justify rebellion to his government, deserves death from the hand of every subject. And should such a time arrive, I shall be as free to act as to say: but till then, my attachment to the person and family of the sovereign shall ever be found more zealous and sincere than that of his flatterers. I would offend the sovereign with as much reluctance as the parent; but if the happiness and security of the whole family made it necessary, so far, and no farther, I would offend him without remorse.

But let us consider a little whether these principles of Junius would lead us. Should Mr. Wilkes once more commission Mr. Thomas Walpole to procure for him a pension of one thousand pounds upon the Irish establishment for thirty years, he must be supported in the demand by the public—because it would mortify the king!

Should he wish to see Lord Rockingham and his friends once more in administration, " unclogged by any stipu-

R

" lations for the people," that he might again enjoy a
" pension of one thousand and forty pounds" a-year, viz.
from the " First Lord of the Treasury" 500l. from the
" Lords of the Treasury," 60l. each; from the " Lords
" of Trade," 40l. each, &c. the public must give up their
attention to points of national benefit, and assist Mr.
Wilkes in his attempt—because it would mortify the
king!

Should he demand the government of Canada, or of
Jamaica, or the embassy to Constantinople, and in case of
refusal, threaten to write them down, as he had before
served another administration, in a year and a half, he must
be supported in his pretensions, and upheld in his insolence
—because it would mortify the king!

Junius may choose to suppose that these things cannot
happen! But that they have happened, notwithstanding
Mr. Wilkes's denial, I do aver. I maintain that Mr.
Wilkes did commission Mr. Thomas Walpole to solicit
for him a pension of 1000l. on the Irish establishment for
thirty years; with which, and a pardon, he declared he
would be satisfied: and that, notwithstanding his letter
to Mr. Onslow, he did accept a clandestine, precarious,
and eleemosynary pension from the Rockingham administration; which they paid in proportion to, and out of
their salaries: and so entirely was it ministerial, that as
any of them went out of the ministry, their names were
scratched out of the list, and they contributed no longer.
I say, he did solicit the governments, and the embassy,
and threatened their refusal nearly in these words :—" It
" cost me a year and a half to write down the last ad-
" ministration; should I employ as much time upon you,
" very few of you would be in at the death." When
these threats did not prevail, he came over to England to
embarrass them by his presence: and when he found that
Lord Rockingham was something firmer, and more manly
than he expected, and refused to be bullied into what he
could not perform, Mr. Wilkes declared, that he could
not leave England without money; and the Duke of
Portland and Lord Rockingham purchased his absence
with 100l. apiece, with which he returned to Paris.
And for the truth of what I here advance, I appeal to the
Duke of Portland, to Lord Rockingham, to Lord John

Cavendish, to Mr. Walpole, &c.—I appeal to the hand-writing of Mr. Wilkes, which is still extant.

Should Mr. Wilkes afterwards (failing in his whole-sale trade) choose, to dole out his popularity by the pound, and expose the city offices to sale, to his brother, his attorney, &c. Junius will tell us, it is only an ambition that he has to make them chamberlain, town-clerk, &c. and he must not be opposed in thus robbing the ancient citizens of their birthright—because any defeat of Mr. Wilkes would gratify the King!

Should he, after consuming the whole of his own fortune, and that of his wife, and incurring a debt of twenty thousand pounds, merely by his own private extravagance, without a single service or exertion all this time for the public, whilst his estate remained; should he at length, being undone, commence patriot, have the good fortune to be illegally persecuted, and in consideration of that illegality, be espoused by a few gentlemen of the purest public principles; should his debts (though none of them were contracted for the public) and all his other encumbrances be discharged; should he be offered 600l. or 1000l. a-year, to make him independent for the future; and should he, after all, instead of gratitude for these services, insolently forbid his benefactors to bestow their own money upon any other subject but himself, and revile them for setting any bounds to their supplies; Junius (who, any more than Lord Chatham, never contributed one farthing to these enormous expences) will tell them, that if they think of converting the supplies of Mr. Wilkes's private extravagance to the support of public measures—they are as great fools as my grandmother: and that Mr. Wilkes ought to hold the strings of their purses—" as long " as he continues to be a thorn in the king's side !"

Upon these principles I never have acted, and I never will act. In my opinion, it is less dishonourable to be the creature of a court, than the tool of a faction. I will not be either. I understand the two great leaders of opposition to be Lord Rockingham and Lord Chatham; under one of whose banners, all the opposing members of both Houses; who desire to get places, enlist. I can place no confidence in either of them, or in any others, unless they will now engage, whilst they are out, to grant certain essential advantages for the security of the public, when they shall be IN administration. These points they refuse to stipulate, because they are fearful lest they should prevent any future overtures from the court. To force them to these stipulations, has been the uniform endeavour of Mr. Sawbridge, Mr. Townsend, Mr. Oliver, &c. and THEREFORE they are abused by Junius. I know no reason but my zeal and industry in the same cause, that should entitle me to the honour of being ranked by his abuse with persons of their fortune and station. It is a duty I owe to the memory of the late Mr. Beckford, to say, that he had no other aim than this, when he provided that sumptuous entertainment at the Mansion-house for the members of both Houses in opposition. At that time he drew up the heads of an engagement, which he gave to me, with a request that I would couch it in terms so cautious and precise, as to leave no room for future quibble and evasion; but to oblige them either to fulfil the intent of the obligation, or to sign their own infamy, and leave it on record: and this engagement he was determined to propose to them at the Mansion-house, that either by their refusal they might forfeit the confidence of the public, or by the engagement lay a foundation for confidence. When they were informed of the intention, Lord Rockingham and his friends flatly refused any engagement; and Mr. Beckford as flatly swore, they should then "eat none of his broth;" and he was determined to put off the entertainment: But Mr. Beckford was prevailed upon by ——— to indulge them in the ridiculous parade of a popular procession through the city, and to give them the foolish pleasure of an imaginary consequence, for the real benefit only of the cooks and purveyors.

It was the same motive which dictated the thanks of the city to Lord Chatham; which were expressed to be given for his declaration in favour of short parliaments; in order thereby to fix Lord Chatham at least to that one constitutional remedy, without which all others can afford no security. The embarrassment, no doubt, was cruel. He had his choice either to offend the Rockingham party, who declared formally against short parliaments; and with the assistance of whose numbers in both houses, he must expect again to be minister; or to give up the confidence of the public, from whom finally all real consequence must proceed. Lord Chatham chose the latter: and I will venture to say that, by his answer to those thanks, he has given up the people, without gaining the friendship or cordial assistance of the Rockingham faction; whose little politics are confined to the making of matches, and extending their family connections, and who think they gain more by procuring one additional vote to their party in the House of Commons, than by adding their languid property and feeble character to the abilities of a Chatham, or the confidence of a public.

Whatever may be the event of the present wretched state of politics in this country, the principles of Junius will suit no form of government. They are not to be tolerated under any constitution. Personal enmity is a motive fit only for the devil. Whoever, or whatever is sovereign, demands the respect and support of the people. The union is formed for their happiness, which cannot be had without mutual respect; and he counsels maliciously, who would persuade either to a wanton breach of it. When it is banished by either party, and when every method has been tried in vain to restore it, there is no remedy but a divorce: But even then he must have a hard and a wicked heart indeed, who punishes the greatest criminal, merely for the sake of the punishment; and who does not let fall a tear for every drop of blood that is shed in a public struggle, however just the quarrel.

JOHN HORNE,

LETTER LIV.

TO THE PRINTER OF THE PUBLIC ADVERTISER.

SIR,.   Aug. 15. 1771.

I OUGHT to make an apology to the Duke of Grafton, for suffering any part of my attention to be diverted from his Grace to Mr. Horne. I am not justified by the similarity of their dispositions. Private vices, however detestable, have not dignity sufficient to attract the censure of the press, unless they are united with the power of doing some signal mischief to the community.

——Mr. Horne's situation does not correspond with his intentions.—In my own opinion, (which, I know, will be
attributed to my usual vanity and presumption), his letter
to me does not deserve an answer. But I understand that
the public are not satisfied with my silence ;—that an answer is expected from me; and that if I persist in refusing
to plead, it will be taken for conviction. I should be Inconsistent with the principles I profess, if I declined an appeal
to the good sense of the people, or did not willingly
submit myself to the judgment of my peers.

If any coarse expressions have escaped me, I am ready
to agree that they are unfit for Junius to make use of;
but I see no reason to admit that they have been improperly
applied.

Mr. Horne, it seems, is unable to comprehend how an
extreme want of conduct and discretion can consist with
the abilities I have allowed him ; nor can he conceive
that a very honest man, with a very good understanding,
may be deceived by a knave. His knowledge of human
nature must be limited indeed. Had he never mixed
with the world, one would think that even his books
might have taught him better. Did he hear Lord Mansfield, when he defended his doctrine concerning libels?
or when he stated the law in prosecutions for criminal
conversation? or when he delivered his reasons for calling the House of Lords together to receive a copy of his
charge to the jury in Woodfall's trial? Had he been present upon any of these occasions, he would have seen how
possible it is for a man of the first talents to confound
himself in absurdities, which would disgrace the lips of
an idiot. Perhaps the example might have taught him
not to value his own understanding so highly. Lord Lyt-
telton's integrity and judgment are unquestionable ; yet
he is known to admire that cunning Scotchman, and verily believes him an honest man. I speak to facts, with
which all of us are conversant. I speak to men, and to
their experience; and will not descend to answer the
little sneering sophistries of a collegian. Distinguished
talents are not necessarily connected with discretion. If
there be any thing remarkable in the character of Mr.
Horne, it is, that extreme want of judgment should be
united with his very moderate capacity. Yet I have not

forgotten the acknowledgement I made him. He owes it to my bounty; and, though his letter has lowered him in my opinion, I scorn to retract the charitable donation.

I said it would be very difficult for Mr. Horne to write directly in defence of a ministerial measure, and not to be detected; and even that difficulty I confined to his particular situation. He changes the terms of the proposition, and supposes me to assert, that it would be impossible for any man to write for the newspapers and not be discovered.

He repeatedly affirms, or intimates at least, that he knows the author of these letters. With what colour of truth, then, can he pretend " that I am no where to be " encountered but in a newspaper ?" I shall leave him to his suspicions. It is not necessary that I should confide in the honour or discretion of a man who already seems to hate me with as much rancour as if I had formerly been his friend. But he asserts that he has traced me through a variety of signatures. To make the discovery of any importance to his purpose, he should have proved, either that the fictitious character of Junius has not been consistently supported, or that the author has maintained different principles under different signatures. I cannot recal to my memory the numberless trifles I have written;—but I rely upon the consciousness of my own integrity, and defy him to fix any colourable charge of inconsistency upon me.

I am not bound to assign the secret motives of his apparent hatred of Mr. Wilkes: nor does it follow that I may not judge fairly of his conduct, though it were true " that I had no conduct of my own." Mr. Horne enlarges with rapture upon the importance of his services; the dreadful battles which he might have been engaged in, and the dangers he has escaped. In support of the formidable description, he quotes verses without mercy. The gentleman deals in fiction, and naturally appeals to the evidence of the poets. Taking him at his word, he cannot but admit the superiority of Mr. Wilkes in this line of service. On one side, we see nothing but imaginary distresses; on the other, we see real prosecutions, real penalties, real imprisonment; life repeatedly hazarded, and, at one moment, almost the certainty of death.

Thanks are undoubtedly due to every man who does his duty in the engagement; but it is the wounded soldier who deserves the reward.

I did not mean to deny that Mr. Horne had been an active partizan. It would defeat my own purpose not to allow him a degree of merit, which aggravates his guilt. The very charge " of contributing his utmost efforts to " support a ministerial measure," implies an acknowledgment of his former services. If he had not at once been distinguished by his apparent zeal in defence of the common cause, he could not now be distinguished by deserting it. As for myself, it is no longer a question, " whe- " ther I shall mix with the throng, and take a single " share in the danger?" Whenever Junius appears, he must encounter an host of enemies.—But is there no honourable way to serve the public, without engaging in personal quarrels with insignificant individuals, or submitting to the drugery of canvassing votes for an election? Is there no merit in dedicating my life to the information of my fellow-subjects? What public question have I declined? What villain have I spared? Is there no labour in the composition of these letters? Mr. Horne, I fear, is partial to me, and measures the facility of my writings by the fluency of his own.

He talks to us in high terms of the gallant feats he would have performed if he had lived in the last century. The unhappy Charles could hardly have escaped him. But living princes have a claim to his attachment and respect. Upon these terms, there is no danger in being a patriot. If he means any thing more than a pompous rhapsody, let us try how well his argument holds together. I presume he is not yet so much a courtier as to affirm that the constitution has not been grossly and daringly violated under the present reign. He will not say, that the laws have not been shamefully broken or perverted; that the rights of the subject have not been invaded; or that redress has not been repeatedly solicited and refused. Grievances like these were the foundation of the rebellion in the last century; and, if I understand Mr. Horne, they would, at that period, have justified him to his own mind in deliberately attacking the life of his sovereign. I shall not ask him to what political constitution this doctrine can be reconciled. But at least it is incumbent upon him to show, that the present King has better excuses than Charles the First for the errors of his government. He ought to demonstrate to us, that the constitution was better understood a hundred years ago than it is at present; that the legal rights of the subject, and the limits of the prerogative, were more accurately defined and more clearly comprehended. If propositions like these cannot be fairly maintained, I do not see how he can reconcile it to his conscience, not to act immediately with the same freedom with which he speaks. I reverence the character of Charles the First, as little as Mr. Horne; but I will not insult his misfortunes by a comparison that would degrade him.

It is worth observing, by what gentle degrees the furious, persecuting zeal of Mr. Horne has softened into moderation. Men and measures were yesterday his objects. What pains did he once take to bring that great state-criminal Macquirk to execution!—To-day, he confines himself to measures only.—No penal example is to be left to the successors of the Duke of Grafton.—To-morrow, I presume, both men and measures will be forgiven. The flaming patriot, who so lately scorched us in the meridian, sinks temperately to the west, and is hardly felt as he descends.

I comprehend the policy of endeavouring to communicate to Mr. Oliver and Mr. Sawbridge a share in the reproaches, with which he supposes me to have loaded him. My memory fails me, if I have mentioned their names with disrespect; unless it be reproachful to acknowledge a sincere respect for the character of Mr. Sawbridge, and not to have questioned the innocence of Mr. Oliver's intentions.

It seems I am a partizan of the great leader of the opposition. If the charge had been a reproach, it should have been better supported. I did not intend to make a public declaration of the respect I bear Lord Chatham. I well knew what unworthy conclusions would be drawn from it. But I am called upon to deliver my opinion; and surely it is not in the little censure of Mr. Horne to deter me from doing signal justice to a man, who, I confess, has grown upon my esteem. As for the common, sordid views of avarice, or any purpose of vulgar ambition, I question whether the applause of Junius would be of service to Lord Chatham. My vote will hardly recommend him to an increase of his pension, or to a seat in the cabinet. But if his ambition be upon a level with his understanding; if he judges of what is truly honourable for himself, with the same superior genius which animates and directs him to eloquence in debate, to wisdom in decision, even the pen of Junius shall contribute to reward him. Recorded honours shall gather round his monument, and thicken over him. It is a solid fabric, and will suppport the laurels that adorn it. I am not conversant in the langage of panegyric. These praises are extorted from me; but they will wear well, for they have been dearly earned.

My detestation of the Duke of Grafton is not founded upon his treachery to any individual: though I am willing enough to suppose, that, in public affairs, it would be impossible to desert or betray Lord Chatham, without doing an essential injury to this country. My abhorrence of the Duke arises from an intimate knowledge of his character; and, from a thorough conviction that his baseness has been the cause of greater mischief to England, than even the unfortunate ambition of Lord Bute.

The shortening the duration of parliaments is a subject on which Mr. Horne cannot enlarge too warmly; nor will I question his sincerity. If I did not profess the same sentiments, I should be shamefully inconsistent with myself. It is unnecessary to bind Lord Chatham by the written formality of an engagement. He has publicly declared himself a convert to triennial parliaments; and though I have long been convinced that this is the only possible resource we have left to preserve the substantial freedom of the constitution, I do not think we have a right to determine against the integrity of Lord Rockingham or his friends. Other measures may undoubtedly be supported in argument, as better adapted to the disorder, or more likely to be obtained.

Mr. Horne is well assured, that I never was the champion of Mr. Wilkes. But though I am not obliged to answer for the firmness of his future adherence to the principles he professes, I have no reason to presume that

he will hereafter disgrace them. As for all those imaginary cases which Mr. Horne so petulantly urges against
me, I have one plain, honest answer to make to him.
Whenever Mr. Wilkes shall be convicted of soliciting a
pension, an embassy, or a government, he must depart
from that situation, and renounce that character which
he assumes at present; and which, in my opinion, entitle
him to the support of the public. By the same act, and
at the same moment, he will forfeit his power of mortifying the King; and, though he can never be a favourite
at St. James's, his baseness may administer a solid satisfaction to the royal mind. The man I speak of has not
a heart to feel for the frailties of his fellow-creatures. It
is their virtues that afflict, it is their vices that console him.

I give every possible advantage to Mr. Horne, when I
take the facts he refers to for granted. That they are the
produce of his invention, seems highly probable ; that they
are exaggerated, I have no doubt. At the worst, what do
they amount to, but that Mr. Wilkes, who never was
thought of as a perfect pattern of morality, has not been
at all times proof against the extremity of distress. How
shameful is it, in a man who has lived in friendship with
him, to reproach him with failings too naturally connected with despair ! Is no allowance to be made for banish-
ment and ruin? Does a two years imprisonment make no
atonement for his crimes ?—The resentment of a priest is
implacable. No sufferings can soften, no penitence can
appease him.—Yet he himself, I think, upon his own system, has a multitude of political offences to atone for. I
will not insist upon the nauseous detail with which he has so
long disgusted the public. He seems to be ashamed of it.
But what excuse will he make to the friends of the constitution for labouring to promote this consummately bad man
to a station of the highest national trust and importance?
Upon what honourable motives did he recommend him to
the livery of London for their representative ;—to the
ward of Faringdon for their alderman ;—to the county of
Middlesex for their knight? Will he affirm, that, at that
time, he was ignorant of Mr. Wilkes's solicitations to the
ministry ?—That he should say so, is indeed very necessary,
for his own justification ; but where will he find credulity
to believe him?

In what school this gentleman learned his ethics I know not. His logic seems to have been studied under Mr. Dyson. That miserable pamphleteer, by dividing the only precedent in point, and taking as much of it as suited his purpose, had reduced his argument upon the Middlesex election to something like the shape of a syllogism. Mr. Horne has conducted himself with the same ingenuity and candour. I had affirmed, that Mr. Wilkes would preserve the public favour " as long as he stood forth against " a ministry and parliament, who were doing every thing " they could to enslave the country, and as long as he " was a thorn in the King's side." Yet, from the exulting triumph of Mr. Horne's reply, one would think that I had rested my expectation, that Mr. Wilkes would be supported by the public upon the single condition of his mortifying the King. This may be logic at Cambrige, or at the Treasury; but among men of sense and honour, it is folly or villany in the extreme.

I see the pitiful advantage he has taken of a single unguarded expression, in a letter not intended for the public. Yet it is only the expression, that is unguarded. I adhere to the true meaning of that member of the sentence, taken separately as he takes it ; and now, upon the coolest deliberation, re-assert, that, for the purposes I referred to, it may be highly meritorious to the public, to wound the personal feelings of the sovereign. It is not a general proposition, nor is it generally applied to the chief magistrate of this or any other constitution. Mr. Horne knows as well as I do, that the best of princes is not displeased with the abuse which he sees thrown upon his ostensible ministers. It makes them, I presume, more properly the objects of his royal compassion ;—neither does it escape his sagacity, that the lower they are degraded in the public esteem, the more submissively they must depend upon his favour for protection. This I affirm, upon the most solemn conviction, and the most certain knowledge, is a leading maxim in the policy of the closet. It is unnecessary to pursue the argument any farther.

Mr. Horne is now a very loyal subject. He laments the wretched state of politics in this country ; and sees, in a new light, the weakness and folly of the opposition. " Whoever, or whatever, is sovereign, demands the re-

" spect and support of the people[d];" it was not so " when " Nero fiddled while Rome was burning:" Our gracious sovereign has had wonderful success in creating new attachments to his person and family. He owes it, I presume, to the regular system he has pursued in the mystery of conversion. He began with an experiment upon the Scotch; and concludes with converting Mr. Horne.—— What a pity it is, that the Jews should be condemned by Providence to wait for a Messiah of their own?

The priesthood are accused of misinterpreting the scriptures. Mr. Horne has improved upon his profession. He alters the text, and creates a refutable doctrine of his own. Such artifices cannot long delude the understanding of the people; and, without meaning an indecent comparison, I may venture to foretel, that the Bible aud Junius will be read, when the commentaries of the Jesuits arc forgotten.

JUNIUS.

LETTER LV.

SIR,   Aug. 26. 1771.

THE enemies of the people, having now nothing better to object to my friend Junius, are at last obliged to quit his politics, and to rail at him for crimes he is not guilty of. His vanity and impiety are now the perpetual topics of their abuse. I do not mean to lesson the force of such charges (supposing they were true); but to show that they are not founded. If I admitted the premises, I should readily agree in all the consequences drawn from them. Vanity indeed is a venial error; for it usually carries its own punishment with it:——but if I thought Junius capable of uttering a disrespectful word of the religion of his country, I should be the first to renounce and give him up to the public contempt and indignation. As a man, I am satisfied that he is a Christian upon the most sincere conviction: as a writer, he would be grossly inconsistent with his political principles, if he dared to attack a religion established by those laws which it seems to be the purpose of his life to defend.——Now for the proofs.——Junius is .ccused of an impious allusion to the holy sacrament, where he says, that " if Lord Weymouth be denied the cup, " there will be no keeping him within the pale of the " ministry." Now, Sir, I affirm, that this passage refers entirely to a ceremonial in the Roman Catholic church, which denies the cup to the laity. It has no manner of relation to the Protestant creed ; and is in this country as fair an object of ridicule as transubstantiation, or any other part of Lord Peter's history in the Tale of a Tub.

But Junius is charged with equal vanity and impiety, in comparing his writings to the holy scripture.—The formal protest he makes against any such comparison avails him nothing. It becomes necessary, then, to show, that the charge destroys itself.—If he be vain, he cannot be impious. A vain man does not usually compare himself to an object which it is his design to undervalue. On the other hand, if he be impious, he cannot be vain ; for his impiety, if any, must consist in his endeavouring to degrade the holy scriptures by a comparison with his own contemptible writings. This would be folly indeed of the grossest nature ; but where lies the vanity ?—I shall now be told,— " Sir, what you say is plausible enough ; but still you must " allow that it is shamefully impudent in Junius to tell " us that his works will live as long as the Bible.' My answer is," Agreed ; but first prove that he has said so." Look at his words, and you will find, that the utmost he expects is, that the Bible and Junius will survive the commentaries of the Jesuits ; which may prove true in a fortnight: The most malignant sagacity cannot show that his works are, in his opinion, to live as long as the Bible. —Suppose I were to foretel, that Jack and Tom would survive Harry—does it follow that Jack must live as long as Tom ? I would only illustrate my meaning and protest against the least idea of profaneness.

Yet this is the way in which Junius is usually answered, arraigned, and convicted. These candid critics never remember any thing he says in honour of our holy religion ; though it is true, that one of his leading arguments is made to rest " upon the internal evidence which the " purest of all religions carries with it." I quote his words ; and conclude from them, that he is a true and hearty Christian, in substance, not in ceremony ; though possibly he may not agree with my reverend lords the bishops, or with the head of the church, " that prayers are " morality ; or that knee.ing is religion."

PHILO JUNIUS.

FROM THE REVEREND MR. HORNE TO JUNIUS.

LETTER LVI.

SIR, Aug. 17. 1771.

I CONGRATULATE you, Sir, on the recovery of your wonted style, though it has cost you a fortnight. I compassionate your labour in the composition of your letters, and will communicate to you the secret of my fluency.——Truth needs no ornament ; and, in my opinion, what she borrows of the pencil is deformity.

You brought a positive charge against me of corruption. I denied the charge, and called for your proofs. You replied with abuse, and re-asserted your charge. I, called again for proofs. You reply again with abuse only, and drop your accusation. In your fortnight's letter there is not one word upon the subject of my corruption.

I have no more to say, but to return thanks to you for your condescension, and to a grateful public and honest ministry for all the favours they have conferred upon me. The two latter, I am sure, will never refuse me any grace I shall solicit; and since you have pleased to acknowledge that you told a deliberate lie in my favour out of bounty, and as a charitable donation, why may I not expect that you will hereafter (if you do not forget you ever mentioned my name with disrespect) make the same acknowledgment for what you have said to my prejudice ?—This second recantation will perhaps be more abhorent from your disposition; but should you decline it, you will only afford one more instance how much easier it is to be generous than just, and that men are sometimes bountiful who are not honest.

At all events, I am as well satisfied with your panegyric as Lord Chatham can be. Monument I shall have none ; but over my grave it will be said, in your own words, " Horne's situation did not correspond with his intentions[e]."

JOHN HORNE.

LETTER LVII.

TO HIS GRACE THE DUKE OF GRAFTON.

MY LORD,   Sept 28. 1771.

THE people of England are not apprised of the full extent of their obligations to you. They have yet no adequate idea of the endless variety of your character. They have seen you distinguished and successful in the continued violation of those moral and political duties by which the little as well as the great societies of life are connected and held together. Every colour, every character became you. With a rate of abilities, which Lord Weymouth very justly looks down upon with contempt, you have done as much mischief to the community as Cromwell would have done, if Cromwell had been a coward; and as much as Machiavel, if Machiavel had not known that an appearance of morals and religion are useful in society.—To a thinking man, the influence of the crown will, in no view, appear so formidable, as when he observes to what enormous excesses it has safely conducted your Grace, without a ray of real understanding, without even the pretensions to common decency or principle of any kind, or a single spark of personal resolution. What must be the operation of that pernicious influence (for which our kings have wisely exchanged the nugatory name of prerogative), that, in the highest stations, can so abundantly supply the absence of virtue, courage, and abilities, and qualify a man to be the minister of a great nation, whom a private gentleman would be ashamed and afraid to admit into his family! Like the universal passport of an ambassador, it supersedes the prohibition of the laws, banishes the staple virtues of the country, and introduces vice and folly triumphantly into all the departments of the state. Other princes, besides his Majesty, have had the means of corruption within their reach; but they have used it with moderation. In former times, corruption was considered as a foreign auxiliary to government, and only called in upon extraordinary emergencies. The unfeigned piety, the sanctified religion, of George the Third, have taught him to new-model the civil forces of the state. The natural resources of the crown are no longer confided in. Corruption glitters in the van;—collects and maintains a standing army of mercenaries, and at the same moment impoverishes and enslaves the country.—His Majesty's predecessors (excepting that worthy family from which you, my Lord, are unquestionably descended) had some generous qualities in their composition, with vices, I confess, or frailties, in abundance. They were kings or gentlemen, not hypocrites or priests. They were at the head of the church, but did not know the value of their office. They said their prayers without ceremony; and had too little priestcraft in their understanding, to reconcile the sanctimonious forms of religion with the utter destruction of the morality of their people.—My Lord, this is fact, not declamation——With all your partiality to the house of Stuart, you must confess, that even Charles the Second would have blushed at that open encouragement, at those eager meretricious caresses with which every species of private vice and public prostitution is received at St. James's.—The unfortunate house of Stuart has been treated with an asperity, which, if comparison be a defence, seems to border upon injustice. Neither Charles nor his brother were qualified to support such a system of measures, as would be necessary to change the government and subvert the constitution of England.—One of them was too much in earnest in his pleasures—the other in his religion. But the danger to this country would cease to be problematical, if the crown should ever descend to a prince, whose apparent simplicity might throw his subjects off their guard,—who might be no libertine in behaviour;—who should have no sense of honour to restrain him,—and who, with just religion enough to impose upon the multitude, might have no scruples of conscience to interfere with his morality. With these honourable qualifications, and the decisive advantage of situation, low craft and falsehood are all the abilities that are wanting to destroy the wisdom of ages, and to deface the noblest monument that human policy has erected. I know such a man;—My Lord, I know you both; and with the blessing of God (for I too am religious), the people of England shall know you as well as I do. I am not very sure that greater abilities would not in effect be an impediment to a design which seems at first sight to require a superior capacity. A better understanding might make 'him sensible of the wonderful beauty of that system he was endeavouring to corrupt. The danger of the attempt might alarm him. The meanness and intrinsic worthlessness of the object (supposing he could attain it), would fill him with shame, repentance, and disgust. But these are sensations which find no entrance into a barbarous contracted heart. In some men, there is a malignant passion to destroy the works of genius, literature, and freedom. The Vandal and the Monk find equal gratification in it.

Reflections like these, my Lord, have a general relation to your grace, and inseparably attend you in whatever company or situation your character occurs to us. They have no immediate connection with the following recent fact, which I lay before the public, for the honour of the best of sovereigns, and for the edification of his people.

A prince (whose piety and self-denial, one would think, might secure him from such a multitude of worldly necessities), with an annual revenue of near a million Sterling, unfortunately wants money.—The navy of England, by an equally strange concurrence of unforeseen circumstances (though not quite so unfortunate for his Majesty), is in equal want of timber. The world knows in what a hopeful condition you delivered the navy to your successor, and in what condition we found it in the moment of distress. You were determined it should continue in the situation in which you left it. It happened, however, very luckily for the privy-purse, that one of the above wants promised fair to supply the other. Our religious, benevolent, generous sovereign, has no objection to selling his own timber to his own admiralty to repair his own ships, nor to putting the money into his own pocket. People of a religious turn naturally adhere to the principles of the church. Whatever they acquire falls into mortmain.—Upon a representation from the admiralty of the extraordinary want of timber for the indispensable repairs of the navy, the surveyor-general was directed to make a survey of the timber in all the royal chases and forests in England. Having obeyed his orders with accuracy and attention, he reported, that the finest timber he had anywhere met with, and the properest in every respect for the purposes of the navy, was in Whittlebury Forest, of which your Grace, I think, is hereditary ranger. In consequence of this report, the usual warrant was prepared at the treasury, and delivered to the surveyor, by which he or his deputy were authorised to cut down any trees in Whittlebury Forest, which should appear to be proper for the purposes above mentioned. The deputy, being informed that the warrant was signed and delivered to his principal in London, crosses the country to Northamptonshire, and, with an officious zeal for the public service, begins to do his duty in the forest. Unfortunately for him, he had not the warrant in his pocket. The oversight was enormous; and you have punished him for it accordingly. You have insisted, that an active, useful officer should be dismissed from his place. You have ruined an innocent man and his family.—In what language shall I address so black, so cowardly, a tyrant;—thou worse than one of the Brunswicks, and all the Stuarts!—To them who know Lord North, it is unnecessary to say, that he was mean and base enough to submit to you.—This, however, is but a small part of the fact. After ruining the surveyor's deputy for acting without the warrant, you attacked the warrant itself. You declared that it was illegal; and swore, in a fit of foaming frantic passion, that it never should be executed. You asserted upon your honour, that in the grant of the rangership of Whittlebury Forest, made by Charles the Second (whom, with a modesty that would do honour to Mr. Rigby you are pleased to call your ancestor), to one of his bastards (from whom I make no doubt of your descent), the property of the timber is vested in the ranger.—I have examined the original grant; and now, in the face of the public, contradict you directly upon the fact. The very reverse of what you have asserted upon your honour is the truth. The grant, " expressly, and by a particular clause," reserves the property of the timber for the use of the crown.—In spite of this evidence, in defiance of the representations of the admiralty,—in perfect mockery of the notorious distresses of the English navy, and those equally pressing and almost equally notorious necessities of your pious sovereign,—here the matter rests. The lords of the treasury recal their warrant; the deputy-surveyor is ruin-

ed for doing his duty;—Mr. John Pitt (whose name I
suppose is offensive to you) submits to be brow-beaten and
insulted;—the oaks keep their ground;—the king is de-
frauded, and the navy of England may perish for want of
the best and finest timber in the island. And all this is
submitted to—to applease the Duke of Grafton!—to gratify the man who has involved the king and his kingdom
in confusion and distress, and who, like a treacherous
coward, deserted his sovereign in the midst of it!

There has been a strange alteration in your doctrines,
since you thought it advisable to rob the Duke of Portland of his property, in order to strengthen the interest
of Lord Bute's son-in-law before the last genesal election.
Nullum tempus occurrit regi, was then your boasted motto,
the cry of all your hungry partizans. Now, it seems, a
grant of Charles the Second to one of his bastards is to
be held sacred and inviolable! It must not be questioned
by the King's servants, nor submitted to any interpretation
but your own.—My Lord, this was not the language you
held, when it suited you to insult the memory of the
glorious deliverer of England from that detested family,
to which you are still more nearly allied in principle than
in blood.—In the name of decency and common sense,
what are your Grace's merits, either with King or ministry, that should entitle you to asssume this domineering
authority over both?—Is it the fortunate consanguinity
you claim with the house of Stuart?—Is it the secret
correspondence you have for so many years carried on
with Lord Bute, by the assiduous assistance of your
cream-coloured parasite?—Could not your gallantry find
sufficient employment for him in those gentle offices by
which he first acquired the tender friendship of Lord
Barrington?—Or is it only that wonderful sympathy of
manners which subsists between your Grace and one of
your superiors, and does so much honour to you both?—
Is the union of Blifil and Black George no longer a ro-
mance?—From whatever origin your influence in this
country arises, it is a phenomenon in the history of human virtue and understanding.—Good men can hardly
believe the fact. Wise men are unable to account for it.
Religious men find exercise for their faith, and make it

the last effort of their piety, not to repine against Providence.

JUNIUS.

LETTER LVIII.

GENTLEMEN,   Sept. 30. 1771.

IF you alone were concerned in the event of the present election of a chief magistrate of the metropolis, it would be the highest presumption in a stranger to attempt to influence your choice, or even to offer you his opinion. But the situation of public affairs has annexed an extraordinary importance to your resolutions. You cannot, in the choice of your magistrate, determine for yourselves only. You are going to determine upon a point in which every member of the community is interested. I will not scruple to say, that the very being of that law, of that right, of that constitution, for which we have been so long contending, is now at stake. They who would ensnare your judgment, tell you, it is a common, ordinary case, and to be decided by ordinary precedent and practice. They artfully conclude from moderate peaceable times, to times which are not moderate, and which ought not to be peaceable—While they solicit your favour, they insist upon a rule of rotation which excludes all idea of election.

Let me be honoured with a few minutes of your attention.—The question, to those who mean fairly to the liberty of the people (which we all profess to have in view), lies within a very narrow compass. Do you mean to desert that just and honourable system of measures which you have hitherto pursued, in hopes of obtaining from parliament, or from the crown, a full redress of past grivances, and a security for the future!—Do you think the cause desperate, and will you declare that you think so to the whole people of England? If this be your meaning and opinion, you will act consistently with it in choosing Mr. Nash.—I profess to be unacquainted with his private character. But he has acted as a magistrate, —as a public man.—As such I speak of him.—I see his name in a protest against one of your remonstrances to the crown.—He has done every thing in his power to destroy the freedom of popular elections in the city, by publishing the poll upon a former occasion; and I know in general, that he has distinguished himself, by slighting and thwarting all those public measures which you have engaged in with the greatest warmth, and hitherto thought most worthy of your approbation.—From his past conduct, what conclusion will you draw, but that he will act the same part as Lord Mayor which he has invariably acted as Alderman and Sheriff; He cannot alter his conduct without confessing that he never acted upon principle of any kind.—I should be sorry to injure the character of a man, who perhaps may be honest in his intention, by supposing it possible that he can ever concur with you in any political measure or opinion.

If, on the other hand, you mean to persevere in those resolutions for the public good, which, though not always successful, are always honourable, your choice will naturally incline to those men who (whatever they be in other respects) are most likely to co-operate with you in the great purposes which you are determined not to relinquish.—The question is not of what metal your instruments are made ; but " whether they are adapted to the " work you have in hand?" The honours of the city, in these times, are improperly, because exclusively, called a reward. You mean not merely to pay, but to employ.—Are Mr. Crosby and Mr. Sawbridge likely to execute the extraordinary as well as the ordinary duties of Lord Mayor?—Will they grant you common-halls when it shall be necessary ?—Will they go up with remonstrances to the King ?—Have they firmness enough to meet the fury of a venal House of Commons?—Have they fortitude enough not to shrink at imprisonment ?—Have they spirit enough to hazard their lives and fortunes in a contest, if it should be necessary, with a prostituted legislature ?—If these questions can fairly be answered in the affirmative, your choice is made. Forgive this passionate language.—I am unable to correct it.—The subject comes home to us all.—It is the language of my heart.

JUNIUS.

LETTER LIX.

TO THE PRINTER OF THE PUBLIC ADVERTISER,

SIR,   Oct. 1. 1771.

No man laments more sincerely than I do, the unhappy differences which have arisen among the friends of the people, and divided them from each other. The cause undoubtedly suffers as well by the diminution of that strength which union carries along with it, as by the separate loss of personal reputation which every man sustains when his character and conduct are frequently held forth in odious or contemptible colours.——These differences are only advantageous to the common enemy of the country.—The hearty friends of the cause are provoked and disgusted.—The lukewarm advocate avails himself of any pretence to relapse into that indolent indifference about every thing that ought to interest an Englishman, so unjustly dignified with the title of moderation.——The false, insidious partizan, who creates or foments the disorder, sees the fruit of his dishonest industry ripen beyond his hopes, and rejoices in the promises of a banquet, only delicious to such an appetite as his own.—It is time for those who really mean well to the Cause and the People, who have no view to private advantage, and who have virtue enough to prefer the general good of the community to the gratification of personal animosities—it is time for such men to interpose.—Let us try whether these fatal dissentions may not yet be reconciled; or, if that be impracticable, let us guard at least against the worst effects of division, and endeavour to persuade these furious partizans, if they will not consent to draw together, to be separately useful to that cause which they all pretend to be attached to.—Honour and honesty must not be renounced, although a thousand modes of right and wrong were to occupy the degrees of morality between Zeno and Epicurus. The fundamental principles of Christianity may still be preserved, though every zealous sectary adheres to his own exclusive doctrine, and pious ecclesiastics make it part of their religion to persecute one another.——The civil constitution too, that legal liberty, that general creed which every Englishman

professes, may still be supported, though Wilkes, and
Horne, and Townsend, and Sawbridge, should obstinately refuse to communicate; and even if the fathers of the
church, if Saville, Richmond, Camden, Rockingham, and
Chatham, should disagree in the ceremonies of their political worship, and even in the interpretation of twenty
texts in Magna Charta.—I speak to the people as one of
the people.—Let us employ these men in whatever departments their various abilities are best suited to, and as
much to the advantage of the common cause as their different inclinations will permit. They cannot serve us,
without essentially serving themselves.

If Mr. Nash be elected, he will hardly venture, after
so recent a mark of the personal esteem of his fellow-
citizens, to declare himself immediately a courtier. The
spirit and activity of the Sheriffs, will, I hope, be sufficient to counteract any sinister intentions of the Lord
Mayor. In collision with their virtue, perhaps he may
take fire.

It is not necessary to exact from Mr. Wilkes the virtues of a Stoic. They were inconsistent with themselves,
who, almost at the same moment, represented him as the
basest of mankind, yet seemed to expect from him such
instances of fortitude and self-denial as would do honour
to an apostle. It is not, however, flattery to say, that he
is obstinate, intrepid, and fertile in expedients. That he
has no possible resource, but in the public favour, is, in
my judgment, a considerable recommendation of him. I
wish that every man, who pretended to popularity, were
in the same predicament. I wish that a retreat to St.
James's were not so easy and open, as patriots have found
it. To Mr. Wilkes there is no access. However he may
be misled by passion or imprudence, I think he cannot be
guilty of a deliberate treachery to the public. The favour
of his country constitutes the shield which defends him
against a thousand daggers. Desertion would disarm him.

I can more readily admire the liberal spirit and integrity, than the sound judgment of any man, who prefers
a republican form of government, in this or any other
empire of equal extent, to a monarchy so qualified and
limited as ours. I am convinced, that neither is it in
theory the wisest system of government, nor practicable

in this country. Yet, though I hope the English constitution will for ever preserve its original monarchical form, I would have the manners of the people purely and strictly republican. I do not mean the licentious spirit of anarchy and riot. I mean a general attachment to the common weal, distinct from any partial attachment to persons or families; an implicit submission to the laws only, and an affection to the magistrate, proportioned to the integrity and wisdom with which he distributes justice to his people, and administers their affairs. The present habit of our political body appears to me the very reverse of what it ought to be. The form of the constitution leans rather more than enough to the popular branch; while, in effect, the manners of the people (of those at least who are likely to take a lead in the country) incline too generally to a dependence upon the crown. The real friends of arbitrary power combine the facts, and are not inconsistent with their principles when they strenuously support the unwarrantable privileges assumed by the House of Commons. In these circumstances, it were much to be desired, that we had many such men as Mr. Sawbridge to represent us in parliament. I speak from common report and opinion only, when I impute to him a speculative predilection in favour of a republic. In the personal conduct and manners of the man, I cannot be mistaken. He has shown himself possessed of that republican firmness which the times require, and by which an English gentlemen may be as usefully and as honourably distinguished as any citizen of ancient Rome, of Athens, or Lacedæmon.

Mr. Townsend complains, that the public gratitude has not been answerable to his deserts. It is not difficult to trace the artifices which have suggested to him a language so unworthy of his understanding. A great man commands the affections of the people. A prudent man does not complain when he has lost them. Yet they are far from being lost to Mr. Townsend. He has treated our opinion a little too cavalierly. A young man is apt to rely too confidently upon himself, to be as attentive to his mistress as a polite and passionate lover ought to be. Perhaps he found her at first too easy a conquest. Yet I fancy she will be ready to receive him whenever he thinks proper to renew his addresses. With all his youth, his spirit, and his appearance, it would be indecent in the lady to solicit his return.

I have too much respect for the abilities of Mr. Horne, to flatter myself that these gentlemen will ever be cordially reunited. It is not, however, unreasonable to expect that each of them should act his separate part with honour and integrity to the public. As for the differences of opinion upon speculative questions, if we wait until they are reconciled, the action of human affairs must be suspended for ever. But neither are we to look for perfection in any one man, nor for agreement among many. When Lord Chatham affirms, that the authority of the British legislature is not supreme over the colonies, in the same sense in which it is supreme over Great Britain; —When Lord Camden supposes a necessity, (which the King is to judge of); and, founded upon that necessity, attributes to the crown a legal power (not given by the act itself) to suspend the operation of an act of the legislature—I listen to them both with diffidence and respect, but without the smallest degree of conviction or assent. Yet, I doubt not, they delivered their real sentiments; nor ought they to be hastily condemned. I too have a claim to the candid interpretation of my country, when I acknowledge an involuntary, compulsive assent to one very unpopular opinion. I lament the unhappy necessity, whenever it arises, of providing for the safety of the state, by a temporary invasion of the personal liberty of the subject. Would to God it were practicable to reconcile these important objects, in every possible situation of public affairs!—I regard the legal liberty of the meanest man in Britain as much as my own, and would defend it with the same zeal. I know we must stand or fall together. But I can never doubt, that the community has a right to command, as well as to purchase, the service of its members. I see that right founded originally upon a necessity, which supersedes all argument. I see it established by usage immemorial, and admitted by more than a tacit assent of the legislature. I conclude there is no remedy, in the nature of things, for the grievance complained of; for, if there were, it must long since have been redressed. Though numberless opportunities have presented themselves highly favourable to public liberty, no successful attempt has ever been made for the relief of the subject in this article. Yet it has been felt and complained of, ever since England had a navy. The conditions which constitute this right must be taken together. Separately they have little weight. It is not fair to argue, from any abuse in the execution, to the legality of the power; much less is a conclusion to be drawn from the navy to the land service. A seaman can never be employed but against the enemies of his country. The only case in which the King can have a right to arm his subjects in general, is that of a foreign force being actually landed upon our coast. Whenever that case happens, no true Englishman will inquire whether the King's right to compel him to defend his country, be the custom of England, or a grant of the legislature. With regard to the press for seamen, it does not follow that the symptoms may not be softened, although the distemper cannot be cured. Let bounties be increased as far as the public purse can support them. Still they have a limit; and when every reasonable expence is incurred, it will be found, in fact, that the spur of the press is wanted to give operation to the bounty.

Upon the whole, I never had a doubt about the strict right of pressing, until I heard that Lord Mansfield had applauded Lord Chatham for delivering something like this doctrine in the House of Lords. That consideration staggered me not a little. But, upon reflection, his conduct accounts naturally for itself. He knew the doctrine was unpopular, and was eager to fix it upon the man who is the first object of his fear and detestation. The cunning Scotchman never speaks truth without a fraudulent design. In council, he generally affects to take a moderate part. Besides his natural timidity, it makes part of his political plan, never to be known to recommend violent measures. When the guards are called forth to murder their fellow subjects, it is not by the ostensible advice of Lord Mansfield. That odious office, his prudence tells him, is better left to such men as Gower and Weymouth, as Barrington and Grafton. Lord Hillsborough wisely confines his firmness to the distant Americans. The designs of Mansfield are more subtle, more effectual, and secure- Who attacks the liberty of the press?—Lord. Mansfield.—Who invades the constitutional power of juries?—Lord Mansfield.—What judge ever challenged a juryman, but Lord Mansfield?—Who was that judge, who, to save the King's Brother, affirmed that a man of the first rank and quality, who obtained a verdict in a suit for criminal conversation, is entitled to no greater damages than the meanest mechanic?—Lord Mansfield.—Who is it makes commissioners of the great seal?—Lord Mansfield.—Who is it forms a decree for those commissioners, deciding against Lord Chatham, and afterwards (finding himself opposed by the judges) declares in parliament, that he never had a doubt that the law was in direct opposition to that decree?—Lord Mansfield.—Who is he that has made it the study and practice of his life, to undermine and alter the whole system of jurisprudence in the Court of King's Bench?—Lord Mansfield. There never existed a man but himself, who answered exactly to so complicated a description. Compared to these enormities, his original attachment to the Pretender (to whom his dearest brother was confidential secretary) is a virtue of the first magnitude. But the hour of impeachment will come, and neither he nor Grafton shall escape me. Now let them make common cause against England and the House of Hanover. A Stuart and a Murray should sympathise with each other.

When I refer to signal instances of unpopular opinions delivered and maintained by men who may well be supposed to have no view but the public good, I do not mean to renew the discussion of such opinions. I should be sorry to revive the dormant questions of Stamp-act, Cornbill, or Press-warrant. I mean only to illustrate one useful proposition, which it is the intention of this paper to inculcate;—" That we should not generally reject the " friendship or services of any man because he differs " from us in a particular opinion." This will not appear a superfluous caution, if we observe the ordinary conduct of mankind. In public affairs there is the least chance of a perfect concurrence of sentiment or inclination. Yet every man is able to contribute something to the common stock; and no man's contribution should be rejected. If individuals have no virtues, their vices may be of use to us. I care not with what principle the new-born patriot is animated, if the measures he supports are beneficial to the community. The nation is interested in his conduct. His motives are his own. The properties of a patriot are perishable in the individual; but there is a quick succession of subjects, and the breed is worth pre-serving. The spirit of the Americans may be an useful example to us. Our dogs and horses are only English upon English ground; but patriotism, it seems, may be improved by transplanting. I will not reject a bill which tends to confine parliamentary privilege within reasonable bounds, though it should be stolen from the house of Ca-vendish, and introduced by Mr. Onslow. The features of the infant are a proof of the descent, and vindicate the noble birth from the baseness of the adoption. I willing-ly accept of a sarcasm from Colonel Barre, or a simile from Mr. Burke. Even the silent vote of Mr. Calcraft is worth reckoning in a division. What though he riots in the plunder of the army, and has only determined to be a patriot when he could not be a peer?—Let us profit by the assistance of such men while they are with us, and place them, if it be possible, in the post of danger, to pre-vent desertion. The wary Wedderburne, the pompous Suffolk, never threw away the scabbard, nor ever went upon a forlorn hope. They always treated the King's ser-vants as men with whom, some time or other, they might possibly be in friendship. When a man who stands forth for the public has gone that length from which there is no practicable retreat,—when he has given that kind of personal offence which a pious monarch never pardons, I then begin to think him in earnest, and that he never will have occasion to solicit the forgiveness of his country. But instances of a determination so entire and unreserved are rarely met with. Let us take mankind as they are. Let us distribute the virtues and abilities of individuals according to the offices they affect; and, when they quit the service, let us endeavour to supply their places with better men than we have lost. In this country, there are always candidates enough for popular favour. The temple of fame is the shortest passage to riches and preferment.

Above all things, let me guard my countrymen against the meaness and folly of accepting of a trifling or moderate compensation for extraordinary and essential injuries. Our enemies treat us as the cunning trader does the unskilful Indian. They magnify their generosity, when they give us baubles of little proportionate value, for ivory and gold. The same House of Commons, who robbed the constituent body of their right of free election; who presumed to make a law, under pretence of declaring it; who paid our good King's debts, without once inquiring how they were incurred; who gave thanks for repeated murders committed at home, and for national infamy incurred abroad; who screened Lord Mansfield; who imprisoned the magistrates of the metropolis for asserting the subject's right to the protection of the laws; who erased a judicial record, and ordered all proceedings in a criminal suit to be suspended;—This very House of Commons have graciously consented, that their own members may be compelled to pay their debts, and that contested elections shall for the future be determined with some decent regard to the merits of the case. The event of the suit is of no consequence to the crown. While parliaments are septennial, the purchase of the sitting member or of the petitioner makes but the difference of a day.—Concessions, such as these are of little moment to the sum of things; unless it be to prove that the worst of men are sensible of the injuries they have done us, and perhaps to demonstrate to us the imminent danger of our situation. In the shipwreck of the state, trifles float and are preserved; while every thing solid and valuable sinks to the bottom, and is lost for ever.

- JUNIUS.

LETTER LX.

SIR,   Oct. 15. 1771.

I AM convinced that Junius is incapable of wilfully misrepresenting any man's opinion, and that his inclination leads him to treat Lord Camden with particular candour and respect. The doctrine attributed to him by Junius, as far as it goes, corresponds with that stated by your correspondent Scævola, who seems to make a distinction without a difference. Lord Camden, it is agreed, did certainly maintain, that, in the recess of parliament, the King (by which we all mean the king in council, or the executive power) might suspend the operation of an act of the legislature ; and he founded his doctrine upon a supposed necessity, of which the King, in the first instance, must be judge. The Lords and Commons cannot be judges of it in the first instance, for they do not exist.— Thus far Junius.

But, says Scævola, Lord Camden made parliament and not the King, judges of the necessity.—That parliament may review the acts of ministers, is unquestionable; but there is a wide difference between saying that the crown has a legal power, and that ministers may act at their peril. When we say that an act is illegal, we mean that it is forbidden by a joint resolution of the three estates. How a subsequent resolution of two of those branches can make it legal *ab initio*, will require explanation. If it could, the consequence would be truly dreadful, especially in these times. There is no act of arbitrary power which the King might not attribute to necessity, and for which he would not be secure of obtaining the approbation of his prostituted Lords and Commons. If Lord Camden admits that the subsequent sanction of parliament was necessary to make the proclamation legal, why did he so obstinately oppose the bill which was soon after brought in for indemnifying all those persons who had acted under it?—If that bill had not been passed, I am ready to maintain, in direct contradiction to Lord Camden's doctrine (taken as Scævola states it), that a litigious exporter of corn, who had suffered in his property in consequence of the proclamation, might have laid his action against the custom-house officers, and would infallibly have recovered damages. No jury could refuse them ; and if I, who am by no means litigious, had been so injured, I would assuredly, have instituted a suit in Westminster-hall, on purpose to try the question of right. I would have done it upon a principle of defiance of the pretended power of either, or both houses to make declarations inconsistent with law ; and I have no doubt that, with an act of parliament on my side, I should have been too strong for them all. This is the way in which an

Englishman should speak and act; and not suffer dangerous precedents to be established; because the circumstances are favourable or palliating.

With regard to Lord Camden, the truth is, that he inadvertently overshot himself, as appears plainly by that unguarded mention of a tyranny of forty days, which I myself heard. Instead of asserting that the proclamation was legal, he should have said, "My Lords, I know the " proclamation was illegal; but I advised it because it " was indispensably necessary to save the kingdom from " famine; and I submit myself to the justice and mercy " of my country."

Such language as this would have been manly, rational, and consistent;—not unfit for a lawyer, and every way worthy of a great man.

PHILO JUNIUS.

P. S. If Scævola should think proper to write again upon this subject, I beg of him to give me a direct answer, that is, a plain affirmative or negative, to the following questions :—In the interval between the publishing such a proclamation (or order of council) as that in question, and its receiving the sanction of the two Houses, of what nature is it?—is it legal or illegal? or is it neither one nor the other?—I mean to be candid, and will point out to him the consequence of his answer either way. If it be legal, it wants no farther sanction; if it be illegal, the subject is not bound to obey it; consequently it is a useless nugatory act, even as to its declared purpose. Before the meeting of parliament, the whole mischief, which it means to prevent, will have been completed.

LETTER LXI.

TO ZENO.

SIR,   Oct. 17. 1771.

THE sophistry of your letter in defence of Lord Mansfield, is adapted to the character you defend. But Lord Mansfield is a man of form, and seldom in his behaviour transgresses the rules of decorum. I shall imitate his Lordship's good manners; and leave you in full posses-sion of his principles. I will not call you liar, jesuit, or villain; but with all the politeness, imaginable, perhaps I may prove you so.

Like other fair pleaders in Lord Mansfield's school of justice, you answer Junius by misquoting his words, and misstating his propositions. If I am candid enough to admit that this is the very logic taught at St. Omer's, you will readily allow that it is the constant practice in the Court of King's Bench.—Junius does not say, that he never had a doubt about the strict right of pressing, " till " he knew Lord Mansfield was of the same opinion."— His words are, " Until he heard that Lord Mansfield had " applauded Lord Chatham for maintaining that doc- " trine in the House of Lords." It was not the accidental concurrence of Lord Mansfield's opinion, but the suspici-ous applause given by a cunning Scotchman to the man he detests, that raised and justified a doubt in the mind of Junius. The question is not, whether Lord Mansfield be a man of learning and abilities (which Junius has never disputed); but, whether or no he abuses and misapplies his talents?

Junius did not say that Lord Mansfield had advised the calling out the guards. On the contrary, his plain meaning is, that he left that odious office to men less cunning than himself.—Whether Lord Mansfield's doctrine con-cerning libels be or be not an attack upon the liberty of the press, is a question which the public in general are very well able to determine. I shall not enter into it at present. Nor do I think it necessary to say much to a man, who had the daring confidence to say to a jury, " Gentlemen, you are to bring in a verdict guilty or not " guilty; but whether the defendant be guilty or inno- " cent, is not matter for your consideration." Clothe it, in what language you will, this is the sum total of Lord Mansfield's doctrine. If not, let Zeno show us the dif-ference.

But it seems, " the liberty of the press may be abused, " and the abuse of a valuable privilege is the certain means " to lose it." The first I admit:—but let the abuse be submitted to a Jury; a sufficient, and indeed the only le-gal and constitutional check upon the licence of the press,

The second I flatly deny. In direct contradiction to Lord Mansfield, I affirm, "that the abuse of a valuable privi-"lege is not the certain means to lose it." If it were, the English nation would have few privileges left; for where is the privilege that has not, at one time or other, been abused by individuals. But it is false in reason and equity, that particular abuses should produce a general forfeiture. Shall the community be deprived of the protection of the laws, because there are robbers and murderers?—Shall the community be punished, because individuals have offended? Lord Mansfield says so, consistently enough with his principles; but I wonder to find him so explicit. Yet for one concession, however extorted, I confess myself obliged to him.—The liberty of the press is, after all, a valuable privilege. I agree with him most heartily, and will defend it against him.

You ask me, What juryman was challenged by Lord Mansfield? I tell you his name is Benson. When his name was called, Lord Mansfield ordered the clerk to pass him by. As for his reasons, you may ask himself, for he assigned none; but I can tell you what all men thought of it. This Benson had been refractory upon a former jury, and would not accept of the law as delivered by Lord Mansfield; but had the impudence to pretend to think for himself.—But you, it seems, honest Zeno, know nothing of the matter. You never read Junius's letter to your patron! You never heard of the intended instructions from the city to impeach Lord Mansfield! You never heard by what dexterity of Mr. Patterson that measure was prevented! How wonderfully ill some people are informed.

Junius did never affirm, that the crime of seducing the wife of a mechanic or a peer, is not the same, taken in a moral or religious view. What he affirmed, in contradiction to the levelling principle so lately adopted by Lord Mansfield, was, " that the damages should be proportion-" ed to the rank and fortune of the parties;" and for this plain reason (admitted by every other judge that ever sat in Westminster-hall), because, what is a compensation or penalty to one man, is none to another. The sophistical distinction you attempt to draw between the person injured, and the person injuring, is Mansfield all over. If you can once establish the proposition, that the injured party is not entitled to receive large damages, it follows pretty plainly, that the party injuring should not be compelled to pay them ; consequectly the King's brother is effectually screened by Lord Mansfield's doctrine. Your reference to Nathan and David come naturally in aid of your patron's professed system of jurisprudence. He is fond of introducing into the Court of King's Bench any law that contradicts or excludes the common law of England ; whether it be canon, civil, *jus gentium*, or Levitical. But, Sir, the Bible is the code of our religious faith, not of our municipal jurisprudence ; and though it was the pleasure of God to inflict a particular punishment upon David's crime (taken as a breach of the divine commands), and to send his prophet to denounce it, an English jury have nothing to do either with David or the prophet. They consider the crime only as it is a breach of order, an injury to an individual, and an offence to society ; and they judge of it by certain positive rules of law, or by the practice of their ancestors. Upon the whole, the man "after God's own heart" is much indebted to you for comparing him to the Duke of Cumberland: That his Royal Highness may be the man after Lord Mansfield's own heart, seems much more probable ; and you, I think, Mr. Zeno, might succeed tolerably well in the character of Nathan. The evil deity, the prophet, and the royal sinner, would be very proper company for one another.

You say Lord Mansfield did not make the commissioners of the Great Seal, and that he only advised the King to appoint. I believe Junius meant no more : and the distinction is hardly worth disputing.

You say he did not deliver an opinion upon Lord Chatham's appeal. I affirm that he did, directly in favour of the appeal.—This is a point of fact, to be determined by evidence only. But you assign no reason for his supposed silence; nor for his desiring a conference with the judges the day before. Was not all Westminster-hall convinced that he did it with a view to puzzle them with some perplexing question, and in hopes of bringing some of them over to him?—You say the commissioners "were "very capable of framing a decree for themselves." By the fact, it only appears, that they were capable of fraing an illegal one; which I apprehend, is not much to the credit either of their learning or integrity.

We are both agreed, that Lord Mansfield has incessantly laboured to introduce new modes of proceeding in the court where he presides; but you attribute it to an honest zeal in behalf of innocence oppressed by quibble and chicane. I say, that he has introduced new law too, and removed the land-marks established by former decisions. I say, that his view is to change a court of common law into a court of equity, and to bring every thing within the *arbitrium* of a prætorian court. The public must determine between us. But now for his merits. *First* then, the establishment of the judges in their places for life (which you tell us was advised by Lord Mansfield), was a concession merely to catch the people. It bore the appearance of royal bounty, but had nothing real in it. The judges were already for life, excepting in the case of a demise. Your boasted bill only provides, that it shall not be in the power of the King's successor to remove them. At the best, therefore, it is only a legacy, not a gift, on the part of his present majesty, since for himself he gives up nothing. —That he did oppose Lord Camden and Lord Northington upon the proclamation against the exportation of corn, is most true, and with great ability. With his talents, and taking the right side of so clear a question, it was impossible to speak ill.—His motives are not so easily penetrated. They who are acquainted with the state of politics at that period, will judge of them somewhat differently from Zeno. Of the popular bills, which you say he supported in the House of Lords, the most material is unquestionably that of Mr. Grenville, for deciding contested elections. But I should be glad to know upon what possible pretence any member of the Upper House could oppose such a bill, after it had passed the House of Commons?—I do not pretend to know what share he had in promoting the other two bills; but I am ready to give him all the credit you desire. Still you will find, that a whole life of deliberate iniquity is ill atoned for, by doing now and then a laudable action upon a mixed or doubtful principle.—If it be unworthy of him, thus ungratefully treated, to labour any longer for the public, in God's name let him retire. His brother's patron (whose health he once was anxious for) is dead; but the son of that unfortunate prince survives, and, I dare say, will be ready to receive him.

PHILO JUNIUS.

LETTER LXII.

TO AN ADVOCATE IN THE CAUSE OF THE PEOPLE.

SIR,   Oct. 18. 1771.

You do not treat Junius fairly. You would not have condemned him so hastily, if you had ever read Judge Foster's argument upon the legality of pressing seamen. A man who has not read that argument, is not qualified to speak accurately upon the subject. In answer to strong facts and fair reasoning, you produce nothing but a vague comparison between two things which have little or no resemblance to each other. General warrants, it is true, had been often issued; but they had never been regularly questioned or resisted until the case of Mr. Wilkes. He brought them to trial; and the moment they were tried, they were declared illegal. This is not the case of press warrants. They have been complained of, questioned, and resisted in a thousand instances; but still the legislature have never interposed, nor has there ever been a formal decision against them in any of the superior courts. On the contrary, they have been frequently recognized and admitted by parliament; and there are judicial opinions given in their favour by judges of the first character. Under the various circumstances stated by Junius, he has a right to conclude for himself, that there is no remedy. If you have a good one to propose, you may depend upon the assistance and applause of Junius. The magistrate who guards the liberty of the individual, deserves to be commended. But let him remember, that it is also his duty to provide for, or at least not to hazard, the safety of the community. If, in the case of a foreign war, and the expectation of an invasion, you would rather keep your fleet in harbour, than man it by pressing seamen who refuse the bounty, I have done.

You talk of disbanding the army with wonderful ease

U

and indifference. If a wiser man held such language, I should be apt to suspect his sincerity.

As for keeping up a much greater number of seamen in time of peace, it is not to be done. You will oppress the merchant, you will distress trade, and destroy the nursery of your seamen. He must be a miserable statesman, who voluntarily by the same act increases the public expence, and lessens the means of supporting it.

PHILO JUNIUS.

LETTER LXIII.

Oct. 22. 1771.

A FRIEND of Junius desires it may be observed, (in answer to A Barrister at law),

1*mo*, That the fact of Lord Mansfield's having ordered a juryman to be passed by (which poor Zeno never heard of) is now formally admitted.

When Mr. Benson's name was called, Lord Mansfield was observed to flush in the face (a signal of guilt not uncommon with him), and cried out, "Pass him by." This I take to be something more than a peremptory challenge. It is an unlawful command, without any reason assigned. That the counsel did not resist, is true; but this might happen either from inadvertence, or a criminal complaisance to Lord Mansfield. You barristers are too apt to be civil to my Lord Chief Justice, at the expence of your clients.

2*do*, Junius did never say that Lord Mansfield had destroyed the liberty of the press. "That his Lordship has " laboured to destroy,—that his doctrine is an attack upon " the liberty of the press,—that it is an invasion of the " right of juries," are the propositions maintained by Junius. His opponents never answer him in point, for they never meet him fairly upon his own ground.

S*tio*, Lord Mansfield's policy, in endeavouring to screen his unconstitutional doctrines behind an act of the legislature, is easily understood.—Let every Englishman stand upon his guard;—the right of juries to return a general verdict, in all cases whatever, is a part of our constitution. *It stands in no need of a bill, either enacting or declaratory, to confirm it.

4*to*, With regard to the Grosvenor cause, it is pleasant to observe, that the doctrine, attributed by Junius to Lord Mansfield, is admitted by Zeno and directly defended. The barrister has not the assurance to deny it flatly; but he evades the charge, and softens the doctrine by such poor contemptible quibbles, as cannot impose upon the meanest understanding.

5*to*,. The quantity of business in the Court of King's Bench proves nothing but the litigious spirit of the people, arising from the great increase of wealth and commerce. These, however, are now upon the decline, and will soon leave nothing but law-suits behind them. When Junius affirms that Lord Mansfield has laboured to alter the system of jurisprudence in the court where his Lordship presides, he speaks to those who are able to look a little farther than the vulgar. Besides, that the multitude are easily deceived by the imposing names of equity and substantial justice, it does not follow that a judge who introduces into his court new modes of proceeding, and new principles of law, intends, in every instance, to decide unjustly. Why should he, where he has no interest!—We say that Lord Mansfield is a bad man, and a worse judge;—but we do not say that he is a mere devil. Our adversaries would fain reduce us to the difficulty of proving too much.—This artifice, however, shall not avail him. The truth of the matter is plainly this. When Lord Mansfield has succeeded in his scheme of changing a court of common law to a court of equity, he will have it in his power to do injustice, whenever he thinks proper. This, though a wicked purpose, is neither absurd nor unattainable.

6*to*, The last paragraph, relative to Lord Chatham's cause cannot be answered. It partly refers to facts of too secret a nature to be ascertained, and partly is unintelligible. " Upon one point, the cause is decided against Lord Chat-" ham.—Upon another point, it is decided for him."——Both the law and the language are well suited to a barrister!—If I have any guess at this honest gentleman's meaning, it is, that, " whereas the commissioners of the great " seal saw the question in a point of view unfavourable " to Lord Chatham, and decreed accordingly,—Lord

"Mansfield, out of sheer love and kindness to Lord Chat-
"ham, took the pains to place it in a point of view more
"favourable to the appellant.—*Credat Judæus Appella.*
So curious an assertion would stagger the faith of Mr. Sylva.

=========================

LETTER LXIV.

Nov. 2. 1771.

We are desired to make the following declaration, in behalf of Junius, upon three material points, on
which his opinion has been mistaken or misrepresented.

1mo, Junius considers the right of taxing the colonies,
by an act of the British legislature, as a speculative right
merely, never to be exerted, nor ever to be renounced.
To his judgement, it appears plain, " That the general
" reasonings which were employed against that power,
" went directly to our whole legislative right, and that one
" part of it could not be yielded to such arguments, with-
" out a virtual surrender of all the rest."

2do, That, with regard to press-warrants, his argument should be taken in his own words, and answered
strictly ;—that comparisons may sometimes illustrate, but
prove nothing ;—and that, in this case, an appeal to the
passions is unfair and unnecessary. Junius feels and acknowledges the evil in the most express terms, and will
show himself ready to concur in any rational plan that
may provide for the liberty of the individual, without hazarding the safety of the community. At the same time,
he expects that the evil, such as it is, be not exaggerated
or misrepresented. In general, it is not unjust, that, when
the rich man contributes his wealth, the poor man should
serve the state in person ;—otherwise the latter contributes nothing to the defence of that law and constitution
from which he demands safety and protection. But the
question does not lie between rich and poor. The laws
of England make no such distinctions. Neither is it true
that the poor man is torn from the care and support of a
wife and family, helpless without him. The single question is, Whether the seaman[f], in times of public danger, shall serve the merchant or the state, in that profession to which he was bred, and by the exercise of which

alone, he can honestly support himself and his family?—
General arguments against the doctrine of necessity, and
the dangerous use that may be made of it, are of no
weight in this particular case. Necessity includes the idea
of inevitable. Whenever it is so, it creates a law to
which all positive laws and all positive rights must give
way. In this sense, the levy of ship-money by the King's
warrant, was not necessary, because the business might
have been as well or better done by parliament. If the
doctrine maintained by Junius be confined within this limitation, it will go but very little way in support of arbitrary power. That the King is to judge of the occasion, is no objection, unless we are told how it can possibly be otherwise. There are other instances, not less important in the exercise, nor less dangerous in the abuse,
in which the constitution relies entirely upon the King's
judgment. The executive power proclaims war and peace,
binds the nation by treaties, orders general embargoes,
and imposes quarantines; not to mention a multitude of
prerogative writs, which, though liable to the greatest
abuses, were never disputed.

3tio, It has been urged as a reproach to Junius, that he
has not delivered an opinion upon the game laws, and
particularly the late dog act. But Junius thinks he has
much greater reason to complain, that he is never assisted by those who are able to assist him; and that almost
the whole labour of the press is thrown upon a single hand,
from which a discussion of every public question whatsoever is unreasonably expected. He is not paid for his
labour, and certainly has a right to choose his employment.—As to the game laws, he never scrupled to declare his opinion, that they are a species of the forest
laws; that they are oppressive to the subject; and that
the spirit of them is incompatible with legal liberty:—
that the penalties imposed by these laws, bear no proportion to the nature of the offence; that the mode of
trial and the degree and kind of evidence necessary to
convict, not only deprive the subject of all the benefits
of a trial by a jury, but are in themselves too summary,
and to the last degree arbitrary and oppressive: that, in
particular, the late acts to prevent dog-stealing, or killing
game between sun and sun, are distinguished by their ab-

surdity, extravagance, and pernicious tendency. If these
terms are weak or ambiguous, in what language can Junius express himself?—It is no excuse for Lord Mansfield
to say, that he happened to be absent when these bills
passed the house of Lords. It was his duty to be present.
Such bills could never have passed the House of Commons without his knowledge. But we very well know by
what rule he regulates his attendance. When that order
was made in the House of Lords, in the case of Lord
Pomfret, at which every Englishman shudders, my honest Lord Mansfield found himself by mere accident, in
the Court of King's Bench:—Otherwise, he would have
done wonders in defence of law and property! The pitiful evasion is adapted to the character. But Junius will
never justify himself by the example of this bad man.
The distinction between doing wrong and avoiding to do
right, belongs to Lord Mansfield. Junius disclaims it.

LETTER LXV.

TO LORD CHIEF JUSTICE MANSFIELD.

Nov. 2. 1771.

At the intercession of three of your countrymen, you have bailed a man who, I presume, is also a
Scotchman, and whom the Lord Mayor of London had
refused to bail. I do not mean to enter into an examination
of the partial, sinister motives of your conduct; but,
confining myself strictly to the fact, I affirm that you
have done that which by law you were not warranted to
do. The thief was taken in the theft;—the stolen goods
were found upon him, and he made no defence. In these
circumstances (the truth of which you dare not deny, because it is of public notoriety), it could not stand indifferent, whether he was guilty or not, much less could
there be any presumption of his innocence; and in these
circumstances, I affirm, in contradiction to You, LORD
CHIEF JUSTICE MANSFIELD, that by the laws of England,
he was not bailable. If ever Mr. Eyre should be brought
to trial, we shall hear what you have to say for yourself;
and I pledge myself, before God and my country, in

proper time and place, to make good my charge against you.

JUNIUS.

LETTER LXVI.

TO THE PRINTER OF THE PUBLIC ADVERTISER.

Nov. 9. 1771.

JUNIUS engages to make good his charge against Lord Chief Justice Mansfield some time before the meeting of parliament, in order that the House of Commons may, if they think proper, make it one article in the impeachment of the said Lord Chief Justice.

LETTER LXVII.

TO HIS GRACE THE DUKE OF GRAFTON.

MY LORD,   Nov. 27. 1771.

WHAT is the reason, my Lord, that when almost every man in the kingdom, without distinction of principles or party, exults in the ridiculous defeat of Sir James Lowther; when good and bad men unite in one common opinion of that baronet, and triumph in his distress, as if the event (without any reference to vice or virtue) were interesting to human nature; your Grace alone should appear so miserably depressed and afflicted? In such universal joy, I know not where you will look for a compliment of condolence; unless you appeal to the tender, sympathetic sorrows of Mr. Bradshaw. That cream-coloured gentleman's tears, affecting as they are, carry consolation with them. He never weeps but, like an April shower, with a lambent ray of sunshine upon his countenance. From the feelings of honest men upon this joyful occasion, I do not mean to draw any conclusion to your Grace. They naturally rejoice when they see a signal instance of tyranny resisted with success;—of treachery exposed to the derision of the world;—an infamous informer defeated, and an impudent robber dragged to the public gibbet.—But, in the other class of mankind, I own I expected to meet the Duke of Grafton. Men who have no regard for justice, nor any sense of honour, seem as heartily pleased with Sir James Lowther's well-deserved punishment, as if he did not constitute an example against themselves. The unhappy baronet has no friends, even among those who resemble him. You, my Lord, are not reduced to so deplorable a state of dereliction. Every villain in the kingdom is your friend; and in compliment to such amity, I think you should suffer your dismal countenance to clear up. Besides, my Lord, I am a little anxious for the consistency of your character. You violate your own rules of decorum, when you do not insult the man whom you have betrayed.

The divine justice of retribution seems now to have begun its progress. Deliberate treachery entails punishment upon the traitor. There is no possibility of escaping it, even in the highest rank to which the consent of society can exalt the meanest and worst of men. The forced, unnatural union of Luttrell and Middlesex was an omen of another unnatural union, by which indefeasible infamy is attached to the house of Brunswick. If one of these acts was virtuous and honourable, the best of princes, I thank God, is happily rewarded for it by the other.—Your Grace, it has been said, had some share in recommending Colonel Luttrell to the King;—or was it only the gentle Bradshaw who made himself answerable for the good behaviour of his friend? An intimate connection has long subsisted between him and the worthy Lord Irnham. It arose from a fortunate similarity of principles, cemented by the constant mediation of their common friend Miss Davis g.

Yet I confess I should be sorry that the opprobrious infamy of this match should reach beyond the family.—We have now a better reason than ever to pray for the long life of the best of princes, and the welfare of his royal issue.—I will not mix any thing ominous with my prayers;—but let parliament look to it.—A Luttrell shall never succeed to the crown of England.—If the hereditary virtues of the family deserve a kingdom, Scotland will be a proper retreat for them.

The next is a most remarkable instance of the goodness of providence. The just law of retaliation has at last overtaken the little contemptible tyrant of the north. To the son-in-law of your dearest friend the Earl of Bute you meant to transfer the Duke of Portland's property; and you hastened the grant with an expedition unknown to the Treasury, that he might have it time enough to give a decisive turn to the election for the county. The immediate consequence of this flagitious robbery was, that he lost the election which you meant to ensure him, and with such signal circumstances of scorn, reproach, and insult (to say nothing of the general exultation of all parties), as (excepting the King's brother-in-law Colonel Luttrell, and old Simon his father-in-law) hardly ever fell upon a gentleman in this country.—In the event, he loses the very property of which he thought he had gotten possession, and after an expence which would have paid the value of the land in question twenty times over.—The forms of villainy, you see, are necessary to its success. Hereafter you will act with greater circumspection, and not drive so directly to your object. To snatch a grace beyond the reach of common treachery, is an exception, not a rule.

And now, my good Lord, does not your conscious heart inform you, that the justice of retribution begins to operate, and that it may soon approach your person?—Do you think that Junius has renounced the Middlesex election?—Or that the King's timber shall be refused to the Royal Navy with impunity;—Or that you shall hear no more of the sale of that patent to Mr. Hine, which you endeavoured to screen by suddenly dropping your prosecution of Samuel Vaughan, when the rule against him was made absolute? I believe, indeed, there never was such an instance in all the history of negative impudence. —But it shall not save you.—The very sunshine you live in is a prelude to your dissolution. When you are ripe, you shall be plucked.

JUNIUS.

P. S. I beg you will convey to our gracious master my humble congratulations upon the glorious success of peerages and pensions, so lavishly distributed as the rewards of Irish virtue.

LETTER LXVIII.

TO LORD CHIEF JUSTICE MANSFIELD.

Jan. 21. 1772.

I HAVE undertaken to prove, that when, at the intercession of three of your countrymen, you bailed John Eyre, you did that which by law you were not warranted to do ; and that a felon, under the circumstances of being taken in the fact, with the stolen goods upon him, and making no defence, is not bailable by the laws of England. Your learned advocates have interpreted this charge into a denial that the Court of King's Bench, or the judges of that court during the vacation, have any greater authority to bail for criminal offences than a justice of peace. With the instance before me, I am supposed to question your power of doing wrong, and to deny the existence of a power at the same moment that I arraign the illegal exercise of it. But the opinions of such men, whether wilful in their malignity, or sincere in their ignorance, are unworthy of my notice. You, Lord Mansfield, did not understand me so ; and, I promise you, your cause requires an abler defence.—I am now to make good my charge against you. However dull my argument, the subject of it is interesting. I shall be honoured with the attention of the public, and have a right to demand the attention of the legislature. Supported as I am by the whole body of the criminal law of England, I have no doubt of establishing my charge. If, on your part, you should have no plain substantial defence, but should endeavour to shelter yourself under the quirk and evasion of a practising lawyer, or under the mere insulting assertion of power without right, the reputation you pretend to is gone for ever ; —you stand degraded from the respect and authority of your office, and are no longer *de jure*, Lord Chief Justice of England. This letter, my Lord, is addressed, not so much to you, as to the public. Learned as you are, and quick in apprehension, few arguments are necessary to satisfy you, that you have done that which by law you were not warranted to do. Your conscience already tells you, that you have sinned against knowledge, and that whatever defence you make contradicts your own internal con-fiction. But other men are willing enough to take the law upon trust. They rely upon your authority, because they are too indolent to search for information; or, conceiving that there is some mystery in the laws of their country, which lawyers only are qualified to explain, they distrust their judgement, and voluntarily renounce the right of thinking for themselves. With all the evidence of history before them, from Tresillian to Jefferies, from Jefferies to Mansfield, they will not believe it possible that a learned judge can act in direct contradiction to those laws, which he is supposed to have made the study of his life, and which he has sworn to administer faithfully. Superstition is certainly not the characteristic of this age. Yet some men are bigotted in politics who are infidels in religion.—I do not despair of making them ashamed of their credulity.

The charge I brought against you is expressed in terms guarded and well considered. They do not deny the strict power of the judges of the Court of King's Bench to bail in cases not bailable by a justice of peace, nor replevisable by the common writ, or *ex officio* by the sheriff. I well know the practice of the court, and by what legal rules it ought to be directed. But, far from meaning to soften or diminish the force of those terms I have made use of, I now go beyond them, and affirm,

I. That the superior power of bailing for felony, claimed by the Court of King's Bench, is founded upon the opinion of lawyers, and the practice of the court;—that the assent of the legislature to this power is merely negative, and that it is not supported by any positive provision in any statute whatsoever.—If it be, produce the statute.

II. Admitting that the judges of the Court of King's Bench are vested with a discretionary power to examine and judge of circumstances and allegations which a justice of peace is not permitted to consider, I affirm that the judges, in the use and application of that discretionary power, are as strictly bound by the spirit, intent, and meaning, as the justice of peace is by the words, of the legislature. Favourable circumstances, alledged before the judge, may justify a doubt whether the prisoner be guilty or not; and, where the guilt is doubtful, a presumption of innocence should in general be admitted. But, when any such probable circumstances are alledged, they alter the state and condition of the prisoner... He is no longer that all-but-convicted felon whom the law intends, and who by law is not bailable at all. If no circumstances whatsoever are alledged in his favour;—if no allegation whatsoever be made to lesson the force of that evidence which the law annexes to a positive charge of felony, and particularly to the fact of being taken with the maner; I then say, that the Lord Chief Justice of England has no more right to bail him than a justice of peace. The discretion of an English judge is not of mere will and pleasure ;—it is not arbitrary ;—it is not capricious :—but, as that great lawyer (whose authority I wish you respected half as much as I do) truly says[h], " Discretion, taken as it ought to be, " is, *discernere per legem quid sit justum.* If it be not di- " rected by the right line of the law, it is a a crooked cord, " and appeareth to be unlawful."—If discretion were arbitrary in the judge, he might introduce whatever novelties he thought proper. But, says Lord Coke, " Novel- " ties, without warrants of precedents, are not to be al- " lowed; some certain rules are to be followed ;—*Quic-* " *quid judicis authoritati subjicitur, novitati non subjicitur :*" and this sound doctrine is applied to the Star-chamber, a court confessedly arbitrary. If you will abide by the authority of this great man, you shall have all the advantage of his opinion, wherever it appears to favour you. Excepting the plain express meaning of the legislature, to which all private opinions must give way, I desire no better judge between us than Lord Coke.

III. I affirm, that, according to the obvious indisputable meaning of the legislature, repeatedly expressed, a person positively charged with feloniously stealing, and taken *in flagrante delicto,* with the stolen goods upon him, is not bailable. The law considers him as differing in nothing from a convict, but in the form of conviction; and (whatever a corrupt judge may do) will accept of no security but the confinement of his body within four walls. I know it has been alledged in your favour, that you have often bailed for murders, rapes, and other manifest crimes. Without questioning the fact, I shall not admit that you are to be justified by your own example. If that were a protection to you, where is the

crime, that as a judge, you might not now securely commit? But neither shall I suffer myself to be drawn aside
from my present argument, nor you to profit by your own
wrong.—To prove the meaning and intent of the legislature, will require a minute and tedious deduction. To
investigate a question of law, demands some labour and
attention : though very little genius or sagacity. As a
practical profession, the study of the law requires but a
moderate portion of abilities. The learning of a pleader
is usually upon a level with his integrity. The indiscriminate defence of right and wrong contracts the understanding, while it corrupts the heart. Subtlety is soon
mistaken for wisdom, and impunity for virtue. If there
be any instances upon record, as some there are undoubtedly, of genius and morality united in a lawyer, they are
distinguished by their singularity, and operate as exceptions.

I must solicit the patience of my readers. This is no light
matter; nor is it any more susceptible of ornament, than
the conduct of Lord Mansfield is capable of aggravation.

As the law or bail, in charges of felony, has been exactly ascertained by acts of the legislature, it is at present
of little consequence to enquire how it stood at common
law before the statute of Westminster. And yet it is worth
the reader's attention to observe, how nearly, in the ideas
of our ancestors, the circumstance of being taken with the
maner approached to the conviction of the felon [i]. It
"fixed the authoritative stamp of verisimilitude upon the
" accusation; and, by the common law, when a thief was
" taken with the maner (that is, with the thing stolen upon
" him; *in manu*), he might, so detected *flagrante delicto*, be
" brought into court, arraigned and tried, without in-
" dictment; as, by the Danish law, he might be taken
" and hanged upon the spot, without accusation or trial."
It will soon appear that our statute-law, in this behalf,
though less summary in point of proceeding, is directed by
the same spirit. In one instance, the very form is adhered
to. In offences relating to the forest, if a man was taken
with vert [k], or venison, it was declared to be equivalent to
indictment. To enable the reader to judge for himself, I
shall state, in due order, the several statutes relative to bail
in criminal cases, or as much of them as may be material

to the point in question, omitting superfluous words. If I misrepresent, or do not quote with fidelity, it will not be difficult to detect me.

The statute of Westminster the first, in 1275, sets forth, that " Forasmuch as sheriffs and others, who have " taken and kept in prison persons detected of felony, " and incontinent have let out by replevin such as were " not replevisable, because they would gain of the one " party and grieve the other; and forasmuch as, before " this time, it was not determined which persons were " replevisable, and which not, it is provided, and by the " king commanded, that such prisoners, &c. as be taken " with the maner, &c: or for manifest offences, shall be in " no wise replevisable by the common writ, nor without " writ ᵐ."—Lord Coke, in his exposition of the last part of this quotation, accurately distinguishes between replevy by the common writ, or *ex officio*, and bail by the King's Bench. The words of the statute certainly do not extend to the judges of that court. But, besides that the reader will soon find reason to think that the legislature, in their intention, made no difference between bailable and replevisable, Lord Coke himself (if he be understood to mean nothing but an exposition of the statute of Westminster, and not to state the law generally, does not adhere to his own distinction. In expounding the other offences, which, by this statute, are declared not replevisable, he constantly uses the words not bailable.——— " That outlaws, for instance are not bailable at all;— " that persons who have abjured the realm, are attainted " upon their own confession, and therefore not bailable " at all by law;—that provers are not bailable;—that " notorious felons are not bailable." The reason why the superior courts were not named in the statute of Westminster, was plainly this, " because anciently most " of the business touching bailment of prisoners for fe- " lony or misdemeanors, was performed by the sheriffs, " or special bailiffs of liberties, either by writ, or *virtute* " *officii* ⁿ ;" consequently the superior courts had little or no opportunity to commit those abuses which the statute imputes to the sheriffs.—With submission to Dr. Blackstone, I think he has fallen into a contradiction; which, in terms at least, appears irreconcileable. After enumerating several offences not bailable; he asserts, without any condition or limitation whatsoever °, " All these are clearly not admissible to bail." Yet, in a few lines after, he says, " it is agreed that the Court of King's " Bench may bail for any crime whatsoever, according " to circumstances of the case." To his first proposition he should have added, by Sheriffs or Justices: otherwise the two propositions contradict each other ; with this difference, however, that the first is absolute, the second limited by a consideration of circumstances. I say this without the least intended disrespect to the learned author. His work is of public utility and should not hastily be condemned.

The statute of 17th Richard II. cap. 1393, sets forth, that " Forasmuch as thieves notoriously defamed, " and others taken with the maner, by their long abiding " in prison, were delivered by charters, and favourable " inquests procured, to the great hinderance of the people, " two men of law shall be assigned, in every commission " of the peace, to proceed to the deliverance of such " felons," &c. It seems by this act, that there was a constant struggle between the legislature and the officers of justice. Not daring to admit felons taken with the maner to bail or mainprise, they evaded the law by keeping the party in prison a long time, and then delivering him without due trial.

The statute of 1st Richard III. in 1483, sets forth, that " Forasmuch as divers persons have been daily arrested " and imprisoned for suspicion of felony, sometime of " malice, and sometime of a light suspicion, and so kept " in prison without bail or mainprise, be it ordained, " that every justice of peace shall have authority, by his " discretion, to let such prisoners and persons so arrested " to bail or mainprise."—By this act it appears, that there had been abuses in matter of imprisonment, and that the legislature meant to provide for the immediate enlargement of persons arrested on light suspicion of felony.

The statute of 3d Henry VII. in 1486, declares, that " under colour of the preceding act of Richard the " Third, persons, such as were not mainpernable, were " oftentimes let to bail or mainprise by justices of the

" peace, whereby many murderers and felons escaped,
" the king, &c, hath ordained, that the justices of the
" peace, or two of them at least (whereof one to be of
" the quorum), have authority to let any such prisoners
" or persons, mainpernable by the law, to bail or main-
" prize."

The statute of 1st and 2d of Philip and Mary, in
1554, sets forth, that, " notwithstanding the preceding
" statute of Henry the Seventh, one justice of peace hath
" oftentimes, by sinister labour and means, set at large
" the greatest and notablest offenders, such as be not re-
" plevisable by the laws of this realm ; and yet, the ra-
" ther to hide their affections in that behalf, have signed
" the cause of their apprehension to be but only for
" suspicion of felony, whereby the said offenders have
" escaped unpunished, and do daily, to the high displea-
" sure of Almighty God, the great peril of the king and
" queen's true subjects, and encouragement of all thieves
" and evil-doers ; for reformation whereof be it en-
" acted, that no justices of peace shall let to bail or
" mainprise any such persons, which, for an offence by
" them committed, be declared not to be replevised, or
" bailed, or be forbidden to be replevised or bailed by
" the statute of Westminster the first ; and furthermore,
" that any persons, arrested for manslaughter, felony,
" being bailable by the law, shall not be let to bail or
" mainprise by any justices of peace, but in the form
" therein after prescribed."—In the two preceding statutes, the words bailable, replevisable, and mainpernable,
are used synonimously q, or promiscuously, to express the
same single intention of the legislature, viz. not to accept of any security but the body of the offender ; and
when the latter statute prescribes the form in which persons arrested on suspicion of felony (being bailable by the
law) may be let to bail, it evidently supposes, that there
are some cases not bailable by the law.—It may be
thought, perhaps, that I attribute to the legislature an appearance of inaccuracy in the use of terms merely to
serve my present purpose. But in truth it would make
more forcibly for my argument, to presume, that the legislature were constantly aware of the strict legal distinction between bail and replevy, and that they always

meant to adhere to it [q]. For if it be true that replevy is by the sheriffs, and bail by the higher courts at Westminster (which I think no lawyer will deny), it follows, that when the legislature expressly says, that any particular offence is by law not bailable, the superior courts are comprehended in the prohibition, and bound by it. Otherwise, unless there was a positive exception of the superior courts (which I affirm there never was in any statute relative to bail), the legislature would grossly contradict themselves, and the manifest intention of the law be evaded. It is an established rule, that when the law is special, and reason of it general, it is to be generally understood; and though by custom a latitude be allowed to the Court of King's Bench (to consider circumstances inductive of a doubt, whether the prisoner be guilty or innocent), if this latitude be taken as an arbitrary power to bail, when no circumstances whatsoever are alledged in favour of the prisoner, it is a power without right, and a daring violation of the whole English law of bail.

The act of the 31st of Charles the Second (commonly called the *Habeas Corpus* act) particularly declares, that it is not meant to extend to treason or felony plainly and specially expressed in the warrant of commitment. The prisoner is therefore left to seek his *habeas corpus* at common law; and so far was the legislature from supposing that persons (committed for treason or felony plainly and specially expressed in the warrant of commitment) could be let to bail by a single judge, or by the whole court, that this very act provides a remedy for such persons, in case they are not indicted in the course of the term or sessions subsequent to their commitment. The law neither suffers them to be enlarged before trial, nor to be imprisoned after the time in which they ought regularly to be tried. In this case the law says, " It shall and may " be lawful to and for the judges of the Court of King's " Bench, and justices of oyer and terminer, or general " gaol delivery, and they are hereby required, upon mo- " tion to them made in open court, the last day of the " term, session, or goal delivery, either by the prisoner, " or any one in his behalf, to set at liberty the prisoner " upon bail; unless it appear to the judges and justices, " upon oath made, that the witnesses for the king could

" not be produced the same term, sessions, or gaol-de-
" livery."—Upon the whole of this article, I observe,
1. That the provision made in the first part of it, would
be, in a great measure, useless and nugatory, if any single
judge might have bailed the prisoner *ex arbitrio* during
the vacation ; or if the court might have bailed him immediately after the commencement of the term or sessions.—2. When the law says, It shall and may be lawful
to bail for felony under particular circumstances, we
must presume, that before the passing of that act, it was
not lawful to bail under those circumstances. The terms
used by the legislature are enacting, not declaratory.—
3. Notwithstanding the party may have been imprisoned
during the greatest part of the vacation, and during the
whole session, the court are expressly forbidden to bail
him from that sesssion to the next, if oath be made that
the witnesses for the king could not be produced that same
term or sessions.

Having faithfully stated the several acts of parliament
relative to bail in criminal cases, it may be useful to the
reader to take a short historical review of the law of bail,
through its various gradations and improvements.

By the ancient common law, before and since the
Conquest, all felonies were bailable, till murder was ex-
cepted by statute ; so that persons might be admitted
to bail, before conviction, almost in every case. The statute of Westminster says, that before that time, it had
not been determined which offences were replevisable,
and which were not, whether by the common writ *de ho-
mine replegiando*, or *ex officio* by the sheriff. It is very remarkable, that the abuses arising from this unlimited
power of replevy, dreadful as they were, and destructive
to the peace of society, were not corrected or taken notice of by the legislature, until the Commons of the kingdom had obtained a share in it by their representatives ;
but the House of Commons had scarce begun to exist,
when these formidable abuses were corrected by the statute of Westminster. It is highly probable, that the mischief had been severely felt by the people, although no remedy had been provided for it by the Norman kings or
barons. " The iniquity of the times was so great [r], as it
" even forced the subjects to forego that, which was in

"account a great liberty, to stop the course of a grow-
"ing mischief." The preamble to the statutes, made
by the first parliament of Edward the First, assigns the
reason of calling it; "because the people had been
"otherwise entreated than they ought to be, the peace
"less kept, the laws less used, and offenders less punish-
"ed, than they ought to be; by reason whereof the
"people feared less to offend;" and the first attempt to
reform these various abuses, was by contracting the power
of replevying felons.

For above two centuries following, it does not appear
that any alteration was made in the law of bail, except
that being taken with vert or venison was declared to be
equivalent to indictment. The legislature adhered firmly
to the spirit of the statute of Westminster. The statute
of 27th of Edward the first, directs the justices of assize
to inquire and punish officers bailing such as were not bailable. As for the judges of the superior courts, it is probable, that in those days they thought themselves bound
by the obvious intent and meaning of the legislature.
They considered not so much to what particular persons
the prohibition was addressed, as what the thing was
which the legislature meant to prohibit; well knowing,
that in law *quando aliquid prohibetur, prohibitur et omne, per
quod devenitur ad illud.* "When any thing is forbidden,
"all the means by which the same thing may be compassed
"or done, are equally forbidden."

By the statute of Richard the third, the power of bailing was a little enlarged. Every justice of peace was authorised to bail for felony; but they were expressly confined to persons arrested on light suspicion; and even
this power, so limited, was found to produce such inconve-
niencies, that, in three years after, the legislature found it
necessary to repeal it. Instead of trusting any longer to a
single justice of peace, the act of 3d Henry VII. repeals
the preceding act, and directs, " that no prisoner (of those
" who are mainpernable by the law) shall be let to bail
" or mainprise by less than two justices, whereof one to
" be of the quorum." And so indispensably necessary was
this provision thought for the administration of justice,
and for the security and peace of society, that at this time
an oath was proposed by the king, to be taken by the

knights and esquires of his household, by the members of the House of Commons, and by the peers spiritual and temporal, and accepted and sworn to *quasi una voce* by them all; which, among other engagements, binds them " not to let any man to bail or mainprise, knowing and " deeming him to be a felon, upon your honour and wor- " ship. So help you God and all saints."

In about half a century, however, even these provisons were found insufficient. The act of Henry the Seventh was evaded, and the legislature once more obliged to interpose. The act of 1st and 2d of Philip and Mary, takes away entirely from the justices all power of bailing for offences declared not bailable by the statute of Westminster.

The illegal imprisonment of several persons who had refused to contribute to a loan exacted by Charles the First, and the delay of the *habeas corpus*, and subsequent refusal to bail them, constituted one of the first and most important grievances of that reign. Yet when the House of Commons, which met in the year 1628, resolved upon measures of the most firm and strenuous resistance to the power of imprisonment assumed by the king, or privy-council, and to the refusal to bail the party on the return of the *habeas corpus*, they did expressly, in all their resolutions, make an exception of commitments, where the cause of the restraint was expressed, and did by law justify the commitment. The reason of the distinction is, that whereas, when the cause of commitment is expressed, the crime is then known, and the offender must be brought to the ordinary trial; if, on the contrary, no cause of commitment be expressed, and the prisoner be thereupon remanded, it may operate to perpetual imprisonment. This contest with Charles the First produced the act of the 16th of that king; by which the Court of King's Bench are directed, within three days after the return to the *habeas corpus*, to examine and determine the legality of any commitment by the king or privy-council, and to do what to justice shall appertain, in delivering, bailing, or remanding the prisoner. Now, it seems, it is unnecessary for the judge to do what appertains to justice. The same scandalous traffic, in which we have seen the privilege of parliament exerted or relaxed, to gratify the present humour, or to serve the immediate purpose of the crown, is introduced into the administration of justice. The magistrate, it seems, has now no rule to follow, but the dictates of personal enmity, national partiality, or perhaps the most prostituted corruption!

To complete this historical inquiry, it only remains to be observed, that the *habeas corpus* act of 31st of Charles the Second, so justly considered as another Magna Charta of the kingdom [b], " extends only to the case of commit- " ments for such criminal charge as can produce no in- " convenience to public justice by a temporary enlarge- " ment of the prisoner." So careful were the legislature, at the very moment when they were providing for the liberty of the subject, not to furnish any colour or pretence for violating or evading the established law of bail in the higher criminal offences. But the exception, stated in the body of the act, puts the matter out of all doubt. After directing the judges how they are to proceed to the discharge of the prisoner upon recognizance and surety, having regard to the quality of the prisoner and nature of the offence, it is expressly added, " unless it shall appear " to the said Lord Chancellor, &c. that the party so " committed is detained for such matters or offences, for " the which, BY THE LAW, THE PRISONER IS NOT BAIL- " ABLE."

When the laws, plain of themselves, are thus illustrated by facts, and their uniform meaning established by history, we do not want the authority of opinions, however respectable, to inform our judgment, or to confirm our belief. But I am determined that you shall have no escape. Authority of every sort shall be produced against you, from Jacob to Lord Coke, from the Dictionary to the Classic. In vain shall you appeal from those upright judges whom you disdain to imitate, to those whom you have made your example. With one voice they all condemn you.

" To be taken with the maner, is where a thief, hav- " ing stolen any thing, is taken with the same about him, " as it were in his hands, which is called *flagrante delicto*. " Such a criminal is not bailable by law."—*Jacob*, under the word *Maner*.

" Those who are taken with the maner are excluded,

" by the statute of Westminster, from the benefit of a
replevin."—*Hawkins, P, C.* ii. 98.

" Of such heinous offences, no one, who is notoriously
" guilty, seems to be bailable by the intent of this statute."
—*Ditto*, ii. 99.

" The common practice and allowed general rule is,
" that bail is only then proper where it stands indifferent
" whether the party were guilty or innocent."—*Ditto,*
ditto

" There is no doubt, but that the bailing of a person,
" who is not bailable by law, is punishable, either at
" common law as a negligent escape, or as an offence
" against the several statutes relative to bail."—*Ditto*, 89.

" It cannot be doubted, but that neither the judges of
" this, nor of any other superior court of justice, are
" strictly within the purview of that statute; yet they
" will always, in their discretion, pay a due regard to it,
" and not admit a person to bail, who is expressly de-
" clared by it irreplevisable, without some particular cir-
" cumstance in his favour; and therefore it seems diffi-
" cult to find an instance, where persons, attainted of fe-
" lony, or notoriously guilty of treason or manslaughter,
" &c. by their own confession, or otherwise, have been
" admitted to the benefit of bail, without some special
" motive to the court to grant it."—*Ditto*, 114.

" If it appears that any man hath injury or wrong by
" his imprisonment, we have power to deliver, and dis-
" charge him; if otherwise, he is to be remanded by us
" to prison again."—*Lord Ch. T. Hyde; State Trials,* xii.
115.

" The statute of Westminster was especial for direc-
" tion to the sheriffs and others; but to say courts of
" justice are excluded from this statute, I conceive it cannot
" be."—*Attorney General Heath, ditto,* 132.

" The court, upon view of the return, judgeth of the
" sufficiency or insufficiency of it. If they think the pri-
" soner in law to be bailable, he is committed to the
" Marshal, and bailed; if not, he is remanded." Through
the whole debate, the objection on the part of the prisoners was, that no cause of commitment was expressed in the
warrant; but it was uniformly admitted by their counsel,
that, if the cause of commitment had been expressed for

treason or felony, the court would then have done right in remanding them.

The Attorney General having urged, before a committee of both Houses, that, in Beckwith's case and others, the lords of the council sent a letter to the Court of King's Bench to bail, it was replied by the managers of the House of Commons, that this was of no moment; " for that ei- " ther the prisoner was bailable by the law, or not bail- " able. If bailable by the law, then he was to be bailed " without any such letter ; if not bailable by the law, " then plainly the judges could not have bailed him up- " on the letter, without breach of their oath, which is, " that they are to do justice according to the law, &c." —State Trials, vii. 175.

" So that in bailing upon such offences of the highest " nature, a kind of discretion, rather than a constant law, " hath been exercised, when it stands wholly indifferent " in the eye of the court whether the prisoner be guilty " or not.'—Selden, St. Tr. vii. 230. 1.

" I deny that a man is always bailable when imprison- " ment is imposed upon him for custody." Attorney Ge- neral Heath, ditto, 238.—By these quotations from the State Trials, though otherwise not of authority, it appears plainly, that, in regard to bailable or not bailable, all par- ties agreed in admitting one proposition as incontrovert- ible.

" In relation to capital offences, there are especially " these acts of parliament that are the common land-marks " touching offences bailable or not bailable." Hale, ii. P. C. 127. The enumeration includes the several acts cited in this paper.

" Persons taken with the manouvre are not bailable, " because it is furtum manifestum."—Hale, ii. P. C. 133.

" The writ of habeas corpus is of a high nature : for if " persons be wrongfully committed, they are to be dis- " charged upon this writ returned ; or, if bailable, they " are to be bailed; if not bailable, they are to be com- " mitted." Hale, ii. P. C. 145. This doctrine of Lord Chief Justice Hale refers immediately to the superior courts from whence the writ issues.—" After the re- " turn is filed, the court is either to discharge, or bail,

" or commit him, as the nature of the cause requires."
—*Hale*, ii. *P. C.* 146.

" If bail be granted otherwise than the law alloweth,
" the party that alloweth the same shall be fined, im-
" prisoned, render damages, or forfeit his place, as the
" case shall require."—*Selden by N. Bacon*, 182.

" This induces an absolute necessity of expressing, upon
" every commitment, the reason for which it is made;
" that the court, upon a *habeas corpus*, may examine into
" its validity, and, according to the circumstances of the
" case, may discharge, admit to bail, or remand the pri-
" soner."—*Blackstone*, iii. 133.

" Marriot was committed for forging indorsements
" upon bank-bills, and upon a *habeas corpus* was bailed,
" because the crime was only a great misdemeanor;—
" for though the forging the bills be felony, yet forging
" the indorsement is not."—*Salkeld*, i. 104.

" Apell de Mahem, &c. ideo ne fuit lesse a baille,
" nient plus que in appell de robbery ou murder; quod
" nota, et que in robry et murder le partie n'est baillable."
—*Bro. Mainprise*, 67.

" The intendment of the law in bail is, *Quod stat in-
" differenter*, whether he be guilty or no; but when he is
" convicted by verdict or confession, then he must be
" deemed in law to be guilty of the felony, and therefore
" not bailable at all."—*Coke*, ii. *Inst.* 188.—iv. 178.

" Bail is *quando stat indifferenter*, and not when the of-
" fence is open and manifest."—ii. *Inst.* 189.

" In this case, *non stat indifferenter* whether he be guilty
" or no; being taken with the *maner*, that is with the thing
" stolen, as it were in his han ."—*Ditto, ditto.*

" If it appeareth that this imprisonment be just and
" lawful, he shall be remanded to the former goaler; but,
" if it shall appear to the court that he was imprisoned
" against the law of the land, they ought, by force of this
" statute, to deliver him; if it be doubtful and under con-
" sideration, he may be bailed."—ii. *Inst.* 55.

It is unnecessary to load the reader with any farther
quotations. If these authorities are not deemed sufficient
to establish the doctrine maintained in this paper, it will
be in vain to appeal to the evidence of law-books, or to the

opinions of judges. They are not the authorities by which Lord Mansfield will abide. He assumes an arbitrary power of doing right; and if he does wrong, it lies only between God and his conscience.

Now, my Lord, although I have great faith in the preceding argument, I will not say that every minute part of it is absolutely invulnerable. I am too well acquainted with the practice of a certain court, directed by your example, as it is governed by your authority, to think there ever yet was an argument, however conformable to law and reason, in which a cunning, quibbling attorney might not discover a flaw. But taking the whole of it together, I affirm, that it constitutes a mass of demonstration, than which nothing more complete or satisfactory can be offered to the human mind. How an evasive, indirect reply will stand with your reputation, or how far it will answer, in point of defence, at the bar of the House of Lords, is worth your consideration. If, after all that has been said, it should still be maintained, that the Court of King's Bench, in bailing felons, are exempted from all legal rules whatsoever, and that the judge has no direction to pursue but his private affections, or mere unquestionable will and pleasure; it will follow plainly, that the distinction between bailable, and not bailable, uniformly expressed by the legislature, current through all our law-Books, and admitted by all our great lawyers without exception, is in one sense a nugatory, in another a pernicious distinction. It is nugatory, as it supposes a difference in the bailable quality of offences, when, in effect the distinction refers only to the rank of the magistrate. It is pernicious, as it implies a rule of law, which yet the judge is not bound to pay the least regard to; and impresses an idea upon the minds of the people, that the judge is wiser and greater than the law.

It remains only to apply the law, thus stated, to the fact in question. By an authentic copy of the *mittimus* it appears, that John Eyre was committed for felony, plainly and specially expressed in the warrant of commitment. He was charged before Alderman Halifax, by the oath of Thomas Fielding, William Holder, William Payne, and William Nash, for feloniously stealing eleven quires of writingpaper, value six shillings, the property of Thomas

Beach, &c.—By the examinations upon oath of the four persons mentioned in the *mittimus*, it was proved, that large quantities of paper had been missed, and that eleven quires (previously marked from a suspicion that Eyre was the thief) were found upon him. Many other quires of paper, marked in the same manner, were found at his lodgings; and after he had been some time in Wood-street Compter, a key was found in his room there, which appeared to be a key to the closet at Guildhall, from whence the paper was stolen. When asked what he had to say in his defence, his only answer was, " I hope you will bail " me." Mr. Holder, the clerk, replied, " That is im- " possible. There never was an instance of it, when the " stolen goods were found upon the thief." The Lord Mayor was then applied to, and refused to bail him.—Of all these circumstances, it was your duty to have informed yourself minutely. The fact was remarkable; and the chief magistrate of the city of London was known to have refused to bail the offender. To justify your compliance with the solicitations of your three countrymen, it should be proved that such allegations were offered to you in behalf of their associate, as honestly and *bona fide* reduced it to a matter of doubt and indifference whether the prisoner was innocent or guilty. Was any thing offered by the Scotch triumvirate that tended to invalidate the positive charge made against him by four credible witnesses upon oath?—Was it even insinuated to you, either by himself or his bail, that no felony was committed;—or that he was not the felon;—that the stolen goods were not found upon him;—or that he was only the receiver, not knowing them to be stolen? Or, in short, did they attempt to produce any evidence of his insanity?—To all these questions I answer for you, without the least fear of contradiction, positively NO. From the moment he was arrested he never entertained any hope of acquital; therefore thought of nothing but obtaining bail, that he might have time to settle his affairs, convey his fortune into another country, and spend the remainder of his life in comfort and affluence abroad. In this prudential scheme of future happiness, the Lord Chief Justice of England most readily and heartily concurred. At sight of so much virtue in distress, your natural benevolence took the alarm.

Such a man as Mr. Eyre, struggling with adversity, must always be an interesting scene to Lord Mansfield.—Or, was it that liberal anxiety, by which your whole life has been distinguished, to enlarge the liberty of the subject?—My Lord, we did not want this new instance of the liberality of your principles. We already knew what kind of subjects they were for whose liberty you were anxious. At all events, the public are much indebted to you for fixing a price at which felony may be committed with impunity. You bound a felon, notoriously worth 30,000l. in the sum of 300l. With your natural turn to equity, and knowing as you are in the doctrine of precedents, you undoubtedly meant to settle the proportion between the fortune of the felon and the fine, by which he may compound for his felony. The ratio now upon record, and transmitted to posterity under the auspices of Lord Mansfield, is exactly one to a hundred.—My Lord, without intending it, you have laid a cruel restraint upon the genius of your countrymen. In the warmest indulgence of their passions, they have an eye to the expence; and if their other virtues fail us, we have a resource in their œconomy.

By taking so trifling a security from John Eyre, you invited and manifestly exhorted him to escape. Although, in bailable cases, it be usual to take four securities, you left him in the custody of three Scotchmen, whom he might have easily satisfied for conniving at his retreat. That he did not make use of the opportunity you industriously gave him, neither justifies your conduct, nor can it be any way accounted for but by his excessive and monstrous avarice. Any other man but this bosom-friend of three Scotchmen, would gladly have sacrificed a few hundred pounds, rather than to submit to the infamy of pleading guilty in open court. It is possible indeed that he might have flattered himself; and not unreasonably, with the hopes of a pardon. That he would have been pardoned, seems more than probable, if I had not directed the public attention to the leading step you took in favour of him. In the present gentle reign, we well know what use has been made of the lenity of the court and of the mercy of the crown. The Lord Chief Justice of England accepts of the hundredth part of the property of a felon taken in the fact, as a recognizance for his appearance. Your brother Smythe browbeats a jury, and forces them to alter their verdict, by which they had found a Scotch sergeant guilty of murder; and though the Kennedies were convicted of a most deliberate and atrocious murder, they still had a claim to the royal mercy.—They were saved by the chastity of their connections.—They had a sister;—yet it was not her beauty, but the pliancy of her virtue, that recommended her to the king.—The holy Author of our religion was seen in the company of sinners; but it was his gracious purpose to convert them from their sins. Another man, who in the ceremonies of our faith might give lessons to the great enemy of it, upon different principles keeps much the same company. He advertises for patients, collects all the diseases of the heart, and turns a royal palace into an hospital for incurables. —A man of honour has no ticket of admission at St. James's.—They receive him like a virgin at the Magdalene's;—"Go thou and do likewise."

My charge against you is now made good. I shall, however, be ready to answer or to submit to fair objections. If, whenever this matter shall be agitated, you suffer the doors of the House of Lords to be shut, I now protest, that I shall consider you as having made no reply. From that moment, in the opinion of the world, you will stand self-convicted. Whether your reply be quibbling and evasive, or liberal and in point, will be matter for the judgment of your peers;—but if, when every possible idea of disrespect to that noble house (in whose honour and justice the nation implicitly confides) is here most solemnly disclaimed, you should endeavour to represent this charge as a contempt of their authority, and move their Lordships to censure the publisher of this paper, I then affirm that you support injustice by violence, that you are guilty of a heinous aggravation of your offence, and that you contribute your utmost influence to promote on the part of the highest court of judicature, a positive denial of justice to the nation.

LETTER LXIX.

TO THE RIGHT HONOURABLE LORD CAMDEN.

MY LORD,

      I TURN with pleasure from that barren waste, in which no salutary plant takes root, no verdure quickens, to a character fertile, as I willingly believe, in every great and good qualification. I call upon you, in the name of the English nation, to stand forth in defence of the laws of your country, and to exert, in the cause of truth and justice, those great abilities with which you were intrusted for the benefit of mankind. To ascertain the facts set forth in the preceding paper, it may be necessary to call the persons mentioned in the *mittimus* to the bar of the House of Lords. If a motion for that purpose should be rejected, we shall know what to think of Lord Mansfield's innocence. The legal argument is submitted to your Lordship's judgment. After the noble stand you made against Lord Mansfield upon the question of libel, we did expect that you would not have suffered that matter to have remained undetermined. But it was said that Lord Chief Justice Wilmot had been prevailed upon to vouch for an opinion of the late Judge Yates, which was supposed to make against you; and we admit of the excuse. When such detestable arts are employed to prejudge a question of right, it might have been imprudent at that time to have brought it to a decision. In the present instance, you will have no such opposition to contend with. If there be a judge, or a lawyer of any note in Westminster-hall, who shall be daring enough to affirm, that, according to the true intendment of the laws of England, a felon, taken with the *maner*, *in flagrante delicto*, is bailable; or that the discretion of an English judge is merely arbitrary, and not governed by rules of law;—I should be glad to be acquainted with him. Whoever he be, I will take care that he shall not give you much trouble. Your Lordship's character assures me that you will assume that principal part which belongs to you, in supporting the laws of England against a wicked judge, who makes it the occupation of his life to misinterpret and pervert them. If you decline this honourable office,

I fear it will be said, that, for some months past, you have kept too much company with the Duke of Grafton. When the contest turns upon the interpretation of the laws, you cannot without a formal surrender of all your reputation, yield the post of honour even to Lord Chatham. Considering the situation and abilities of Lord Mansfield, I do not scruple to affirm, with the most solemn appeal to God for my sincerity, that, in my judgement, he is the very worst and the most dangerous man in the kingdom. Thus far I have done my duty in endeavouring to bring him to punishment. But mine is an inferior, ministerial office in the temple of justice:—I have bound the victim, and dragged him to the altar.

JUNIUS.

THE Reverend Mr. John Horne having, with his usual veracity and honest industry, circulated a report that Junius, in a letter to the supporters of the bill of rights, had warmly declared himself in favour of long parliaments and rotten boroughs, it is thought necessary to submit to the public the following extract from his letter to John Wilkes, Esq. dated the 7th of September 1771, and laid before the society on the 24th of the same month.

" With regard to the several articles, taken separately,
" I own I am concerned to see, that the great condition
" which ought to be the *sine qua non* of parliamentary
" qualification——which ought to be the basis (as it
" assuredly will be the only support) of every barrier rais-
" ed in defence of the constitution, I mean a declaration
" upon oath to shorten the duration of parliaments, is re-
" duced to the fourth rank in the esteem of the society;
" and, even in that place, far from being insisted on
" with firmness and vehemence, seems to have been parti-
" cularly slighted in the expression, ' You shall endeavour
" to restore annual parliaments !'—Are these the terms
" which men, who are in earnest, make use of, when the *sa-*
" *lus reipublicæ* is at state?—I expected other language from
" Mr. Wilkes.—Besides my objection in point of form,
" I disapprove highly of the meaning of the fourth article

" as it stands. Whenever the question shall be seriously
" agitated, I will endeavour (and if I live, will assuredly
" attempt it) to convince the English nation, by argu-
" ments to my understanding unanswerable, that they
" ought to insist upon a triennial, and banish the idea of
" an annual parliament. . . . . I am
" convinced, that if shortening the duration of parliaments
" (which in effect is keeping the representative under the
" rod of the constituent) be not made the basis of our
" new parliamentary Jurisprudence, other checks or im-
" provements signify nothing. On the contrary, if this
" be made the foundation, other measures may come in aid,
" and, as auxiliaries, be of considerable advantage. Lord
" Chatham's project, for instance, of increasing the num-
" ber of knights of shires, appears to me admirable. . . .
" . . . . As to cutting away the rotten boroughs, I am
" as much offended as any man at seeing so many of
" them under the direct influence of the crown, or at the
" disposal of private persons. Yet, I own, I have both
" doubts and apprehensions in regard to the remedy you
" propose. I shall be charged, perhaps, with an unusual
" want of political intrepidity, when I honestly confess
" to you, that I am startled at the idea of so extensive an
" amputation.—In the first place, I question the power
" de jure, of the legislature to disfranchise a number of
" boroughs, upon the general ground of improving the
" constitution. There cannot be a doctrine more fatal
" to the liberty and property we are contending for, than
" that which confounds the idea of a supreme and an ar-
" bitary legislature. I need not point out to you the
" fatal purposes to which it has been, and may be, ap-
" plied. If we are sincere in the political creed we pro-
" fess, there are many things which we ought to affirm
" cannot be done by the King, Lords, and Commons.
" Among these I reckon the disfranchising of boroughs
" with a general view to improvement. I consider it as equi-
" valent to robbing the parties concerned, of their freehold,
" of their birthright. I say, that although this birthright
" may be forfeited, or the exercise of it suspended in par-
" ticular cases, it cannot be taken away by a general law,
" for any real or pretended purpose of improving the
" constitution. Supposing the attempt made, I am per-

" suaded you cannot mean that either King or Lords,
" should take an active part in it. A bill, which only
" touches the representation of the people, must originate
" in the House of Commons. In the formation and
" mode of passing it, the exclusive right of the Commons
" must be asserted as scrupulously as in the case of a mo-
" ney bill. Now, Sir, I should be glad to know by what
" kind of reasoning it can be proved, that there is a pow-
" er vested in the representative to destroy his immediate
" constituent. From whence could he possibly derive it?
" A courtier, I know, will be ready to maintain the af-
" firmative. The doctrine suits him exactly, because it
" gives an unlimited operation to the influence of the
" crown. But we, Mr. Wilkes, ought to hold a diffe-
" rent language. It is no answer to me to say that the
" bill, when it passes the House of Commons, is the act
" of the majority, and not the representatives of the par-
" ticular boroughs concerned. If the majority can dis-
" franchise ten boroughs, why not twenty, why not the
" whole kingdom? Why should not they make their
" own seats in parliament for life?—When the septen-
" nial act passed, the legislature did what, apparently and
" palpably, they had no power to do: but they did more
" than what people in general were aware of; they, in
" effect, disfranchised the whole kingdom for four years."

" For argument's sake, I will now suppose that the ex-
" pediency of the measure and the power of parliament
" are unquestionable. Still you will find an unsurmounta-
" ble difficulty in the execution. When all your instru-
" ments of amputation are prepared, when the unhappy
" patient lies bound at your feet without the possibility of
" resistance, by what infalliable rule will you direct the ope-
" ration? When you propose to cut away the rotten parts,
" can you tell us what parts are perfectly sound?—Are there
" any certain limits in fact or theory, to inform you at
" what point you must stop, at what point the mortifica-
" tion ends? To a man so capable of observation and
" reflection as you are, it is unnecessary to say all that
" might be said upon the subject. Besides that I approve
" highly of Lord Chatham's idea of infusing a portion
" of new health into the constitution, to enable it to bear
" its infirmities (a brilliant expression, and full of intrin-

" sic wisdom), other reasons concur in persuading me to " adopt it." I have no objection, &c.

The man who fairly and completely answers this argument shall have my thanks and my applause. My heart is already with him.—I am ready to be converted.—I admire his morality, and would gladly subscribe to the articles of his faith.—Grateful as I am to the GOOD BEING whose bounty has imparted to me this reasoning intellect, whatever it is, I hold myself proportionably indebted to him, from whose enlightened understanding another ray of knowledge communicates to mine. But neither should I think the most exalted faculties of the human mind a gift worthy of the Divinity, nor any assistance in the improvement of them a subject of gratitude to my fellow-creature, if I were not satisfied, that really to inform the understanding, corrects and enlarges the heart.

JUNIUS.

NOTES.

DEDICATION. *a* This positive denial, of an arbitary power being vested in the legislature, is not in fact a new doctrine. When the Earl of Lindsay, in the year 1675, brought a bill into the House of Lords; " To prevent the dangers which might arise from persons disaffected " to government," by which an oath and penalty was to be imposed upon the members of both Houses, it was affirmed, in a protest signed by twenty-three lay peers (my lords the bishops were not accustomed to protest), " That the privilege of sitting and voting in parliament " was an honour they had by birth, and a right so inherent in them, " and inseparable from them, that nothing could take it away, but " what, by the law of the land, must withat take away their lives, and " corrupt their blood." These noble peers (whose names are a reproach to their posterity) have, in this instance, solemnly denied the power of parliament to alter the constitution. Under a particular proposition, they have asserted a general truth, in which every man in England is concerned.

PREFACE. *b* The following quotation from a speech delivered by Lord Chatham on the 11th of December 1770, is taken with exactness. The reader will find it curious in itself, and very fit to be inserted here. " My Lord, The verdict given in Woodfall's trial was,—guilty of " printing and publishing only :—upon which two motions were made " in court ; one, in arrest of judgement, by the defendant's counsel, " grounded upon the ambiguity of the verdict ; the other, by the " counsel for the crown, for a rule upon the defendant to show cause " why the verdict should not be entered up according to the legal " import of the words. On both motions a rule was granted, and " soon after the matter was argued before the Court of King's Bench. " The noble judge, when he delivered the opinion of the court upon " the verdict, went regularly though the whole of the proceedings at " *nisi prius*, as well as the evidence that had been given, as his own ', charge to the jury. This proceeding would have been very proper, " had a motion been made on either side for a new trial; because either " a verdict given contrary to evidence, or an improper charge by the " judge at *nisi prius*, is held to be a sufficient ground for granting a " new trial. But when a motion is made in arrest of judgment, or " for establishing the verdict by entering it up according to the legal " import of the words, it must be on the ground of something appearing on the face of the record : and the court, in considering " whether the verdict shall be established or not, are so confined to " the record, that they cannot take notice of any thing that does not " appear on the face of it; in the legal phrase, they cannot travel out " of the record: The noble judge did travel out of the record ; and " I affirm that his discourse was irregular, extrajudicial, and un-" precedented. His apparent motive for doing what he knew to be " wrong was, that he might have an opportunity of telling the public " extrajudicially, that the other three judges concurred in the doc-" trine laid down in his charge."

c Parliamentary History, Vol. VII. p. 406.

d Monsieur de Lolme.

LETTERS. *a* The Duke of Grafton took the office of Secretary of State, with an engagement to support the Marquis of Rockingham's administration. He resigned, however, in a little time, under pretence that he could not act without Lord Chatham, nor bear to see Mr. Wilkes abandoned; but that, under Lord Chatham, he would act in any office. This was the signal of Lord Rockingham's dismission. When Lord Chatham came in, the duke got possession of the Treasury. Reader, mark the consequence!

b This happened frequently to poor Lord North.

c Yet Junius has been called the partizan of Lord Chatham!

d That they should retract one of their resolutions, and erase the entry of it.

e It was pretended that the Earl of Rochford, while ambassador in France, had quarrelled with the Duke of Choiseuil; and that therefore he was appointed to the Northern department, out of compliment to the French minister.

f The late Lord Granby.

g This man, being committed to the court of King's Bench for a contempt, voluntarily made oath, that he would never answer interrogatories, unless he should be put to the torture.

h It has been said, I believe truly, that it was signified to Sir William Draper, as the request of Lord Granby, that he should desist from writing in his Lordship's defence. Sir William Draper certainly drew Junius forward to say more of Lord Granby's character than he originally intended. He was reduced to the dilemma of either being totally silenced, or of supporting his first letter. Whether Sir William had a right to reduce him to this dilemma, or to call upon him for his name, after a voluntary attack on his side, are questions submitted to the candour of the public.—The death of Lord Granby was lamented by Junius. He undoubtedly owed some compensations to the public, and seemed determined to acquit himself of them. In private life, he was unquestionably that good man who, for the interest of his country, ought to have been a great one. *Bonum virum facile dixeris;—magnum libenter.* I speak of him now without partiality:—I never spoke of him with resentment. His mistakes, in public conduct, did not arise either from want of sentiment, or want of judgment, but in general from the difficulty of saying NO to the bad people who surrounded him.

As for the rest, the friends of Lord Granby should remember, that he himself thought proper to condemn, retract, and disavow, by a most solemn declaration in the House of Commons, that very system of political conduct which Junius had held forth to the disapprobation of the public.

i Les rois ne se sont reservé que les graces. Ils renvoient les condamnations vers leurs officiers. *Montesquieu.*

k *Whitehall, March* 11. 1769. His Majesty has been graciously pleased to extend his royal mercy to Edward M'Quirk, found guilty of the murder of George Clarke, as appears by his royal warrant to the tenor following:

GEORGE R.

Whereas a doubt had arisen in our Royal breast concerning the evidence of the death of George Clarke, from the representations of William Bloomfield, Esq. surgeon, and Solomon Starling, apothecary; both of whom, as has been represented to Us, attended the deceased before his death, and expressed their opinions that he did not die of the blow he received at Brentford: and whereas it appears to Us, that neither of the said persons were produced as witnesses upon the trial, though the said Solomon Starling had been examined before the Coroner; and the only person called to prove that the death of the said George Clarke was occasioned by the said blow, was John Foot, surgeon, who never saw the deceased till after his death: We thought fit thereupon to refer the said representations, together with the report of the Recorder of Our City of London, of the evidence given by Richard and William Beale, and the said John Foot, on the trial of Edward Quirk, otherwise called Edward Kirk, otherwise called Edward M'Quirk, for the murder of the said Clarke, to the master, wardens, and the rest of the court of examiners of the Surgeons Company, commanding them likewise to take such further examination of the said persons so representing, and of said John Foot, as they might think necessary, together with the premises above mentioned, to form and report to Us their opinion, " Whether it did or did not appear to " them, that the said George Clarke died in consequence of the blow " he received in the riot at Brentford, on the 8th of December last." And the said court of examiners of the Surgeons Company having thereupon reported to Us their opinion, " That it did not appear to " them that he did;" We have thought proper to extend Our Royal mercy to him the said Edward Quirk, otherwise Edward Kirk, otherwise called Edward M'Quirk, and to grant him Our free pardon for the murder of the said George Clarke, of which he has been found guilty. Our will and pleasure therefore is, that he the said Edward Quirk, otherwise called Kirk, otherwise called Edward M'Quirk, be inserted for the said murder in Our first and next general pardon that shall come out for the poor convicts of Newgate, without any condition whatsoever; and that in the mean time you take bail for his appearance, in order to plead Our said pardon. And for so doing, this shall be your warrant.

Given at Our Court at St. Jame's, the 10th day of March 1769, in the ninth year of Our reign.

By his Majesty's command,
ROCHFORD.

To our trusty and well-beloved James Eyre, Esq. Recorder of our city of London, the Sheriffs of Our said City and County of Middlesex, and all others whom it may concern.

This unfortunate person had been persuaded by the Duke of Grafton to set up for Middlesex, his Grace being determined to seat him in the House of Commons, if he had but a single vote. It happened unluckily that he could not prevail upon any one freeholder to put him in nomination.

m Sir Fletcher Norton, when it was proposed to punish the sheriffs, declared in the House of Commons, that they, in returning Mr. Wilkes, had done no more than their duty.

n The reader is desired to mark this prophecy.

o The Duke, about this time, had separated himself from Ann Parsons; but proposed to continue united with her, on some Platonic terms of friendship, which she rejected with contempt. His baseness to this woman is beyond description or belief.

p To understand these passages, the reader is referred to a noted pamphlet, called, " The History of the Minority."

q His Grace had lately married Miss Wrottesly, niece of the Good Gertrude, Duchess of Bedford.

r Miss Liddel, after her divorce from the Duke, married Lord Upper Ossory.

s The wise Duke, about this time, exerted all the influence of government to procure addresses to satisfy the King of the fidelity of his subjects. They came in very thick from Scotland; but, after the appearance of this letter, we heard no more of them.

t It is hardly necessary to remind the reader of the name of Bradshaw.

u Sir John Moore.

v The reader will observe, that these admissions are made, not as of truths unquestionable, but for the sake of argument, and in order to bring the real question to issue.

w Precedents, in opposition to principles, have little weight with Junius; but he thought it necessary to meet the ministry upon their own ground.

x Case of the Middlesex Election considered, p. 38.

y This is still meeting the ministry upon their own ground; for, in truth, no precedents will support either natural injustice, or violation of positive right.

z Mr. Grenville had quoted a passage from the Doctor's excellent Commentaries, which directly contradicted the doctrine maintained by the Doctor in the House of Commons.

a (page 77.) If, in stating the law upon any point, a judge deliberately affirms that he has included every case, and it should appear that he has purposely omitted a material case, he does in effect lay a snare for the unwary.

b It is well worth remarking, that the compiler of a certain quarto, called " The case of the last election for the county of Middlesex; con-
" sidered," has the impudence to recite this very vote in the following
terms, *vide* page 11. " Resolved, that Robert Walpole, Esq. having
" been that session of parliament expelled the House, was and is in-
" capable of being elected a member to serve in the present parlia-
" ment." There cannot be a stronger positive proof of the treachery
of the compiler, nor a stronger presumptive proof that he was convinced that the vote, if truly recited, would overturn his whole argument.

SIR,   May 22. 1777.

VERY early in the debate upon the decision of the Middlesex election, it was observed by Junius, that the House of Commons had not only exceeded their boasted precedent of the expulsion and consequent incapacitation of Mr. Walpole, but that they had not even adhered to it strictly as far as it went. After convicting Mr. Dyson of giving a false quotation from the Journals, and having explained the purpose which that contemptible fraud was intended to answer, he proceeds to state the vote itself by which Mr. Walpole's supposed incapacity was declared, viz.—" Resolved, That Robert Walpole,
" Esq. having been this session of parliament committed a prisoner
" to the Tower, and expelled this House for a high breach of trust in
" the execution of his office, and notorious corruption when Secretary
" at War, was and is incapable of being elected a member to serve in
" the present parliament :"—and then observes, that, from the terms of the vote, we have no right to annex one incapacitation to the expulsion only; for that, as the proposition stands it must arise equally from the expulsion and the commitment to the Tower. I believe Sir, no man who knows any thing of Dialectics, or who understands English, will dispute the truth and fairness of this construction. But Junius has a great authority to support him, which, to speak with the Duke of Grafton, I accidentally met with this morning in the course of my reading. It contains an admonition, which cannot be repeated too often. Lord Sommers, in his excellent tract upon the rights of the people, after reciting the votes of the convention of the 28th of January 1687, viz.—" That King James the second having endeavour-
" ed to subvert the constitution of this kingdom, by breaking the
" original contract between king and people, and by the advice of
" Jesuits, and other wicked persons, having violated the fundamental
" laws, and having withdrawn himself out of this kingdom, hath
" abdicated the government," &c.—makes this observation upon it:
" The word abdicated relates to all the clauses aforegoing, as well as
" to his deserting the kingdom, or else they would have been wholly
" in vain." And that there might be no pretence for confining the abdication merely to the withdrawing, Lord Sommers farther observes,
" That King James, by refusing to govern us according to that law
" by which he held the crown, implicitly renounced his title to it."
If Junius's construction of the vote against Mr. Walpole be now admitted (and indeed I cannot comprehend how it can honestly be disputed), the advocates of the House of Commons must either give up their precedent entirely, or be reduced to the necessity of maintaining one of the grossest absurdities imaginable, viz. " That a
" commitment to the Tower is a constituent part of, and contributes
" half at least to, the incapacitation of the person who suffers it."
I need not make you any excuse for endeavouring to keep alive the attention of the public to the decision of the Middlesex election. The more I consider it, the more I am convinced that, as a fact, it is indeed highly injurious to the rights of the people; but that, as a precedent, it is one of the most dangerous that ever was established

against those who are to come after us. Yet I am so far a moderate man, that I verily believe the majority of the House of Commons, when they passed this dangerous vote, neither understood the question, nor knew the consequence of what they were doing. Their motives were rather despicable than criminal, in the extreme. One effect they certainly did not foresee. They are now reduced to such a situation, that if a member of the present House of Commons were to conduct himself ever so improperly, and in reality deserve to be sent back to his constituents with a mark of disgrace, they would not dare to expel him; because they know that the people, in order to try again the great question of right, or to thwart an odious House of Commons, would probably overlook his immediate unworthiness, and return the same person to parliament.—But, in time, the precedent will gain strength. A future House of Commons will have no such apprehensions; consequently will not scruple to follow a precedent, which they did not establish. The miser himself seldom lives, to enjoy the fruit of his extortion; but his heir succeeds him of course and takes possession without censure. No man expects him to make restitution; and no matter for his title, he lives quietly upon the estate.

PHILO JUNIUS.

d The Duke lately lost his only son, by a fall from his horse.

e At this interview, which passed at the house of the late Lord Eglington, Lord Bute told the Duke that he was determined never to have any connection with a man who had so basely betrayed him.

f In an answer in Chancery, in a suit against him to recover a large sum paid him by a person whom he had undertaken to return to parliament for one of his Grace's boroughs, he was compelled to repay the money.

g Of Bedford; where the tyrant was held in such contempt and detestation, that, in order to deliver themselves from him, they admitted a great number of strangers to the freedom. To make his defeat truly ridiculous, he tried his whole strength against Mr. Horne, and was beaten upon his own ground.

h Mr. Heston Homphrey, a country attorney, horsewhipped the Duke, with equal justice, severity, and preseverance, on the course at Litchfield. Rigby and Lord Trentham were also cudgelled in a most exemplary manner. This gave rise to the following story: " When the late King heard that Sir Edward Hawke had given the " French a drubbing, his Majesty, who had never received that kind " of chastisement, was pleased to ask Lord Chesterfield the meaning " of the word.—Sir, says Lord Chesterfield, the meaning of the word " —but here comes the Duke of Bedford, who is better able to ex- " plain it to your Majesty than I am."

i This man, notwithstanding his pride and Tory principles, had some English stuff in him. Upon an official letter he wrote to the Duke of Bedford, the Duke desired to be recalled, and it was with the utmost difficulty that Lord Bute could appease him.

k Mr. Grenville, Lord Halifax, and Lord Egremont.

l The ministry having endeavoured to exclude the Dowager out of the regency bill, the Earl of Bute determined to dismiss them. Upon this the Duke of Bedford demanded an audience of the—; reproached him in plain terms with his duplicity, baseness, falsehood, treachery hypocrisy—repeatedly gave him the lie, and left him in convulsions

m He received three thousand pounds for plate and equipage money.

n When Earl Gower was appointed President of the Council, the King, with his usual sincerity, assured him that he had not had one happpy moment since the Duke of Bedford left him.

o Lords Gower, Weymouth and Sandwich.

p Was Brutus an ancient bravo and dark assassin ? or does Sir W. D. think it criminal to stab a tyrant to the heart ?

q " Measures and not men," is the common cant of affected moderation ;—a base, counterfeit language, fabricated by knaves, and made current among fools. Such gentle censure is not fitted to the present degenerate state of society. What does it avail, to expose the absurd contrivance or pernicious tendency of measures, if the man who advises or executes, shall be suffered not only to escape with impunity, but even to preserve his power, and insult us with the favour of his sovereign ! I would recommend to the reader the the whole of Mr. Pope's letter to Dr. Arburthnot, dated July 26, 1734, from which the following is an extract: " To reform, and " not to chastise, I am afraid is impossible ; and that the best pre-" cepts, as well as the best laws, would prove of small use, if " there were no examples to enforce them. To attack vices in the " abstract, without touching persons, may be safe fighting indeed, " but it is fighting with shadows. My greatest comfort and en-" couragement to proceed, has been to see that those who have no " shame, and not fear of any thing else, have appeared touched by " my satires."

r Sir William gives us a pleasant account of men, who, in his opinion at least, are the best qualified to govern an empire.

s This gentleman is supposed to have the same idea of blushing, that a man, blind from his birth, has of scarlet or sky-blue.

t If Sir W. D. will take the trouble of looking into Torcy's Memoirs, he will see with what little ceremony a bribe may be offered to a Duke, and with what little ceremony it was only not accepted.

u Within a fortnight after Lord Tavistock's death, the venerable Gertrude had a route at Bedford House. The good Duke (who had only sixty thousand pounds) a-year ordered an inventory to be taken of his son's wearing apparel, down to his slippers, sold them all, and put the money in his pocket. The amiable Marchioness, shocked at such brutal, unfeeling avarice, gave the value of the clothes to the Marquis's servant, out of her own purse. That incomparable woman did not long survive her husband. When she died, the Duchess of Bedford treated her as the Duke had treated his only son. She ordered every gown and trinket to be sold, and pocketed the money.—These are the monsters whom Sir William Draper comes forward to defend !—May God protect me from doing any thing that may require such defence, or to deserve such friendship ?

v Major-General Gansel.

w Lieutenant Dodd.

x Lieutenant Garth.

y A few of them were confined.

z. A little before the publication of this and the preceding letter, the chaste Duke of Grafton had commenced a prosecution against Mr. Samuel Vaughan, for endeavouring to corrupt his integrity, by an offer of five thousand pounds for a patent place in Jamaica. A rule to show cause why an information should not be exhibited against Vaughan for certain misdemeanors, being granted by the Court of King's Bench, the matter was solemnly argued on the 27th of November 1769, and, by the unanimous opinion of the four judges, the rule was made absolute. The pleadings and speeches were accurately taken in short-hand, and published. The whole of Lord Mansfield's speech, and particularly the following extracts from it, deserve the readers attention. "A practice of the kind " complained of here, is certainly dishonourable and scandalous.— " If a man standing under the relation of an officer under the king, " or of a person in whom the king puts confidence, or of a minis- " ter, takes money for the use of that confidence the king puts in " him, he basely betrays the king,—he basely betrays his trust.— " If the king sold the office, it would be acting contrary to the " trust the constitution hath reposed in him. The constitution " does not intend the crown should sell those offices, to raise a re- " venue out of them.—Is it possible to hesitate, whether this " would not be criminal in the Duke of Grafton—contrary to his " duty as a privy counsellor—contrary to his duty as a minister— " contrary to his duty as a subject?—His advice should be free, " according to his judgment.—It is the duty of his office;—he " hath sworn to it."—Notwithstanding all this, the chaste Duke of Grafton certainly sold a patent place to Mr. Hine, for three thousand five hundred pounds; and, for so doing, is now Lord Privy Seal to the chaste George, with whose piety we are perpetu- ally deafened. If the House of Commons had done their duty, and impeached the black Duke for this most infamous breach of trust, how woefully must poor honest Mansfield have been puzzled! His embarrassment would have afforded the most ridiculous scene that ever was exhibited. To save the worthy judge from this perplexity, and the no less worthy Duke from impeachment, the prosecution against Vaughan was immediately dropped upon my discovery and publication of the Duke's treachery. The suffering this charge to pass without any inquiry, fixes shameless prostitution upon the face of the House of Commons, more strongly than even the Mid- dlesex election:—Yet the licentiousness of the press is complained of!

a (page 126.) From the publication of the preceding to this date, not one word was said in defence of the infamous Duke of Grafton. But vice and impudence soon recovered themselves, and the sale of the royal favour was openly avowed and defended. We acknow- ledge the piety of St. James's; but what has become of its morality?

b And by the same means preserves it to this hour.

c Tommy Bradshaw.

d Mr. Taylor. He and George Ross (the Scotch agent, and worthy confident of Lord Mansfield) managed the business.

e The plan of tutelage and future dominion over the heir-apparent, laid many years ago at Carlton-house, between the Princess Dowager and her favourite the Earl of Bute, was as gross and palpable as that which was concerted between Anne of Austria and Cardinal Mazarin, to govern Lewis the Fourteenth, and in effect to prolong his minority until the end of their lives. That Prince had strong natural parts, and used frequently to blush for his own ignorance and want of education, which had been willfully neglected by his mother and her minion. A little experience, however, soon showed him how shamefully he had been treated, and for what infamous purposes he had been kept in ignorance. Our great Edward too, at an early period, had sense enough to understand the nature of the connection between his abandoned mother and the detested Mortimer. But, since that time, human nature, we may observe, is greatly altered for the better. Dowagers may be chaste, and minions may be honest. When it was proposed to settle the present King's household, as Prince of Wales, it is well known that the Earl of Bute was forced into it, in direct contradiction to the late king's inclination. That was the salient point, from which all the mischiefs and disgraces of the present reign took life and motion. From that moment Lord Bute never suffered the Prince of Wales to be an instant out of his sight.—We need not look farther.

f One of the first acts of the present reign, was to dismiss Mr. Legge, because he had some years before refused to yield his interest in Hampshire to a Scotchman recommended by Lord Bute. This was the reason publicly assigned by his Lordship.

g Viscount Townshend sent over on the plan of being resident governor. The history of his ridiculous administration shall not be lost to the public.

h In the King's speech of 8th November, 1768, it was declared, " That the spirit of faction had broken out afresh in some of the " colonies, and, in one of them, proceeded to acts of violence and " resistance to the execution of the laws ;—that Boston was in a state " of disobedience to all law and government, and had proceeded to " measures subversive of the constitution, and attended with circum- " stances that manifested a disposition to throw off their dependence " on Great Britain."

i The number of commissioned officers in the guards, are to the marching regiments as one to eleven; the number of regiments given to the guards, compared with those given to the line, is about three to one, at a moderate computation ; consequently the partiality in favour of the guards is as thirty-three to one.—So much for the officers.—The private men have four-pence a day to subsist on, and five hundred lashes if they desert. Under this punishment they frequently expire. With these encouragements, it is supposed, they

may be depended upon, whenever a certain person thinks it necessary to butcher his *fellow-subjects.*

——*k Sacro tremuere timore.* Every coward pretends to be planet-
struck.

l There was something wonderfully pathetic in the mention of the
horned cattle.

m The Bedford party.

n The most secret particulars of this detestable transaction shall
in due time be given to the public. The people shall know what
kind of man they have to deal with.

o Mr. Stewart Mackenzie.

p A pension of 1500l. per annum, insured upon the 4 1-half per
cents. (he was too cunning to trust in Irish security) for the lives of
himself and all his sons. This gentleman, who a very few years ago
was a clerk to a contractor for forage, and afterwards exalted to a
petty post in the War Office, thought it necessary (as soon as he was
appointed Secretary to the Treasury) to take that great house in
Lincoln's-Inn-Fields, in which the Earl of Northington had resided
while he was Lord High Chancellor of Great Britain. As to the
pension, Lord North very solemnly assured the House of Commons,
that no pension was ever so well deserved as Mr. Bradshaw's.—
N. B. Lord Camden and Sir Jeffery Amherst are not near so well
provided for; and Sir Edward Hawke, who saved the state, retires
with two thousand pounds a-year on the Irish establishment, from
which he in fact receives less than Mr. Bradshaw's pension.

q This eloquent person has got as far as the discipline of Demost-
henes. He constantly speaks with pebbles in his mouth, to improve
his articulation.

r When his Majesty had done reading his speech, The Lord
Mayor, &c. had the honour of kissing his Majesty's hand; after
which, as they were withdrawing, his Majesty instantly turned round
to his courtiers, and burst out a laughing.—

"Nero fiddled, while Rome was burning." JOHN HORNE.

s This graceful minister is oddly constructed. His tongue is a
little too big for his mouth, and his eyes a great deal too big for their
sockets. Every part of his person sets natural proportion at defiance.
At this present writing, his head is supposed to be much too heavy
for his shoulders.

t About this time the courtiers talked of nothing but a bill of
pains and penalties against the Lord Mayor and sheriffs, or impeachment at the least. Little Manniken Ellis told the King, that, if the
business were left to his management, he would engage to do wonders. It was thought very odd, that a motion of so much importance
should be intrusted to the most contemptible little piece of machinery in the whole kingdom. His honest zeal however, was disappointed. The minister took fright; and, at the very instant that
little Ellis was going to open, sent him an order to sit down. All
their magnanimous threats ended in a ridiculous vote of censure, and
a still more ridiculous add ess to the King. This shameful desertion
so afflicted the generous mind of George the Third, that he was

obliged to live upon potatoes for three weeks, to keep off a malignant fever.—Poor man!—*Quis talia fando temperet a lachrymis!*

u After a certain person had succeeded in cajolling Mr. Yorke, he told the Duke of Grafton, with a witty smile, " My Lord, you " may kill the next Percy yourself."—N .B. He had but that instant wiped the tears away which overcame Mr. Yorke.

v Every true friend of the House of Brunswick sees with affliction, how rapidly some of the principal branches of the family have dropped off.

w This extravagant resolution appears in the votes of the House; but in the minutes of the committees, the instances of resolutions contrary to law and truth, or of refusals to acknowledge law and truth, when proposed to them, are innumerable.

x When the King first made it a measure of his government to destroy Mr. Wilkes, and when for this purpose it was necessary to run down privileges, Sir Fletcher Norton, with his usual prostituted effrontery, assured the House of Commons, that he should regard one of their votes no more than a resolution of so many drunken porters. This is the very lawyer whom Ben Johnson describes in the following lines:

" Gives forked counsel; takes provoking gold,
" On either hand, and puts it up.
" So wise, so grave, of so perplex'd a tongue,
" And loud withal, that would not wag, nor scarce
" Lie still without a fee."

y The man who resists and overcomes this iniquitous power, assumed by the Lords, must be supported by the whole people. We have the laws on our side, and want nothing but an intrepid leader. When such a man stands forth, let the nation look to it. It is not his cause, but our own.

z The examination of this firm, honest man, is printed for Almon. The reader will find it a most curious and most interesting tract. Dr. Musgrave, with no other support but truth and his own firmness, resisted and overcame the whole House of Commons.

a (page 164.) " An ignorant, mercenary, and servile crew; unani- " mous in evil, diligent in mischief, variable in principles, constant to " flattery, talkers for liberty, but slaves to power;—stiling them- " selves the court party, and the prince's only friends." *Davenant.*

b Miss Kennedy.

c He now says that his great object is the rank of Colonel, and that he will have it.

d This infamous transaction ought to be explained to the public. Colonel Gisborne was Quarter-Master-General in Ireland. Lord Townshend persuades him to resign to a Scotch officer, one Fraser; and gives him the government of Kinsale.—Colonel Cunninghame was Adjutant-General in Ireland. Lord Townshend offers him a pension, to induce him to resign to Luttrell. Cunninghame treats the offer with contempt. What's to be done? Poor Gisborne must move once more.—He accepts of a pension of 500l. a year, until a government of greater value shall become vacant. Colonel Cuninghame is made Governor of Kinsale: and Luttrell, at last, for whom the whole machinery is put in motion, becomes Adjutant-General, and in effect takes the command of the army in Ireland.

e This man was always a rank Jacobite. Lord Ravensworth produced the most satisfactory evidence of his having frequently drank the Pretender's health upon his knees.

f Confidential Secretary to the late Pretender. This circumstance confirmed the friendship between the brothers.

g The oppression of an obscure individual gave birth to the famous *Habeas Corpus* Act of 31st Car. II. which is frequently considered as another Magna Charta of the kingdom.　　　*Blackstone*, iii. 135.

h Bingley was committed for contempt, in not submitting to be examined. He lay in prison two years, until the Crown thought the matter might occasion some serious complaint; and therefore he was let out, in the same contumelious state he had been put in, with all his sins about him, unanointed and unannealed.—There was much coquetry between the Court and the Attorney-General, about who should undergo the ridicule of letting him escape.—*Vide* another Letter to Almon, p. 189.

i The philosophical poet doth notably describe the damnable and damned proceedings of the judge of hell,—

　　" Gnossius hæc Rhadamanthus habet durissima regma,
　　", Castigatque, auditque dolos, subigitque fateri."

Frst he punisheth, and then he heareth, and lastly compelleth to confess, and makes and mars laws at his pleasure; like as the Centurion, in the holy history, did to St. Paul; for the text saith " Centu-" rio apprehendi Paulum jussit, et se catenis eligari; et tunc INⁿ" TERROGABAT, quis fuisset, et quid fecisset." But good judges abhor these courses.　　　　　　　　　　　　　　*Coke*, 2 *Inst.* 55.

k Directly the reverse of the doctrine he constantly maintained in the House of Lords, and elsewhere, upon the decision of the Middlesex election. He invarably asserted, that the decision must be legal, because the court was competent; and never could be prevailed on to enter farther into the question.

l These iniquitous prosecutions cost the best of princes six thousand pounds, and ended in the total defeat and disgrace of the prosecutors. In the course of one of them, Judge Aston had the unparralleled impudence to tell Mr. Morris (a gentleman of unquestionable honour and integrity, and who was then giving his evidence on oath), that " he should pay very little regard to any affidavit he should make.".

m He said in the House of Lords, that he believed he should carry his opinion with him to the grave. It was afterwards reported that he had intrusted it, in special confidence, to the ingenious Duke of Cumberland.

n This paragraph gagged poor Leigh. I really am concerned for the man, and wish it were possible to open his mouth.—He is a very pretty orator.

o The King's acceptance of the Spanish ambassador's declaration is drawn up in babarous French, and signed by the Earl of Rochford. This diplomatic Lord has spent his life in the study and practice of etiquettes, and is supposed to be a profound master of ceremonies. I will not insult him by any reference to grammar or common sense; if he were even acquainted with the common forms of his office, I should think him as well qualified for it as any man in his Majesty's service.—The reader is requested to observe Lord Rochford's method of authenticating a public instrument. " En foi de quoi, moi " soussigné, un des principaux Secretaires d'Etat S. M. B. ai signé " la presente de ma signature ordinaire, et icelle fait apposer le " cachet de nos Armes."—In three lines there are no less than seven false concords But the man does not even know the style of his office. If he had known it, he would have said, " nous soussigné Secretaire " d'Etat de S. M. B. avons signé," &c.

p A mistake. He appears before them every day with the mark of a blow upon his face.—*Proh pudor!*

q The necessity of securing the House of Commons against the King's power, so that no interruption might be given either to the attendance of the members in parliament, or to the freedom of debate, was the foundation of parliamentary privilege ; and we may observe, in all the addresses of new appointed Speakers to the Sovereign, the utmost privilege they demand, is liberty of speech, and freedom from arrests. The very word privilege means no more than immunity, or a safeguard to the party who possesses it, and can never be construed into an active power of invading the rights of others.

r In the years 1593—1597—and 1601.

s Upon their own principles, they should have committed Mr. Wilkes, who had been guilty of a greater offence than even the Lord Mayor or Alderman Oliver. But after repeatedly ordering him to attend, they at last adjourned beyond the day appointed for his attendance ; and by this mean, pitiful evasion, gave up the point.—Such is the force of conscious guilt!

t " If it be demanded, in case a subject should be committed by " either House for a matter manifestly out of their jurisdiction, what " remedy can he have ? I answer, That it cannot well be imagined " that the law which favours nothing more than the liberty of the " subject, should give us a remedy against commitments by the King " himself, appearing to be illegal, and yet give us no manner of redress " against our commitment by our fellow subjects, equally appearing " to be unwarranted. But as this is a case which I am persuaded " will never happen, it seems needless over-nicely to examine it."— *Hawkins,* ii. 110.—N. B. He was a good lawyer, but no prophet.

u That their practice might be every way conformable to their principles, the House proceeded to advise the Crown to publish a proclamation, universally acknowledged to be illegal. Mr. Moreton publicly protested against it before it was issued ; and Lord Mansfield, though not scrupulous to an extreme, speaks of it with horror. It is remarkable enough, that the very men who advised the proclamation, and who hear it arraigned every day both within doors and without, are not daring enough to utter one word in its defence; nor have they ventured to take the least notice of Mr. Wilkes for discharging the persons apprehended under it.

v Lord Chatham very properly called this the act of a mob, not of a senate.

w When Mr. Wilkes was to be punished, they made no scruple about the privileges of parliament: and although it was as well known as any matter of public record and uninterrupted custom could be, " that the members of either House are privileged, ex- " cept in case of treason, felony, or breach of peace," they declared, without hesitation, " that privilege of parliament did not extend to " the case of a seditious libel;" and undoubtedly they would have done the same, if Mr. Wilkes had been prosecuted for any other misdemeanor whatsoever. The ministry are of a sudden grown won- derfully careful of privileges, which their predecessors were as ready to invade. The known laws of the land, the rights of the subject, the sanctity of charters, and the reverence due to our magistrates, must all give way, without question or resistance, to a privilege of which no man knows either the origin or the extent. The House of Commons judge of their own privileges without appeal; they may take offence at the most innocent action, and imprison the person who offends them during their arbitrary will and pleasure. The party has no remedy; he cannot appeal from their jurisdiction; and if he questions the privilege which he is supposed to have violated, it becomes an aggravation of his offence. Surely this doctrine is not to be found in Magna Charta. If it be admitted without limitation, I affirm that there is neither law nor liberty in this kingdom. We are the slaves of the House of Commons; and through them we are the slaves of the King and his ministers.—*Anonymous.*

x If there be in reality any such law in England as the law of par- liament, which (under the exceptions stated in my letter on privi- lege), I confess, after long deliberation, I very much doubt, it cer- tainly is not constituted by, nor can it be collected from, the resolu- tions of either House, whether enacting or declaratory. I desire the reader will compare the above resolution of the year 1704 with the following of the third of April 1628.—" Resolved, That the writ of " Habeas Corpus cannot be denied, but ought to be granted to every " man that is committed or detained in prison, or otherwise restrained " by the command of the King, the Privy Council, or any other, he " praying the same."

y The Duke was lately appointed Lord Privy Seal.

z A superb villa of Colonel Burgoyne, about this time advertised for sale.

a (page 203.) It will appear by a subsequent letter, that the Duke's precipitation proved fatal to the grant. It looks like the hurry and con- fusion of a young highwayman, who takes a few shillings, but leaves the purse and watch behind him:—And yet the Duke was an old offender!

b By an intercepted letter from the Secretary of the Treasury, it appeared, " that the friends of government were to be very active" in supporting the ministerial nomination of sheriffs.

c I beg leave to introduce Mr. Horne to the character of the Double Dealer. I thought they had been better acquainted.—" Another very " wrong objection has been made by some, who have not taken leisure " to distinguish the characters. The hero of the play (meaning Mell- " font, is a gull, and made a fool, and cheated—Is every man a gull " and a fool that is deceived?—At that rate, I am afraid the two " classes of men will be reduced to one, and the knaves themselves " be at a loss to justify their title. But if an open honest-hearted " man; who has an entire confidence in one whom he takes to be " his friend, and who (to confirm him in his opinion), in all appear- " ance, and upon several trials, has been so; if this man be de- " ceived by the treachery of the other, must he of necessity com- " mence fool immediately; only, because the other has proved a " villain?"—Yes, says Parson Horne; No, says Congreve; and he, I think, is allowed to have known something of human nature.

d The very soliloquy of Lord Suffolk before he passed the Rubicon.

e The epitaph would not be ill suited to the character; at the best, it is but equivocal.

f I confine myself strictly to seamen;—if any others are pressed, it is a gross abuse, which the magistrate can and should correct.

g There is a certain family in this country, on which nature seems to have entailed an hereditary baseness of disposition. As far as their history has been known, the son has regularly improved upon the vices of his father, and has taken care to transmit them pure and undiminished into the bosom of his successor. In the senate, their abilities have confined them to those humble, sordid services in which the scavengers of the ministry are usually employed. But, in the memoirs of private treachery, they stand first and unrivalled. The following story will serve to illustrate the character of this respectable family, and to convince the world that the present pos- sessor has as clear a title to the infamy of his ancestors as he has to their estate. It deserves to be recorded for the curiosity of the fact, and, should be given to the public as a warning to every honest member of society.

The present Lord Irnham, who is now in the decline of life, lately cultivated the acquaintance of a younger brother of a family with which he had lived in some degree of intimacy and friendship The young man had long been the dupe of a most unhappy attachment to a common prostitute. His friends and relations foresaw the conse- quences of this connection, and did every thing that depended upon them to save him from ruin. But he had a friend in Lord Irnham, whose advice rendered all their endeavours ineffectual. This hoary leacher, not contented with the enjoyment of his friend's mistress, was base enough to take advantage of the passions and folly of a young man, and persuaded him to marry her. He descended even to per- form the office of father to the prostitute. He gave her to his friend, who was on the point of leaving the kingdom, and the next night lay with her himself.

A a

Whether the depravity of the human heart can produce any thing more base and detestable than this fact, must be left, undetermined, until the son shall arrive at the fathers age and experience.

h 4 Inst. 41. 66.

i Blackstone, 4. 303.

k 1 Ed. III. cap. 8. and 7 Rich. II. cap. 4.

" *l* Videtur que le statute de mainprise n'est que rehersal del " menley."—*Bro. Mainp.* 61.

m " There are three points to be considered in the construction of " all remedial statutes;—the old law, the mischief, and the re- " medy;—that is, how the common law stood at the making of the " act, what the mischief was for which the common law did not pro- " vide, and what remedy the parliament hath provided to cure this " mischief. It is the business of the judges so to construe the act " as to suppress the mischief and advance the remedy."—*Blackstone,* i. 87.

n 2 Hale. P. C. 128. 136.

o Blackstone, iv. 296.

p 2 Hale, P. C. ii. 124.

q Vide 2d Inst. 150. 186.—The word *replevisable* never signifies *bail-* " *able.* *Bailable* is in a court of record by the King's justices; but " *replevisable* is by the Sheriff."—*Selden,* State Tr. vii. 149.

r Selden, by N. Bacon, 182.

s Parliamentary History, i. 82.

t Parliamentary History, ii. 419.

u Blackstone, iv. 137.

x It has been the study of Lord Mansfield to remove landmarks.

INDEX.

that he deals in fiction, and therefore naturally appeals to the evidence of the poets, ib.; is allowed a degree of merit which aggravates his guilt, 244; his furious persecuting zeal has by gentle degrees softened into moderation, 225; shameful for him who has lived in friendship with Mr. Wilkes, to reproach him for failings naturally connected with despair, 227.

HUMPHREY, Mr. his treatment of the Duke of Bedford on the course at Litchfield (h) 292.

I.

IRELAND, the people of, have been uniformly plundered and oppressed, 135.

IRNHAM, Lord, father of Colonel Luttrell, (g) 301.

JUDGE, one may be honest enough in the decision of private causes, yet a traitor to the public, 23.

JUNIUS, letter from, to the Printer of the Public Advertiser, on the state of the nation, and the different departments of the state, 17; to Sir William Draper, 28; approves of Sir William's spirit in giving his name to the public, but that it was a proof of nothing but spirit, ib.; requires some instances of the military skill and capacity of Lord Granby 29; puts some queries to Sir William, as to his own conduct, 31; called upon by Sir William to give his real name, 32; another letter to Sir William Draper, 37; explains Sir William's bargain with Colonel Gisborne, 38; letter to Sir William Draper, 40; declares himself to be a plain unlettered man, ib.; calls upon Sir William to justify his declaration of the sovereign's having done an act in his favour, contrary to law, 41; takes his leave of Sir William,

ib.; letter to the Duke of Grafton, ib.; that the only act of mercy to which the Duke advised his Majesty, meets with disapprobation, 42; that it was hazarding too much to interpose the strength of prerogative between such a felon as M'Quirk and the justice of his country, ib.; the pardoning of this man, and the reasons alledged for so doing, considered, 44; to the Duke of Grafton, ib.; that one fatal mark seems to be fixed on every measure of his Grace, whether in a personal or political character, ib.; that a certain ministerial writer does not defend the minister as to the pardoning M'Quirk upon his own principles, 45; that his Grace can best tell for which of Mr Wilkes's good qualities he first honored him with his friendship, 46; to Mr. Edward Weston, 47; a citation from his pamphlet in defence of the pardoning of M'Quirk, with remarks, ib.; to the Duke of Grafton, 48; that his Grace was at first scrupulous of even exercising those powers with which the executive power of the legislature is invested, ib.; that he reserved the proofs of his intrepid spirit for trials of greater hazard, 49; that he balanced the non-execution of the laws with a breach of the constitution, ib.; to the Duke of Grafton, 52; that his Grace addresses himself simply to the touch, ib.; his character resembles that of his royal ancestors, 53; to the Duke of Grafton, 63; if his Grace's talents could keep pace with the principles of his heart, he would have been a most formidable minister, ib.; that he became the leader of an administration collected from the deserters of all parties, 65; to the Printer of the Public Advertiser, 68; the question arising

not brought to a trial, the Duke of Grafton shall hear from him again, ib.; leaves it to his countrymen to determine whether he is moved by malevolence, or animated by a just purpose of obtaining a satisfaction to the laws of the country, 125; to his Grace the Duke of Grafton, ib.; Junius gives his Grace credit for his discretion, in refusing Mr. Vaughan's proposals, ib.; asks what was the price of Mr. Hine's patent, ib.; and whether the Duke dares to complain of an attack upon his own honour, while he is selling the favours of the crown, 126; to his Grace the Duke of Grafton, ib.; Junius is surprised at the silence of his Grace's friends to the charge of having sold a patent place, ib.; the price at which the place was knocked down, ib. 127; that there is none of all his Grace's friends hardy enough to deny the charge, 127; that Mr. Vaughan's offer amounted to a high misdemeanor, 128; the opinion of a learned judge on this matter (z) 294; to the Printer of the Public Advertiser, 128; Junius supposes a well-intentioned prince asking advice for the happiness of his subjects, 129; and an honest man, when permitted to approach a king, in what terms he would address his sovereign, ib.; he separates the amiable prince from the folly and treachery of his servants, 130; and that the king should distinguish betwixt his own dignity and what serves only to promote the interest and ambition of a minister, ib.; that he should withdraw his confidence from all parties, and consult his own understanding, ib.; that there is an original bias in his education, 131; that a little personal motive was able to remove the ablest servants

of the crown, ib.; that Mr. Wilkes, though he attacked the favourite, was unworthy of a king's personal resentment, 132, that the destruction of one man has been for years the sole object of government, ib,; that his ministers have forced the subjects from wishing well to the cause of one man to unite with him in their own, 133; that nothing less then a repeal of a certain resolution, can heal the wound given to the constitution, ib.; if an English king be hated or despised, he must be unhappy, ib.; that the prince takes the sense of the army from the conduct of the guards, as he does that of the people from the representations of the ministry, 137; that the House of Commons have attributed to their own vote an authority equal to an act of the legislature, 139; to the Duke of Grafton, 141; in his public character, he has injured every subject of the empire, 142; at the most active period of life, he must quit the busy scene, and conceal himself from the world, ib.; that the neglect of the remonstrances and petitions was part of his original plan of government, 143; the situation in which he abandoned his royal master, ib.; that he either differed from his colleagues, or thought the administration no longer tenable, 145: that he began with betraying the people, and concluded with betraying the king, ib.; Junius takes leave of the Duke, 147; to the Printer of the Public Advertiser, 148; the king's answer to the city remonstrance considered, ib.; the grievances of the people aggravated by insults, 149; if any part of the representative body be not chosen by the people, that part vitiates and cor-

out confessing that he never acted upon principle of any kind,
238; to the Printer of the Public Advertiser, 239; Junius laments the unhappy differences
which have arisen among the
friends of the people, ib. ; the insidious partizan who foments the
disorder, sees the fruit of his industry ripen beyond his hopes,
ib. ; that Mr. Wilkes has no resource but in the public favour,
240; that Mr. Sawbridge has
shewn himself possessed of that
republican firmness which the
times require, 241; the right of
pressing founded originally upon
a necessity which supersedes all
argument, 242; the designs of
Lord Mansfield, subtle, effectual,
and secure, 243, 244; we should
not reject the services or friendship of any man, because he differs from us in a particular opinion, 244; patriotism, it seems,
may be improved by transplanting, 245; Junius defended in three
material points, 256; charges
Lord Mansfield with doing what
was illegal in bailing Eyre, 258;
engages to make good his charge,
259; to the Duke of Grafton, ib.;
the miserable depression of his
Grace, when almost every man
in the kingdom was exulting in
the defeat of Sir James Lowther,
260; that he violates his own
rules of decorum, when he does
not insult the man whom he has
betrayed, ib. ; to Lord Chief-
Justice Mansfield, 262; Junius
undertakes to prove the charge
against his Lordship, ib. ; that
the superior power of bailing for
felony, claimed by the Court of
King's Bench, has only the negative assent of the legislature, 263;
that a person positively charged
with feloniously stealing, and taken with the stolen goods upon
him, is not bailable, 264; autho-

rities quoted to support this opinion, 265; the several statutes
relative to bail in criminal cases,
stated in due order, ib.; the law,
as stated, applied to the case of
John Eyre, who was committed
for felony, 277; to the Right Honourable Lord Camden, 281; Junius calls upon his Lordship to
stand forth in defence of the laws
of his country, ib. ; extract of a
letter from Junius to Mr. Wilkes,
282.

L

LIGONIER, Lord, the army
taken from him, much against
his inclination, 31.

LONDON, City of, has given an
example in what manner a king
of this country should be addressed, 149.

LOTTERY, the worst way of
raising money upon the people,
20.

LOYALTY, what it is, 17.

LUTTRELL, Mr. patronized by
the Duke of Grafton with success, 49; the assertion, that two-
thirds of the nation approve of
his admission into parliament,
cannot be maintained nor confuted by argument, 60; the appointment of, invades the foundations of the laws themselves, 66;
a strain of prostitution in his
character admired for its singularity, 166.

LYNN, burgesses of, re-elect
Mr. Walpole, after being expelled, 70.

M

M'QUIRK, the king's warrant
for his pardon (k) 288; the pardoning of him much blamed, and
the reasons alleged for so doing,
refuted, 43.

MANILLA ransom dishonoura-
bly given up, 29; the ministers
said to be desirous to do justice
in this affair, but their efforts in
vain, 36.

B b

STATE, the principal departments of, when improperly bestowed, the cause of every mischief, 19.

T.

TOWNSHEND, Mr. complains
that the public gratitude has not
been equal to his deserts, 241.

TOUCHET, Mr. in his most
prosperous fortune, the same
man as at present, 205.

V.

VAUGHAN, Mr. sends propo-
sals to the Duke of Grafton,
125; his offers to the Duke
amounted to a high misdemeanor, 128; a prosecution commenced against him (z) 294;
the matter solemnly argued in
the Court of King's Bench, ib.;
Junius does justice to this
injured man, 146.

W.

WESTON, Edward, a letter to
him from Junius, 47; quotations
from this pamphlet, in defence
of the pardoning M'Quirk, with
remarks, ib.

WALPOLE, Mr. his case supposed to be strictly in point, to
prove expulsion creates incapacity of being re-elected, 80; the
vote of expulsion, as expressed
in the votes, 86; remarks upon
its meaning and extent (b),
290; the election was declared
void, 87.

WEYMOUTH, Lord, appointed
one of the Secretaries of State,
22; nominated to Ireland, 98.

WHITTLEBURY Forest, the
Duke of Grafton hereditary
ranger of, 234; the right to the
timber claimed by his Grace,
235.

WILKES, Mr. his conduct
often censured by Junius, 46;
suffered to appear at large, and
to canvass for the city and
county, with an outlawry hanging
over him, 48; his situation and
private character gave the ministry advantages over him, 50;
it is perhaps the greatest misfortune of his life, that the Duke
of Grafton had so many compensations to make in the closet
for his former friendship with
him, 54; said more than moderate men would justify, 132;
hardly serious at first, he became
an enthusiast, ib.; commissions
Mr. Thomas Walpole to solicit
a pension for him, 218; comes
over from France to England,
where he gets 200l. from the
Duke of Portland and Lord
Rockingham, ib.

WOOLASTON, Mr. expelled,
re-elected, and admitted into the
same parliament, 88; the public
left to determine whether this
be a plain matter of fact, 90.

Y.

YATES, Mr. Justice, quits the
Court of King's Bench, 171.

THE END.

CONTENTS.